THE LIFE AND WORKS OF
MARIE-CATHERINE DESJARDINS
(*Mme de Villedieu*)
1632-1683

BY

BRUCE ARCHER MORRISSETTE
ASSOCIATE PROFESSOR OF ROMANCE LANGUAGES
WASHINGTON UNIVERSITY

WASHINGTON UNIVERSITY STUDIES — NEW SERIES

LANGUAGE AND LITERATURE — NO. 17

SAINT LOUIS, 1947

TO MY MOTHER

.

PREFACE

Mlle Marie-Catherine Desjardins, who preferred to sign herself "Mme de Villedieu,"—a name to which she had a sentimental if not a legal right—was one of the first women in France to live by her literary productions alone. She achieved fame and notoriety not only through her poetry, letters, drama, and fiction, but also by leading an independent and bohemian existence which shocked and amused her contemporaries. Her colorful literary career coincided with the quarter of a century which saw the production of many of the greatest works of the classical period, upon two of which (Molière's *Les Précieuses ridicules* and Mme de La Fayette's *La Princesse de Clèves*) some of her own writings cast important side lights. Mlle Desjardins was, and remains, a minor author; no attempt has been made to "rehabilitate" her, or to discover among her productions any forgotten masterpieces. On the other hand, no author who enjoyed a popularity comparable to that of Mlle Desjardins, in a period of such literary taste as that which prevailed under Louis XIV, should be, or can be, neglected, in the summing up toward which literary historians endlessly work. A complete picture of the literary past must show, in addition to a sequence of masterpieces, the trends and processes of second- and third-rate writing from which the masterpieces emerge. Moreover, the historian of taste may discover, in certain mediocre and forgotten works of the past, viewpoints, sentimentalities, or ideals which to the society of the time seemed equally as significant and important as those which they found in contemporary masterpieces. In literary history, whatever is, is of a certain importance.

It has been my object to give as complete an account as possible of the life and works of Mlle Desjardins. 1 have sought to study her novels, stories, plays, verse, and letters from the standpoint of their composition, style, sources, and originality, or lack of it, pointing out those elements of her work which represented currents of opinion and taste among the readers of the time, and discussing the relationship of certain of her works to those of more famous authors. The importance of her psychological-historical novels and stories in the development of French fiction—perhaps her most lasting claim to scholarly interest—has been emphasized. Lastly, I have studied her influence and fortune, and have attempted a "final" evaluation of her status, which may at least serve for the *état présent*.

For much material concerning Mlle Desjardins' life I am indebted to the entertaining biography by Émile Magne, *Mme de Villedieu*.[1] Documents published subsequently, together with a detailed study of her works and other sources, have enabled me to correct and amplify some of the biographical data of this fine work. The two modern studies which have attempted to give an account of Mlle Desjardins' literary production, A. Kretschmar's *Mme de Villedieu, Leben, Romane und Erzählungen*[2] and Henri Chatenet's *Le Roman et les romans d'une femme de lettres au XVIIe siècle, Mme de Villedieu*,[3] have little scholarly importance, and contain chiefly analyses of plots. Mlle Desjardins' three plays have received definitive study in H. C. Lancaster's *History of French Dramatic Literature in the Seventeenth Century*.[4] In dealing with them I have been able to add only supplementary material and to recount more fully the part played by Mlle Desjardins' *Manlius* in the quarrel of Corneille, the abbé d'Aubignac, and de Visé over *Sophonisbe* and *Sertorius*.

Mlle Desjardins knew personally Molière, Gilles Boileau, the Dutch poet and diplomat Huygens, the minister Hugues de Lionne, the *libertins* Des Barreaux and Saint-Pavin, and many other notable personages of her time. Louis XIV accepted the dedication of her *Fables* (1670), had her play *Le Favory* presented before him at Versailles by Molière's troupe (1665), and granted her a pension. She was twice married, only to discover each time, according to Goujet, that her husband already had a wife. High priestess of *la galanterie*, she suffered late in life an emotional crisis which led her to the convent; but her reputation followed her and caused her to be dismissed. Gay, passionate, versatile, she tried her hand at all the literary genres of her period, succeeding best in the creation of characters like herself, women of sensibility afflicted with faithless lovers. Romantic in her private life, she was an arch-conservative in letters, blindly following what she understood to be tradition; yet she left her stamp on the novel by shortening it and by increasing

---

[1] In the series *Femmes galantes du XVIIe siècle*, Paris, 1907. Other biographical references will be found in Ch. I, below, and in the Bibliography.

[2] Inaugural-Dissertation, Leipzig, 1907.

[3] Paris, 1911.

[4] Baltimore, 1936. See Ch. IV, below.

its emotional and psychological intensity.[5] Never wholly forgotten by critics and literary historians, some of whom, in the nineteenth century, went so far as to form a cult of admirers, she has never been definitely "placed" in French literary history. It is the assignment of such a "place" which the present work seeks to achieve. In this intent the author's effort has taken, as it were, a double direction: externally, to establish the greatest possible number of relationships between the works of Mlle Desjardins and the literary *Gestalt* of her times, and, internally, to attain—to the limits of his ability—completeness, accuracy, and critical objectivity.

I owe to Professor H. C. Lancaster of The Johns Hopkins University a large debt of gratitude, not only for his initial suggestion of Mlle Desjardins as a topic for investigation, but also for his generous and wise counsel over a period of years. It was under his direction that I wrote my Ph.D. thesis on Mlle Desjardins, from which the present study is derived. I would also thank Mrs. Carleton S. Hadley for her assistance in typing much of the manuscript of this work. The task of editing and checking it for publication has been cheerfully and expertly handled by Professor Thomas Shearer Duncan, Editor of the Washington University Studies, and Miss Annie Louise Carter, Associate Editor, to whom I would express the greatest appreciation. My wife Dorothy Morrissette has been of inestimable assistance, in ways too numerous to mention. Professor Duncan, Miss Carter, Mrs. Kendall W. Venable, and Miss Helen Barnard have borne most of the tedious burden of reading and correcting proofs.

B. A. M.

[5] Anatole de Gallier, in his *Mme de Villedieu*, Paris, 1883, p. 13, attributes to Voltaire the statement, "Elle a fait perdre le goût des romans longs." The remark was probably made, however, by Voisenon (cf. Ch. V, n. 21, below).

TABLE OF CONTENTS

CHAPTER I

LIFE OF MARIE-CATHERINE DESJARDINS (1632-1683)

In her *Mémoires de la vie de Henriette-Sylvie de Molière,* a novel with a certain autobiographical flavor, Mlle Desjardins has her heroine exclaim:

Pour commencer, je n'ai jamais bien sçu qui j'étois; je sçai seulement que je ne suis pas une personne qui ait de communes destinées, que ma naissance, mon éducation et mes mariages ont été l'effet d'autant d'avantures extraordinaires.[1]

The Rousseauesque tone of this passage is in keeping with many of the episodes of the author's own life. She was to some extent, as Pierre Brun has styled her, "une sorte de George Sand de son époque."[2] But despite her preromantic tendencies, she cannot be placed among those "héroïnes du préromantisme" of which M. Monglond writes (*Le Préromantisme*). George Sand put on men's clothes to become a critic of society; Mlle Desjardins disguised herself as a man, if indeed the anecdote recorded in the eighteenth century is true, only to rival the *femmes déguisées* of the *Astrée* or of any *roman d'aventures*.[3] Mlle Desjardins' works are traditional, conservative, classical, only hinting at a latent originality never fully developed. If her life seems at times bohemian or romantic, such a

[1] *Œuvres de Mme de Villedieu,* ed. 1741, VII, 3. Unless otherwise indicated, *Œuvres* refers to this edition throughout the text and footnotes.

[2] Pierre Brun, *Autour du XVIIe siècle,* Grenoble, 1901, p. 380.

[3] *Bibliothèque universelle des romans (BUR),* February, 1776, pp. 194 ff. The heroine of the *Mémoires de Henriette-Sylvie de Molière* also disguises herself as a man, but under different circumstances from those referred to in the *BUR.* For the reasons set forth in Ch. VII, below, I am unable to agree with Émile Magne that the *Mémoires* constitute "une autobiographie volontairement embrouillée" which may be cited as a "référence indiscutable." Magne's *Mme de Villedieu* (1907) is nevertheless a fully documented, brilliant attempt to reconstruct year by year both the factual events of Mlle Desjardins' life and her emotional reactions to them. The date of her death accepted by Magne, 1692, arrived at by a confusion with the date of the death of Catherine Ferrand, her mother, has, however, led the author to invent nine years of life for Mlle Desjardins which she unhappily failed to enjoy. Magne deals with her works only in passing, or when some biographical relevance may be established, making a number of misstatements which I have attempted to rectify at the proper places in this study. Magne's exhaustive footnotes were an invaluable point of departure for research on Mlle Desjardins. As another work has proved (Chatenet's *Le Roman d'une femme de lettres au XVIIe siècle, Mme de Villedieu,* Paris, 1911), there are few additions or improvements possible as far as Magne's biography is concerned (except, of course, for its final pages). At most I have tried to separate the facts from the conjectures, and make corrections and amplifications in the light of new evidence. Kretschmar's Inaugural-Dissertation, *Mme de Villedieu,* written in 1907, may from a scholarly viewpoint be dismissed as almost worthless.

contrast must not be considered unusual or especially significant. The realistic, *roman comique* aspects of life during the reign of Louis XIV are not always easy to reconcile with the literary dignity of classical tragedy, the baroque religious oratory of a Bossuet, or the surface manifestations of salon conduct. In the *terre-à-terre* world of Tallemant des Réaux, who speaks of Mlle Desjardins at length, she seems not at all remarkable, unrestrained, or immoral. If her love affairs and independent behavior shocked some of her contemporaries, she was at least, to judge by Tallemant's roster, in a numerous and notable company.[4]

Marie-Catherine Desjardins was born at Alençon, probably in 1632.[5] The name "Hortense" which figures in many present-day references was first added to "Marie-Catherine" by Beauchamps, a theatrical historian, in 1735.[6] Her parents, lately from Paris, were Catherine Ferrand, a former lady-in-waiting to the Duchesse de Montbazon, and Guillaume Desjardins, a former "avocat du Parlement" who became in 1659 "prévôt de la maréchaussée" of Alençon.[7] Apparently the child was taken to Paris on visits; Tallemant relates that Voiture commented on the young

[4] Tallemant des Réaux, *Historiettes*, ed. Monmerqué and Paris, Paris, 1854-1860, VII, 243 ff. and *passim*.

[5] Odolant Desnos, *Mémoires historiques sur la ville d'Alençon, et sur ses seigneurs*, 1787, II, 617, states that the birth registers of Alençon carry 1632 as the year of Mlle Desjardins' birth. Chatenet, *op. cit.*, states that these registers, which begin in 1630, contain no mention of her, but that certain portions, from 1631 on, are missing. The *Annuaire d'Alençon*, 1808, gives 1632. Mlle Desjardins' *Lettres* (1667) refer twice to her age as twenty-seven, but vanity had no doubt subtracted several years from her count.

[6] Cf. "le Capitaine" Derome, "Mme de Villedieu inconnue," in *Revue historique et archéologique du Maine*, 1911, pp. 224-236. P.-F. G. de Beauchamps' *Recherches sur les théâtres de France*, Paris, 1735, p. 235, refers for the first time to Marie-Catherine Hortense Desjardins. Magne, Chatenet, and all contemporary library catalogues in and outside of France, concur in perpetuating this addition, which is, as far as I can discover, based on no ascertainable evidence. Derome, *loc. cit.*, first reproduced the true death certificate of Mlle Desjardins, dated 1683, proving Magne's mistaken date of 1692 to be that of Mlle Desjardins' mother Catherine. Derome also claimed, but without evidence, that Mlle Desjardins was born "à Paris en 1640, rue St.-Thomas-du-Louvre, dans la maison où mourut Voiture." Her death certificate terms her "agée de 45 ans," a figure which would put her birth in the year 1638. Magne gives a list of the dates and places which had been assigned to her birth by various authors; the dates range from 1631 to 1640, and the places from Alençon to Clinchemaure and Saint-Remi-du-Plain (*op. cit.*, p. 17, note). Cf. also the *Asmodée Cenoman*, 1822 (see Bibliography).

[7] Cf. Magne, *op. cit.*, pp. 405-410, for the document of Guillaume Desjardins' appointment. Tallemant, *loc. cit.*, mentions Marie-Catherine's parents. I shall attempt in this recapitulation of Mlle Desjardins' biography to give detailed and complete references to all controversial points. Statements made without substantiation in notes may be taken to represent facts agreed upon by all biographers, or completely demonstrated by Magne in his extensive work.

girl's wit, predicting that she would, however, "devenir folle."[8] We know
nothing about her education; the *BUR* states that her father instructed
her in the rudiments of literature. In one of her *Lettres* of 1667 she dis-
claims all knowledge of writers earlier than d'Urfé and Gomberville, but
the evidence of her works shows that she knew classical historians (perhaps in translation) well enough to use their writings as sources.[9]
Whatever her early instruction may have been, she began to write verses
at an early age, and, according to her own claim, had begun at the age
of sixteen her first novel, *Alcidamie.*[10]

Before it was completed, Mlle Desjardins became involved in a love
affair, probably with a cousin in Alençon, and apparently fled *enceinte*
to Paris, where Magne fancifully pictures her seeking refuge with Mme
de Montbazon, formerly her mother's employer, and there giving birth
to a child which soon died.[11]

The next period of her life cannot be accurately reconstructed. Until
the year 1657, date of the death of the *président* Bellièvre (subject of the
earliest extant writing of Mlle Desjardins), it is impossible to affirm
whether she was, as seems likely, living with her mother in Paris (as we
know from Tallemant's account that she did a year or two later), or
whether she was engaged in the series of romanesque adventures ascribed
to her by Magne, pursuing her lover through the provinces, and even
joining Molière's troupe, the *Illustre Théâtre,* as a successful actress.[12]

[8] *Loc. cit.* Brun, *op. cit.,* p. 379, writes: "Prognostic assez juste, mais sa folie, que
je crois, fut de la démence hystérique." This seems an unwarrantedly severe judgment.

[9] This letter is discussed in Ch. II, below. For her use of classical sources, cf. below,
passim.

[10] Cf. Tallemant, *op. cit.,* VII, 245; Jean Loret, *La Muze historique* of May 27,
1662. Mlle Desjardins' claim concerning *Alcidamie* is discussed in Ch. III, below.

[11] It is difficult to be sure of these facts. Magne, *op. cit.,* pp. 50 ff., builds on the
assertions of the frères Parfaict in their *Théâtre françois,* Amsterdam, 1735-1749, IX,
123. Cf. also l'abbé Claude-Pierre Goujet, *Bibliothèque françoise,* Paris, 1741-1756,
XVIII, 118 ff. Tallemant says nothing to support the story, nor does Pierre Richelet,
who in his *Vie des auteurs françois,* Paris, 1699, article "Desjardins," does not mince
words concerning other real or imaginary "galanteries" of Marie-Catherine. The
abbé de Voisenon in his life of Mlle Desjardins (*Œuvres,* Paris, 1781, IV, 94) is likewise silent on the point of Mlle Desjardins' early fall from grace. Pierre Bayle
in the article "Jardins" in his *Dictionnaire historique et critique,* Paris, 1820, says,
in attempting to refute Richelet's charge that Mlle Desjardins was extremely immoral during her later years, that it was during the first part of her life only that her
conduct was reprehensible, and that during her last years she led a reformed and
chastened existence.

[12] Magne's reconstruction of these early years is based on his theory, mentioned

In any event, we find Mlle Desjardins in Paris in 1657 or shortly thereafter. Her first publication, a maidenly sonnet on "Les plaisirs que l'on n'a point goustez," appeared in the *Muses illustres* of 1658.[13] In 1659 the *Recueil de portraits* of Sercy published portraits in prose by Mlle Desjardins of a certain "Daphnis," of Mlle Gaboury, and of herself. Her self-portrait, which is quite long, contains some interesting passages:

> Je dirai donc que j'ai la phisionomie heureuse et spirituelle, les yeux noirs et petits, mais pleins de feu; la bouche grande, mais les dents belles, pour ne pas rendre son ouverture désagréable; le teint aussi beau que peut l'être un reste de petite vérole maligne; le tour du visage ovale, les cheveux châtins . . . et la gorge et les mains disposées à être belles, quand j'aurai l'embonpoint, que jusqu'ici mon âge et la grandeur de ma taille m'ont empêché d'avoir. . . . J'aime fort Paris, et passe pourtant assez bien mon temps à la campagne pour y demeurer toute ma vie sans chagrin. . . . J'aime fort à railler et ne me fâche jamais qu'on me raille. . . . Ce qui me divertissoit un jour, m'ennuye un autre, sans que j'en puisse donner d'autre raison, que celle de mon tempérament. . . . Voilà comme je suis faite, ou du moins comme je le crois.[14]

The picture of Mlle Desjardins sketched by herself may be compared with the engravings reproduced by Magne and by Derome. The prettiest portrait is that from the *Recueil de poésies* of 1664. That of Desrochers in 1740 shows an older woman, already running to flesh. Another, by Dewrits, reproduced from the collection *Les Poètes normands* of 1840, is a romantic beautification in keeping with the exaggerated tributes and

earlier, that the *Mémoires de Henriette-Sylvie de Molière* are a dependable autobiography. Arguments against this view are presented in Ch. VII, below. Magne's statement that in the *Mémoires* "toutes les étapes de l'Illustre théâtre sont . . . marquées" is astonishing in view of the fact that no theatre whatever is mentioned in the work. One anecdote related by Tallemant has, however, suggested to some critics that Mlle Desjardins must have played in Molière's troupe in the provinces. Recounting an exchange of words between Molière and Marie-Catherine over the billing to be given her name at the time of the presentation of her *Favory* in 1665, Tallemant quotes her as saying to Molière: "Allez! vous êtes un ingrat; quand vous jouiez à Narbonne, on n'allait à votre théâtre que pour me voir" (*op. cit.*, VII, 256). Writers of the *Moliériste* have taken various positions in the discussion whether Mlle Desjardins actually played in Molière's troupe; the obvious inference from Tallemant's account is that she did, but her name does not appear in any of the documents concerning the *Illustre Théâtre*, and it is impossible to find other evidence to settle the question.

[13] See Frédéric Lachèvre, *Bibliographie des recueils collectifs de poésie*, Paris, 1901-1905, II, 246. Cf. Ch. II, below.

[14] Reproduced in the frères Parfaict, *op. cit.*, IX, 126. The description of Henriette-Sylvie de Molière recalls this self-portrait: "Au reste, je suis grande et de bonne mine; j'ai les yeux noirs et brillans, bien ouverts, bien coupés, et qui marquent assez d'esprit. On jugera si j'en ai. Ma bouche est grande quand je ris, fort petite quand je ne ris point; mais par malheur pour elle, je ris toujours. J'ai les dents belles, le nez bien fait, la gorge comme le teint, c'est-à-dire, admirable. . . ." (*Œuvres*, VII, 7.)

praise of the text. In none is Mlle Desjardins portrayed as beautiful; her figure, as she implies, may have been good, but she must indeed have pleased society by her charm and animation, rather than by her beauty of face.[15]

Literary Paris soon became aware of Mlle Desjardins' presence. As early as June, 1660, Loret wrote of her:

> Ces dames qu'on tient fort belles
> Entrent chez une d'entre elles,
> Savoir l'aimable des Jardins
> Qui plaît à bien des citadins
> Comme ayant de rares lumières
> Et des grâces particulières. . . .[16]

Two years later, Tallemant wrote the sketch of her preserved in the *Historiettes*.[17] It seems clear that during this early period Mlle Desjardins lived with her mother in a furnished room near the Arsenal.[18] There she turned out numerous sonnets, portraits, and epigrams, dedicated to an increasingly important circle of admirers. The *Mss. Conrart* of this period contain many of her pieces, indicating that Mlle de Scudéry had taken notice of her work. Evidence of her popularity as early as the year 1661 is found in the newly published journal of Christian Huygens, the Dutch scientist and savant.[19]

Verse did not long satisfy the growing creative urge of Mlle Desjardins. Year by year her productions grew more varied and more numerous. In 1659 appeared the *Récit* in prose and verse of Molière's *Précieuses ridicules*, a work which still evokes contention among *moliéristes*. Her

[15] Cf. Magne, *op. cit.*, frontispiece, and Derome, *loc. cit.* The source of Desrochers' portrait, on which Dewrits based his romanticized version, is unknown.

[16] Loret, *Gazette*, June 26, 1660 (in *La Muze historique*).

[17] *Op. cit.*, VII, 257 ff. Monmerqué dates the article as of 1662. Tallemant speaks of Mlle Desjardins' "long séjour en province" and says that she has been in Paris for "trois ans ou environ."

[18] Baudeau de Somaize, *Dictionnaire des précieuses*, ed. Charles Livet, Paris, 1856, article "Dinamise" (Mlle Desjardins), which states that the authoress is "logée près du palais de Jupiter," or, according to the *clef*, the Arsenal. Tallemant also mentions a furnished room shared with her mother.

[19] Henri C. Brugmans, *Le Séjour de Christian Huygens à Paris*, Paris, 1935, p. 160. On Mar. 17, 1661, Huygens wrote: "Esté avec Montconis chez le duc de Luines à qui je montray ma lunette d'approche et le microscope. Vismes Chaliot et le mont Valerien . . . ad. d. vu M. Justel qui me donna les clefs de Cyrus et Clélie et des vers de Mlle des Jardins." For Mlle Desjardins' relations with Huygens' father, cf. below and Ch. II.

first novel, *Alcidamie,* appeared in 1661.[20] The accusation that it dealt in *roman à clef* fashion with a notorious scandal in the Rohan family led to the temporary suppression of the work and to numerous complications dealt with elsewhere. In 1662, on the occasion of a "carrousel" given by Louis XIV, Mlle Desjardins devised a child's *Carrousel* for the baby Dauphin. The first *Recueil de poésies de Mlle Desjardins* appeared in 1662. Turning to the theatre, Mlle Desjardins composed a play, *Manlius,* drawing her subject from Livy and receiving some assistance from the abbé d'Aubignac, the lawgiver of the *Pratique du théâtre.* It was presented at the Hôtel de Bourgogne in May, 1662, and occasioned a literary battle involving d'Aubignac, Donneau de Visé, de Villiers, and even Corneille. A second play, *Nitétis,* based on Herodotus' account, was presented at the same theatre on April 27, 1663, attracting little attention. A third, the tragi-comedy *Le Favory,* drawn from a Spanish source, was performed by Molière's troupe in Paris, beginning April 24, 1665, and later at Versailles before the King.[21] The first of her short prose *nouvelles,* a *genre* in which she came to excel, had appeared by this time (*Lisandre*).

Dedications and familiar references in the works of this first period of literary activity give evidence of an ever-widening circle of social and literary relationships. She refers to Mlle de Montbazon, the *président* Bellièvre, Gilles Boileau, Mlle Gaboury, Mme de Morangis, Saint-Aignan, the minister Hugues de Lionne, the Duchesse de Montpensier, the *chancelier* Séguier, Mme de Montglas, Guillaume de Bautru, the abbé du Buisson, d'Aubignac, the Duc and Duchesse de Montausier, M. de Nanteuil, Colbert, and the Comte de Séry. External evidence of her popularity, which became great enough to secure for her a royal pension, permits the list of her admirers to be extended even further.[22]

In the winter of 1660, according to Tallemant's account, Mlle Desjardins met Boesset de Villedieu, a captain in the Dauphin's regiment, and member of a family of court musicians.[23] Mlle Desjardins, already known for her *coquetteries* and *galanteries,* was now to taste the "plaisirs

[20] All these works are discussed in detail in later chapters. Christian Huygens in his *Journal* (see Brugmans, *op. cit.,* p. 155) mentions buying a copy of *Alcidamie* (Feb. 23, 1661). Cf. Ch. III, below.

[21] Mlle Desjardins herself wrote a description of the Versailles presentation. For her dramatic works, see Ch. III, below.

[22] Cf. below, *passim.*

[23] *Op. cit.,* VII, 246. Auguste Jal's *Dictionnaire critique de biographie et d'histoire,* Paris, 1867 (article "Boesset") contains information concerning the family.

que l'on n'a point goustez." The circumstances were curious. The two met at a ball. Villedieu took his leave, only to reappear shortly to say he had forgotten his key and had been unable to awaken his concierge. Mlle Desjardins took him home with her and offered him her bed, going to sleep, presumably, with her mother. During the night Villedieu fell ill, and the next day could not be moved. Before he was well the two had fallen in love, and after Villedieu's recovery they began to live together openly. This is the period of Marie-Catherine's first real experience of passion:

Aujourd'hui dans tes bras j'ay demeuré pâmée;
Aujourd'hui, cher Tircis, ton amoureuse ardeur
Triomphe impunément de toute ma pudeur
Et je cède aux transports dont mon âme est charmée. . . .[24]

Eventually the question of marriage arose. The major difficulty confronting the couple was Villedieu's previous marriage to a certain Mlle de Fez, or Faïs, daughter of a Paris notary. Villedieu, apparently, expected to obtain an annulment, and caused the banns for his marriage to Marie-Catherine to be published, when he was suddenly recalled to his regiment. There are many versions of what happened at this point. The frères Parfaict state that Mlle Desjardins followed Villedieu to his garrison in Flanders and there lived with him. The *BUR* alleges that Marie-Catherine pursued her lover disguised as a man. Hauréau has them married by a "pasteur hollandais." Desnos pictures the jealous Villedieu killed in a duel with a rival for his mistress' affections. At all events, when the lovers reappeared in Paris, Mlle Desjardins had adopted the name of Mme de Villedieu and claimed to be his legal wife.[25] Though they were separated from time to time before Villedieu's death, Marie-Catherine's feeling for Boesset seems indeed to have been "la seule vraiment sincère et durable [affection] de sa vie."[26]

[24] From the *Recueil de Sercy* of 1660; not in the *Œuvres*. Reproduced in the notes to Monmerqué's edition of Tallemant, in Brun, *op. cit.*, and in Magne. Somaize (*loc. cit.*) wrote: "Elle a fait du bruit dans Athènes par des *Jouissances* qui passent pour estre fort agréables." There is another sonnet with the title "Jouissance" in Mlle Desjardins' *Journal amoureux*. The form was a popular one at the time. The *Mss. Conrart* contain "Jouissances" by various authors, many of the poems "nettement pornographiques" (Magne).

[25] Tallemant, *op. cit.*, VII, 248; frères Parfaict, *op. cit.*, X, 132. *BUR*, February, 1776, p. 194. Desnos, *op. cit.*, II, 621. B. Hauréau, *Histoire littéraire du Maine*, Paris, 1870-1877, IV, article "Desjardins." Cf. also Titon du Tillet, Richelet, Bayle, Goujet, Clogenson, Brun, Magne, Chatenet, and Gallier (see the Bibliography).

[26] Magne, *op. cit.*, p. 168. A curious side light on the affair is thrown by several

The *"histoire intérieure"* of the relationship may be pieced together from the verses composed at this time. Mlle Desjardins, despite her real passion for Villedieu, was forced gradually to feign a pose of inconstancy and insouciance which became characteristic. There were infidelities on the part of the lover, separations, reunions, reproaches, and

interesting passages, not hitherto mentioned by historians of Mlle Desjardins' career, in the *Archives de la Bastille*, ed. Fr.-N. Ravaisson, Paris, 1866-1891, regarding Mlle de Faïs, Villedieu's legitimate wife. Vol. VI, 8 ff., gives the following testimony by the notorious la Voisin, "sorceress" and dealer in abortive powders and poisons (it was she who accused Racine of causing the death of la Du Parc, his mistress). The inquiry is dated Oct. 10, 1679, and proceeds:

"—Si elle (la Voisin) connaît Mme de Villedieu?

"—Oui, elle la connaît depuis longtemps. . . . Elle lui a dit qu'elle n'avait pas trop d'amitié pour son mari. . . .

"—Si elle ne sait pas que V. avait dessein de s'en défaire? (Non.)" ["V." here evidently means *Mme* de Villedieu, *passim.*]

"—Si V. ne lui a point parlé du dessein qu'elle avait d'empoisonner M. de Loynes, président à Metz?

"—Non, mais elle se souvient bien qu'un jour V., se peignant, étant lors logée vers les Petits-Frères, parla en colère d'un homme qu'elle ne nomma point, et lui dit que si elle pouvait le faire crever, elle le ferait. V. est un esprit pernicieux, et menteuse. . . ."

Later (p. 121) appears a "Ms. écrit par Desgrez, sous la dictée de Lesage, 13 janvier, 1680, à Vincennes," in which the foregoing Mlle de Faïs is apparently confused with Mlle Desjardins. The questions still refer to la Voisin:

"Si, pendant les affaires qu'elle avait entreprises pour ces dames de Polignac et d'Artigny contre la dame de la Vallière, si elle ne s'est pas servie de la Defays [*sic*, for "de Faïs"] dite la Villedieu, qui fait des vers, laquelle disait en avoir présenté au Roi, qui les avait agréés par son frère, qui est musicien de la musique du Roi, et si elle, Voisin, ne lui a pas donné des placets pour lui présenter, afin d'avoir entrée chez madame de la Vallière.

"Si la Villedieu n'était pas du parti de cette robe d'empereur pour couvrir leur malice, et si elle n'a pas été, la Villedieu, elle y compris le chevalier de Bernières et Ravetot qui allèrent chez MM de Riantz et d'Effita, dénoncer contre Lesage pour lui empêcher de parler, afin de le faire périr par le crédit de la Villedieu, comme étant leur putain et maquerelle.

"Sur ce sujet, je n'en parlerai plus jamais, mais croyez-moi, tirez de la cour la Villedieu, si aimez votre Roi; elle se retire d'ordinaire chez Pietre, vendeur de marée. . . . La V. et la Voisin sont de société dès il y a plus de vingt ans avec la Courtin, *distillateuse.* . . ."

On July 29 of the same year (p. 252) appears the questioning of "Marg. de Faïs, veuve de M. de Villedieu, âgée de 34-35 ans." The editors of the *Archives* add the following note: "Le père de M. de Faïs était notaire à Paris—elle épousa en 1660 Boesset de Villedieu, fils du surintendant de la musique du roi, et mort en 1669. . . . Nous n'avons pas pu découvrir s'il avait suivi le cours ordinaire de la nature, ou si l'habileté de sa femme avait précipité le dénouement de l'intrigue [with Mlle Desjardins]. . . . Mme de Villedieu, la femme légitime, qui était plus jeune et plus riche que sa rivale, paraît avoir supporté héroïquement la trahison et la mort de son époux. . . ." This is the interrogatory:

". . . Despuis quand elle a connu la Voisin?

"—Elle n'a été qu'une seule fois chez la Voisin, et pour se faire regarder à la main.

"Si elle ne sait pas que Duverger est morte après avoir pris des poudres qui lui furent données par Javotte [*femme de chambre* of Marguerite de Faïs] de sa part, pour se faire avorter?

forgivenesses.[27] We cannot be certain how long they lived together, nor do we know when Villedieu died. It seems likely that a semi-permanent separation took place sometime in 1664, and that Villedieu died in 1667, or shortly thereafter.[28]

Contemporary accounts credit Mlle Desjardins with other suitors, if not lovers: the abbé du Buisson, the archaeologist Sauval, an unidentified *mousquetaire*, among others.[29] Sometime about the year 1664, the author-ess made the acquaintance of René Le Pays, a native of Grenoble, *intendant des gabelles*, and man of letters. The relationship seems to have been entirely literary and intellectual; Le Pays sent Marie-Catherine books to read, and received in turn a copy of "cette agréable *Sylvie*" which appears to be the first draft of at least a portion of the *Mémoires de la vie de Henriette-Sylvie de Molière*, evidently begun at this time.[30] The work refers to Grenoble as the home of many of the heroine's friends, a fact which suggests that Marie-Catherine may have spent some time in that city. The *Mémoires* also refer to an encounter, on the way to Paris

"Non, et il y a 12 ans que Javotte est hors d'auprès d'elle, et ne sait pas de quoi est morte la Duverger."
And so on. Marguerite de Faïs denied another charge that she had sought to further the advantageous marriage of a man whose wife had died mysteriously. On p. 385 of the same volume she is accused by Mariette, one of la Voisin's group, of plotting the death of Lesage and of Mme de Loynes. Lesage accused her of buying poisons from Mariette.
The records of the affair end here. Obviously Mlle Desjardins was not in any way connected with la Voisin or with the *affaire des poisons*, but the slight involvement of the real Mme de Villedieu has led to some confusion on this point. Magne attempted to investigate the matter, but his mistaken version of the name of the real witness, which he gives as Marguerite de *Saye*, prevented his realization that Ville-dieu's legitimate wife was the one indicted (cf. *op. cit.*, p. 389, note).
[27] Cf. especially the first *Recueil de poésies* (*Œuvres*, II, 159 ff.) and see Ch. II, below.
[28] Jean Robinet's *Lettre* of Sept. 4, 1667, reproduced in Baron James de Roth-schild's *Les Continuateurs de Loret*, Paris, 1833, mentions the death of a Villedieu at the siege of Lille. At the same time Mlle Desjardins deplores the death of a person dear to her (*Recueil de lettres*, ed. 1669, pp. 207 ff.). Jal writes: "Je n'ai pas pu savoir quand mourut ce Villedieu." The *privilège* of the *Amours des grands hommes* (dated Dec. 4, 1670) is accorded to "la dame des Jardins, veuve du feu sieur de Villedieu." (Reproduced by Derome, *op. cit.*) Gallier (*op. cit.*, p. 34) repeats Desnos' story that Villedieu was killed in a duel.
[29] Cf. the letter in *Œuvres*, II, 229 ff.; Somaize, *op. cit.* Magne, *op. cit.*, p. 178, mentions an accusation of lesbianism brought against Mlle Desjardins, a charge based on two poems written as if by a man, but fails to state the source of the allega-tion. The *Lettres* refer to the attentions of various suitors.
[30] Cf. René Le Pays, *Nouvelles œuvres de M. Le Pays*, Paris, 1715, and Magne, *op. cit.*, pp. 250 ff., where Le Pays' letters are reproduced. Le Pays was aware of Mlle Desjardins' interest in Villedieu, whom he terms her "amant," and seems to have felt no jealousy. The *Mémoires* appeared anonymously in 1672, and Le Pays' letter is the clearest evidence of their authorship. Cf. Ch. IX, below.

from Grenoble, with the eccentric poet Des Barreaux. The notorious *esprit fort* is depicted as talkative, cynical about women, full of gossip, and outspoken in his opinions.[31]

Evidences of Mlle Desjardins' popularity appear with increasing frequency at this period. Saint-Pavin, freethinker and friend of Des Barreaux, wrote this tribute to the authoress:

MADRIGAL

Plus je relis ce que vous faites,
Plus je connois ce que vous êtes,
Il ne faut que vous mettre en train.
Tout le monde, Iris, vous admire,
Si les Dieux se mêloient d'écrire
Ils emprunteroient votre main,
Vous faites des choses si belles,
Si justes et si naturelles,
Que votre style est sans égal:
Sans cesse je vous estudie,
Qui peut estre votre copie
Passe pour un original.[32]

The *recueils* of the day clamored for her verses; scarcely one, from the *Recueil de Sercy* to Corbinelli's alphabetical anthology (with poems grouped under *absence, beauté, colère, crainte,* etc.), appeared without a contribution from her hand.[33] Jean de la Forge in his *Cercle des femmes sçavantes* (1663) lauds in this fashion the "aimable Aréthuse," whom he identifies as Mlle Desjardins:

J'ai dit dans mes Vers qu'elle estoit une dixième Muse, mais quant ie considère tous ses divers Ouvrages, son Roman, ses pièces de Theatre, ses Eglogues, ses Lettres, et tant d'autres œuvres galantes, i'ose dire qu'elle a surpassé toutes les Muses ensemble.[34]

---

[31] *Œuvres*, VII, 264. Magne places this meeting in 1664, as does Lachèvre in his *Disciples et successeurs de Théophile de Viau (Des Barreaux et Saint-Pavin)*, Paris, 1911. The heroine of the *Mémoires*, however, on her arrival in Paris hears of the death of Hugues de Lionne, which occurred early in 1671. Tallemant (*op. cit.*, VII, 256) puts Marie-Catherine's return to Paris "vers Pasques" in 1665. Perhaps the authoress juggled her chronology a bit: another indication that the *Mémoires* must not be regarded as reliable autobiography.

[32] In Lachèvre, *Disciples et successeurs de Théophile . . .*, p. 418. Also in Richelet, *op. cit.*, Brun, *op. cit.*, and Hauréau, *op. cit.*, where it is mistakenly assigned to Titon du Tillet. A similar tribute by Étienne Pavillon appears in his *Œuvres*, Paris, 1750, II, 2 ("Madrigal").

[33] Cf. Lachèvre, *Bibliographie des recueils . . .* and see Ch. II, below.

[34] Jean de la Forge, *Cercle des femmes sçavantes*, Paris, 1663, p. 14. Cf. also the poem in the same place.

In the same year, Guéret's guide to celebrities of the court speaks of her as "l'une des grâces."[35] Sorel in 1664 cites her among the lesser authors of the day.[36] In 1668 her name appeared on the list of possible pensioners drawn up by the abbé de Pure.[37] In various connections, her name and works are mentioned by numerous writers, including Tallemant, Huygens, Somaize, d'Aubignac, Donneau de Visé, Brébeuf, Gilles Boileau, Voiture, and René Le Pays.[38] Brueys in his play *Le Muet* has one of the characters quote four lines from her *Fables*.[39] Boursault in a letter refers at length to her novel *Alcidamie*.[40] A treatise on style which appeared in 1668 contains a eulogy of her "invention belle et hardie," her "prose magnifique et éloquente," and her "très-belle mémoire."[41] Huet refers to her in his history of the novel, published as a preface to *Zaïde* in 1670. Martin de Pinchesne wrote:

> Reçoy, célèbre des Jardins,
> Dont les talents sont tous divins
> En fait de vers et d'écriture
> Ceux-ci qui, te venant de moy,
> Viennent du neveu de Voiture,
> Et, pour les agréer, c'est assez dire à toy.[42]

Samuel Chappuzeau's *Théâtre françois* of 1674 praises her plays. Her celebrity is attested in 1677 by a eulogy in the *Quatrains* of Michel de Marolles.[43] Richelet, Titon du Tillet, and Pierre Bayle are among her

[35] Gabriel Guéret, *La Carte de la Cour*, Paris, 1663, p. 35. Mlle Desjardins is "Pomone."

[36] Charles Sorel, *Bibliothèque françoise*, Paris, 1664, p. 187. Mlle Desjardins is placed beside Quinault, Boyer, and Gilbert. Sorel also mentions Mlle Desjardins in his *De la connoissance des bons livres*, Amsterdam, 1672.

[37] Lancaster, *op. cit.*, III (I), 15, and the abbé de Pure, *Idée des spectacles*, Paris, 1668, p. 165. Mlle Desjardins is listed with Desmaretz, Molière, and Racine, "qui ont droit aux plus justes louanges qu'on ait jamais données."

[38] Cf. below, *passim*. Georges de Brébeuf's *Œuvres*, Paris, 1664, II, 108, contain a laudatory *Lettre de Mlle Desjardins*, with an acknowledgment. Magne states (*op. cit.*, p. 123) that Mlle Desjardins' *Annales galantes de Grèce* (1687) contain a reference to Brébeuf, but I cannot find it in the novel as printed in the *Œuvres complètes* (cf. Ch. VIII, below).

[39] David-A. de Brueys, *Œuvres de M. Brueys*, Paris, 1735, II, 170; cf. Ch. II, below.

[40] E. Boursault, *Lettres de Babet*, Lyons, 1715-1720, III, 59; cf. Ch. III, below.

[41] Marguerite Buffet, *Nouvelles observations sur la langue françoise*, Paris, 1668, pp. 274-275, "Éloge de Mlle Desjardins."

[42] *Œuvres de Martin de Pinchesne* (*additions de quelques pièces nouvelles faites depuis l'impression*), Paris, n.d., p. 37; reproduced by Magne, *op. cit.*, p. 362.

[43] Cf. Magne, *op. cit.*, p. 364.

early biographers.[44] Her patronesses included, at least at one time, so great a personage as Henriette d'Angleterre.[45]

At the beginning of spring, 1667, in the midst of this growing fame and popularity, Mlle Desjardins suddenly left France for the Low Countries. Her extensive trip is described fully in the *Recueil de quelques lettres ou relations galantes,* which her publisher Barbin issued in 1668, with a dedication to Mlle de Sévigné.[46] The motive for the trip cannot be definitely established. Most of the letters suggest travel for its own sake, but several references to a lawsuit at Amsterdam imply a more practical reason.[47] Twenty of the thirty letters are dated from specific places (covering the period from "Bruxelles le 1 Avril" to "Huy le 12 Octobre"). The remaining ten contain internal evidence of time and place. The bare facts of her visit may be reconstructed as follows: Arriving in Brussels on April 1, she spends a month enjoying the sights of the city in company with Gourville, formerly attached to the disgraced Fouquet, and others. She tutors the son of the Comtesse de Marcin in the *galanteries* of polite conduct, and composes a long defence of Boileau's satires, then under attack in Paris.[48] Hearing that the "Dames de la Cour de Bruxelles" have expressed some astonishment at her behavior, and much curiosity concerning her literary talents, she rapidly sets down a prose *nouvelle*

---

[44] Cf. below, Bayle's *Dictionnaire,* and his reviews in the *Journal des sçavans* and the *Nouvelles de la république des lettres,* referred to in the following chapters.

[45] The Bibliothèque de la Rochelle contains a Ms. entitled "Noël, Mme le fit faire à Mlle des Jardins en sa présence." Cited by Magne, *op. cit.,* p. 220.

[46] Cf. Ch. II, below. Barbin claims to be printing the letters "en son absence," but Mlle Desjardins appears already to have returned to Paris, since the last letters are written from that city. Bayle in his *Dictionnaire* makes the curious mistake of confusing Mlle Desjardins with a homonym in the Low Countries (cf. n. 50, below). He writes: "Il y a eu dans les Pais-Bas Espagnol une Demoiselle des Jardins contemporaine de celle-là." Bayle had not known the authoress personally, and his article was written after 1699, but it seems strange that he was unfamiliar with the *Recueil de lettres* and with the fact that Marie-Catherine had visited Flanders. Since later editions of the *Œuvres complètes* all failed to contain the *Recueil de lettres,* Bayle doubtless had never seen a copy of the work.

[47] Cf. *Recueil de lettres,* p. 82 ("mon procez d'Amsterdam va . . . lentement," etc.). Magne states that research through the French consul at Amsterdam failed to reveal records of any suit or litigation involving Mlle Desjardins (*op. cit.,* p. 327). The heroine of the *Mémoires* goes to Flanders to sue for a contested heritage, but the *Lettres* give no hint that such was the case with Mlle Desjardins herself. One letter (p. 209) refers to "la perte de mon bien," a possible reference to loss of a lawsuit.

[48] Only Mlle Desjardins' itinerary and experiences of biographical interest are presented here; the *Lettres* are discussed more fully in Ch. II, below. No page references are given for statements based directly on the *Recueil de lettres;* but collateral or supplementary material is cited in the notes.

entitled *Anaxandre,* dedicating it to the ladies with the hope that they will think less harshly of her.[49]

Her next sojourn is in Antwerp, where she is entertained and escorted by the Prince d'Aremberg, the Duc d'Arschot, the Baron d'Ysola, and the Marquis de Castel-Rodrigo, Spanish governor of the Pays-Bas. "Monsieur de la N. . . ," probably Pierre Tissier de la Nogerette, brother-in-law of Gourville, arranges her trip to Holland "jusqu'à pourvoir aux meubles de ma Barque." By May 25, she is in Amsterdam, where she announces she will stay until the end of her "procez." The next letter finds her at The Hague on June 7, brimming over with impressions of Rotterdam, Leiden, Delft, the collections of Rubens and Weenix at The Hague, its library of rare books, etc.

At last able to meet "l'Alexandre de mon Idée," the elder Huygens, Sieur de Zuylichem, she establishes a friendship with him, stops for a while at his estate, and visits the curiosities of The Hague in his company.[50] She overflows in praise of his munificence and learning. Returning to Belgium by way of the military fortress of Breda, she proceeds to Liége, stopping with the Comte and Comtesse de Marcin at their estate of Modave, near by. The bourgeois of Liége seem to have shared the suspicions formerly expressed by the ladies of Brussels concerning the character of the Parisian authoress, for she is forced to produce letters from the minister Lionne "sur l'intégrité de mes sentiments, pour dissiper le nuage que la vivacité de mon esprit avoit élevé

---

[49] *Anaxandre* is not mentioned in the *Recueil de lettres;* these facts appear in the dedicatory epistle of the *rarissime* copy in the Library of Congress. See Ch. VI, below. Mlle Desjardins had left the society of the "prudes" of Brussels before the appearance of the story (*achevé,* June 20, 1667).

[50] Cf. Ch. II, below. Magne assumes that the elder Zuylichem, poet and diplomat, being at the time too old to guide Mlle Desjardins about, turned her over to Christian Huygens, with whom she became friendly (*op. cit.,* pp. 317 ff.). This hypothesis is disproved by a letter from Christian, in Paris at the time, to his brother Lodewijk, apparently in answer to a letter of inquiry concerning Mlle Desjardins. He writes: "Je n'ay encore rien à vous dire touchant ce que vous me demandez de Madame de Villedieu, mais je m'informeray." (Letter dated Paris, May 20, 1667, in *Œuvres de Christian Huygens,* La Haye, 1888, VI, 130.) Unfortunately no further mention of the matter occurs, although in 1669 Christian mentions her name again, apparently in reference to an unpaid debt dating from her stay with his father: "Ces commissions sont aisée, et je voudrois que celles du Signor Padre fussent de cette sorte au lieu qu'il m'envoie icy à redemander 10 pistoles qu'il a prestées à la des Jardins lors qu'elle estoit à la Haye" (*ibid.,* p. 471, letter dated Paris, July 5, 1669). The annotator of Huygens' works identifies "la des Jardins" with a certain Marie Cadenne, wife of a sculptor sometimes known by the name Desjardins. The reasons for this identification are not given; it seems more likely that the person referred to was Mlle Desjardins the authoress.

dans le leur." She speaks of working for six weeks on a tragedy entitled *Agis*, the first act of which she has completed.[51]

On July 1 Mlle Desjardins reached the famous watering place of Spa, where she appears to have gone through a spell of depression and melancholia, even entertaining fancifully the possibility of having her doctor poison her in a sort of mercy killing, leaving her epitaph to be read by "quelque Perse caterreux, ou . . . quelque Armenien tourmenté de Nefretique." It is impossible to divine the reasons for her mood. Gradually her spirits improve, and within the month we find the letters once more full of *galanterie* and banter on amorous topics. Mlle Desjardins congratulates herself on ending her affair with Gourville "sans avoir appris à dissimuler." Two letters protest to a lady of Spa against her constant efforts to force upon Marie-Catherine the attentions of a "redoutable Garçon" for whom she has no taste. A large number of verses appear, written apparently in order to repay social obligations incurred at Spa.

By October she has transferred her residence to Huy. Here serious thoughts again occupy her mind; she devotes one letter to the discussion of Divine Providence and the Last Judgment, and another to her grief over the loss of certain *biens de famille* and of persons dear to her, one of whom may have been Villedieu.[52] Her associations continue with the Comtesse de Marcin. She composes verses for the "Marquise de F * * *" and other ladies, attends a carnival, and writes an account in verse of its pastoral ballet.

The last three letters are obviously written in Paris, but no dates are given, and her return to France cannot be dated with absolute certainty. One letter concerns the quarrel over the attempt to suppress Mlle Desjardins' first novel, *Alcidamie*, which the Rohan family took to be a *roman à clef* dealing with the scandalous story of Tancrède de Rohan's sequestration.[53] The collection ends with an unimportant note to a "demoiselle" forced to live away from her lover.

A new period of literary fertility followed Mlle Desjardins' return to Paris. After the *Recueil de lettres* came one of her longest novels,

---

[51] Whatever *Agis* may have been, no trace of it is left. Magne (*op. cit.*, p. 337) makes the strange error of identifying *Agis* with *Anaxandre*, the *nouvelle* mentioned above.

[52] It is hard to be sure how many deaths Marie-Catherine is mourning. Evidently her father's is one, for one passage mentions "la mort de mon Pere, et . . . les autres trépas que vous sçavez que je dois pleurer." (*Recueil de lettres*, p. 209.)

[53] See Ch. III, below.

Carmante (1668), dedicated to the Duchesse de Nemours. The next year yielded the *Nouveau recueil de pièces galantes,* containing a large number of new poems dedicated to court celebrities, *Cléonice, nouvelle,* and the first of her historical novels, the *Journal amoureux.* Towards the end of the year 1669, the minister Hugues de Lionne succeeded in obtaining for Marie-Catherine a pension of 1500 livres from the King. In 1670 the *Annales galantes* appeared, dedicated to Lionne as a gesture of gratitude. To Louis XIV Mlle Desjardins addressed the volume of *Fables* issued in the same year, and duly prefaced it with a pompous dedicatory epistle in the usual style:

> Mais, grand Monarque, ma puissance
> S'accorde mal à ma reconnaisance;
> Je fais ce que je puis, et non ce que je dois. . . .[54]

In 1671, her protector Hugues de Lionne died. A passage in the *Mémoires de la vie de Henriette-Sylvie de Molière* (1672) reads: "Ah, Madame, quelle perte pour moy! Le généreux et puissant protecteur que j'avois en ce digne ministre. . . ."[55]

Seeking to continue in Louis' favor, Mlle Desjardins dedicated to him the *Amours des grands hommes* (1671), referring in the dedication to the "manière obligeante" in which the monarch had received the "offrande" of the *Fables* in 1670.

At this point a new edition of the *Journal amoureux* made its appearance, containing between two of the volumes an unusual statement by the authoress concerning the authenticity of various works currently attributed to her. She presents the public with the following check list of authentic works:

> Alcidamie
> Recueil de poésies diverses
> trois pièces de théâtre
> Lisandre
> Cléonice
> Anaxandre
> Carmante
> quelques lettres sur la Flandre
> deuxième recueil de poésies

---

[54] *Œuvres,* I, *Fables* (p. 336). A later "Placet" to Colbert, requesting payment of her pension, suggests that Mlle Desjardins found it rather difficult to collect her award. The list of pensioners for the period 1664-1683, given by Clément in *Lettres, instructions et mémoires de Colbert,* Paris, 1868, V, 466 ff., fails to mention Mlle Desjardins.

[55] *Œuvres,* VII, 280.

le Carrousel
trois Parties (II, V, VI) du Journal amoureux
les Annales galantes (I, II, III, IV)
deux tomes des Amours des grands hommes[56]

Except for its failure to mention the *Récit de la farce des Précieuses* (1659) and the *Fables* (1670), both of which are certainly hers, the list appears to be quite accurate. Her contention that certain portions of the *Journal amoureux* and other works are not hers is perhaps questionable.[57] Mlle Desjardins does not mention the titles falsely attributed to her, but it is possible through the use of external evidence to compile a list of about ten works which have been wrongly included among her productions. Some of these appeared before 1671, others at later dates, one or two persistently recurring in editions of her *Œuvres complètes*.[58]

Although the *privilège* of the *Mémoires de la vie de Henriette-Sylvie de Molière* is of the same year as the works mentioned above, the novel was not published until 1672, and hence does not appear on the list.[59] In 1672 one of the most widely circulated of Mlle Desjardins' novels, the

[56] List as transcribed by Derome, *loc. cit.*, as it appears between *Parties V* and *VI* of the 1671 edition of the *Journal amoureux*, a *rarissime* edition not available in this country or in the Bib. Nat. A reference to the above list appears in Bayle's *Nouvelles lettres sur le calvinisme*, Amsterdam, 1715, II, 735: "Une de nos amies . . . s'emporta un peu contre le *Journal amoureux* . . . et nous dit qu'il estoit fort scandaleux qu'une femme fît imprimer de telles histoires. Nous lui montrâmes pour l'apaiser la préface d'un tome de ce *Journal* où Mme de Villedieu renonce pour une de ses productions un des tomes précédents dans lequel il y avoit des choses un peu trop libres." In the earliest editions each *Partie* formed one *tome*.

[57] See Ch. V, below.

[58] De Visé's *Jaloux par force*, mistakenly attributed to Mlle Desjardins by Magne, probably because it appeared in a *recueil* of Bontemps in 1668 along with a poem by her entitled *La Revue des Troupes d'amour*, mentioned in Lachèvre's *Bibliographie des recueils* . . .; Vaumorière's *Comte de Dunois*, also called *Mlle d'Alençon*; Deschamps' *Mémoires du sérail*; *Astérie, ou Tamerlan*, by Mlle de la Roche; *Dom Carlos* by Saint-Réal; Vaumorière's *Mlle de Tournon*; Boursault's *Prince de Condé*; *L'Illustre Parisienne*, by Préchac; Mlle de la Roche's *Journal amoureux d'Espagne*; *Les Nouvelles et galanteries chinoises*, anonymous (Lyons, Baritel, 1712). Cf. Derome, *loc. cit.*, and the article in the *Journal des sçavans* of Dec. 17, 1703, on attributions to Mlle Desjardins. These works are mentioned in the appropriate chapters below. As recent a critic as Chatenet devotes many pages to a discussion of Préchac's *Illustre Parisienne*. Mlle Desjardins' list offers additional evidence that the date assigned by Magne to the *Annales galantes de Grèce* (1668, taken from J. G. Theodor Graesse's *Trésor de livres rares*, Berlin, 1922, VI [II], 321) is incorrect, since the work is not mentioned (see Ch. VIII, below). The same is true of *Le Portefeuille*, which is dated by Magne 1668, but contains a reference to the death of Chapelain, which did not occur until 1674. It would also seem that the date of the first edition of *Les Désordres de l'amour*, which has a certain importance in the problem of the source of Mme de La Fayette's *Princesse de Clèves*, cannot be 1670, as given by Graesse, but is probably the next earliest date mentioned, 1675 (see Ch. V, below).

[59] Derome, *loc. cit.*, reproduces the *privilège*, dated June 29, 1671.

Exilez de la cour d'Auguste, was published. The *Galanteries grenadines,* a novel in the style of Scudéry's *Almahide,* appeared in 1673. A *nouvelle* in letter form, *Le Portefeuille,* may be dated late 1674 or early 1675. *Les Désordres de l'amour* made its appearance in 1675.

Suddenly Mlle Desjardins ceased, if not to write, at least to publish. Her remaining works all appeared posthumously: the *Portrait des foiblesses humaines* in 1685, the *Annales galantes de Grèce* in 1687, and the *Nouvelles africuaines* at some uncertain date after 1685.

The reason for this withdrawal from an active literary career may be found in the events of the last phase of her life. Shortly after 1675 one of her friends, a certain Mme Thévart, dissatisfied with her widow's state, and possessing a small fortune, persuaded Marie-Catherine to find a likely youth who would be willing to marry her. In the midst of the transaction Mme Thévart suddenly died. Mlle Desjardins was overcome by shame and misgiving. At the suggestion of a monk, she requested and obtained from Monseigneur de Harlay, Archbishop of Paris, permission to enter a convent. Hardly was she inside when the brother of a nun recognized her and complained to the Mother Superior of the presence in her cloisters of a woman notorious for her scandalous writings and for her affairs with men. Monseigneur de Harlay was prevailed upon to order her dismissal from the convent.[60]

Mme de Saint-Romain, Villedieu's sister-in-law, offered her refuge. Shortly thereafter she met the Marquis Claude-Nicholas de Chaste, Seigneur de Chaalons, a poverty-stricken noble who, according to one account, was already married to the daughter of a rich shoemaker. After a brief acquaintance, Mlle Desjardins and the Marquis decided to be married. If indeed Chaste already had a wife, the difficulty was in some way surmounted, for the marriage of Claude-Nicholas de Chaste and Marie-Catherine Desjardins was celebrated with the permission of Monseigneur de Harlay at Notre-Dame in Paris on August 17, 1677.[61]

[60] Barbin's *Recueil* of 1692 and Richelet's *Les Plus belles lettres françoises,* Paris, 1698, mention this incident briefly. It was expanded by the frères Parfaict (*op. cit.,* IX, 132) and Goujet (*op. cit.,* XVIII, 128 ff.). Hauréau, Desnos, Clogenson, Gallier, Magne, and others repeat the account.

[61] Goujet (*loc. cit.*) states that Chaste had abandoned the shoemaker's daughter when the amount promised as her dowry was not paid. He also writes that the "deux Amans" concealed their marriage, which took place "à dix ou douze lieues de Paris." Anatole de Gallier (*op. cit.,* pp. 44-50) affirms that Claude-Nicholas was unmarried at the time he met Mlle Desjardins, and cites the notarized record of their marriage in Paris on the date given above. Mlle Desjardins' death certificate, as reproduced by Derome, *loc. cit.,* speaks of her as the legitimate wife of de Chaste. Magne

A son was soon born to Marie-Catherine, now Marquise de Chaste, but while the child was still in swaddling clothes, the Marquis died. In her misfortune Marie-Catherine turned to the Marquis' aged father, suggesting to him in a letter that he come to Paris and spend his remaining days with her.[62] Chaalons answered from his estate in Dauphiné proposing instead that she bring her child to live with him, and Marie-Catherine accepted the invitation. It seems indeed rather more than likely that she expected something of the kind. The old man made a new will leaving his fortune to her, to be turned over in due time to "l'enfant nommé de Chaste." The child, however, did not long survive its father, and the elder Marquis de Chaste appears to have annulled his will.[63] Marie-Catherine soon left her father-in-law, and, after passing through Paris, went to live with her mother on their little property of Clinchemaure, near Alençon. Titon du Tillet, Goujet, and other biographers relate that she re-established relations with the cousin with whom she had had her first affair, and finally married him, but this legend is demonstrably false.[64]

(op. cit., pp. 385-387) accepts Goujet's account of the defaulting shoemaker's daughter. Gallier traces the ancestry of the Chaste family as far back as Aiman de Chaste (governor of Dieppe in 1589, later ambassador to England under Henri IV in 1603) whose bastard son, legitimized by the King in 1615, married Catherine du Port du Mourier, by whom he had Claude-Nicholas de Chaste, Seigneur de Chaalons.

[62] This letter was discovered by Gallier and first published in the *Bulletin de la Société archéologique de la Drôme*, April, 1883, p. 119. Gallier was accused of falsification by Augustin Gazier in an article, "Mme de Villedieu," *Bulletin du comité des travaux historiques et scientifiques*, 1883, No. 1, p. 50, but answered the charge in his own *Mme de Villedieu* of the same year. Magne reproduces the letter (op. cit., p. 387). It reads in part: À Paris, le 9 janvier 1679

Hélas, monsieur, de quels termes et de quelle encre me servirai-je pour vous annoncer la triste nouvelle que j'ay à vous dire. Le pauvre M. de Chaalons mourut jeudi. . . . Il est temps de vous dire que je l'épousay par permission extraordinaire de Mgr l'archivesque de Paris, le 16 [sic] d'aoust de l'année 1677 . . . et que pendant ce temps Dieu nous a donné un fils qui a presentement six mois. . . .

Venez achever vos jours avec moi. . . . S'il ne tient qu'à vous aller chercher moy-mesme pour vous faire faire le voyage avec moins d'incommodité, je partiray aussitôt après votre reponse.

There seems to be no reason to doubt the authenticity of the letter. Its orthographic peculiarities (*moi, moy, servirai, partiray*, etc.) merely reflect the uncertainty and indifference of the period in such matters. The phrase "Il est temps de vous dire que je l'épousay" would seem to add some weight to Goujet's allegation that the marriage was kept secret because of Chaste's first wife.

[63] Cf. Gallier, *op. cit.*, p. 49.

[64] Titon du Tillet, *Description du parnasse françois*, Paris, 1727, p. 360; Goujet, *op. cit.*, XVIII, 131. Magne, *op. cit.*, pp. 390 ff., depicts her as resuming her former affair without marriage. As Lancaster first pointed out (*op. cit.*, III [II], 559), her death certificate proves that she was publicly recognized as the widow of de Chaste, and could not have married her cousin.

The last years of Mlle Desjardins' life were spent quietly at Clinche-maure. To divert herself Marie-Catherine composed several new works, but it is doubtful whether she intended to publish them. The "Avis du libraire" which serves as preface to her posthumous *Portrait des foiblesses humaines* (1685) confirms this opinion:

> Quelques amis de Mme de Châte, qui étoit autrefois Mme de Villedieu, sçachant sa resolution de ne plus rien faire imprimer, et n'ignorant pas toutefois que par une espèce de délassement d'esprit elle composoit encore quelque Ouvrages, ont en son absence volé son cabinet, et m'ont apporté les Ouvrages nouveaux que je vous présente. Elle me voudra sans doute du mal. . . .[65]

Hauréau describes the study, at the top of a tower, where she withdrew to work, and relates that it was still pointed out (around 1852) by the people of Alençon.[66]

On October 20, 1683, Mlle Desjardins died. She was buried in the nearby parish of Saint-Remy-du-Plain. The death certificate published by Derome removes all doubt concerning this much disputed date.[67]

Within a month, Donneau de Visé announced her death in the *Mercure galant*, extolling her "manière d'écrire aussi galante que tendre," and stating that her publisher Barbin still had manuscript works of hers which he intended to publish.[68] Pierre Bayle in October, 1684, published an article praising the works of "la défunte Dame des Jardins."[69] At about the same time, the Ricovrati Academy of Padova, known as the

---

[65] Ed. of Desbordes, Amsterdam, 1686. I assume this "Avis" was the work of Barbin who first published the novel in 1685 (Derome, *loc. cit.*, gives the *privilège* as of Aug. 14, 1685, and accorded to "*feue* Mme de Villedieu"), though I have not seen Barbin's edition. The phrase "Elle me voudra sans doute du mal" clashes with the fact of her death in 1683, and can only be explained by the assumption that the notice was written before that date. The "theft" of Mss. from Mlle Desjardins' desk may be regarded as a conventional publisher's exaggeration.

[66] *Op. cit.*, IV, 224.

[67] Derome, *loc. cit.* The document is folio No. 3 of the records of Saint-Remy-du-Plain for 1683. It is clear that the date of 1692 which Desnos assigns to Mlle Desjardins' death (alleging documentary evidence) must have been the date of the death of her mother, Catherine Ferrand Desjardins. (Desnos, article "Orne," in *La France*, 1834.)

[68] *Mercure galant*, November, 1683. De Visé specifically refers to the *Portrait des foiblesses humaines* as one of these Mss., a fact which renders wholly plausible the suggestion made above that its preface, referring to Mlle Desjardins as still alive, was written before her death, and left unchanged upon later publication.

[69] *Œuvres*, La Haye, 1737, I, 157. Bayle's *Dictionnaire* (article "Jardins") also gives the correct date of her death, 1683.

"Real Academia di Scienze, Lettere ed Arti," seems to have elected her to membership.[70]

Catherine Ferrand Desjardins took over the administration of her daughter's literary estate, supervising Barbin's publication of her posthumous works.[71] After the mother's death in 1692, various publishers began to issue editions of earlier novels and stories. The *Œuvres de Mme de Villedieu*, in many editions, continued to enjoy wide popularity far into the eighteenth century, but the "avantures extraordinaires" of a charming and talented woman were long since ended.[72]

---

[70] From the documents preserved it is not clear whether the Ricovrati intended to elect Mlle Desjardins, Mme Deshoulières, or both. The entry on the original list, dated Sept. 14, 1684, reads "La signora des Houlières de Châte, francese." Magne, *op. cit.*, pp. 402-404, reproduces the original Ms. and cites an explanatory letter addressed to him by the secretary of the Ricovrati in 1906, stating that the words "de Châte" were inserted "spora la riga tra le parole *Houlières* e *francese*," in another hand, "ma del tempo." M. E. Storer, who does not mention Mlle Desjardins, states that Mme Deshoulières was received into the Ricovrati on Mar. 15, 1688 ("Mme Deshoulières jugée par ses contemporains," *RR*, XXV [1934], 371). One might assume that, since "de Châte" was inserted between the lines, no intent to elect Mlle Desjardins ever existed, the Ricovrati being confused about the exact name of Mme Deshoulières and mistakenly adding the last name of another well-known French woman writer. But Mlle Desjardins was not widely known under the name "Châte," and the date conflicts with that assigned by Storer to Mme Deshoulières' election. Moreover, Vertron, a writer of the period, referred to Mlle Desjardins as among the deceased members of the Academy (in *La Nouvelle Pandore*, 1698, article "Châte"). Lack of documentary evidence for Storer's date prevents the drawing of a positive conclusion from these puzzling inconsistencies.

[71] Cf. Derome, *loc. cit.* The *privilège* of the *Annales galantes de Grèce*, 1687, was accorded to Catherine Ferrand. Later editions of earlier works were issued under her direction. See Ch. VIII, below.

[72] Editions of individual works are listed as each appears in succeeding chapters. I have identified the following collections of *Œuvres complètes*, some lacking in certain works and some containing works by other authors: Lyons, Baritel et Besson, 1696-1713, 12 vols.; Paris, Veuve Barbin, 1702, 10 vols.; Toulouse, 1703, 6 vols.; Paris, Compagnie des Libraries, 1720-1721, 12 vols.; Paris, Roslin, 1741, 12 vols.; Paris, Pierre Gandouin, 1741, 12 vols.; and Paris, Le Breton, 1741 (evidence for which is a single volume "10" containing the *Journal amoureux*, in the Washington University Library).

CHAPTER II

VERSE, LETTERS, *RÉCITS*, AND *MÉLANGES*

Le Récit en prose et en vers de la farce des Précieuses (1659)

Édouard Fournier in 1858 first recognized the importance of Mlle Desjardins' account of the *Précieuses ridicules;* since that date each successive *moliériste* has attempted to discover the true relationship between Molière's play and the *Récit* of it.[1] Despite the quantity of scholarly research, the chief questions raised by Mlle Desjardins' *compte-rendu* remain unsolved, and it appears unlikely that it will ever be known whether some of the deductions which have been made from the *Récit* are true or false.

The *données* of the problem may be summarized briefly. In her preface to the first edition of the *Récit* (1660), Mlle Desjardins states that her account of Molière's play is based "sur le rapport d'autrui," that the order of scenes is slightly different from that of the play, and that the *Récit* circulated in manuscript form until the publisher Luynes brought out an unauthorized edition, forcing her to publish a correct version herself with Barbin.[2] What scholars have sought to ascertain is whether the differences between the *Récit* and the *Précieuses ridicules* can be attributed to Mlle Desjardins, or whether they must be explained by changes made by Molière between the time Mlle Desjardins or her informant saw the play and the time when it was published in the version known today.

The *Mss. Conrart* text of the *Récit*, which varies slightly from Barbin's

---

[1] Fournier republished the *Récit* and studied it in *Variétés historiques et littéraires,* Paris, 1858. See Eugène Despois, *Œuvres de Molière,* Paris, 1875, II; Brun, *op. cit.* The *Récit* was also published by Damase Jouast, in *Nouvelle collection moliéresque,* Paris, 1879; by J. Baur, *Un Compte-rendu de Précieuses,* Paris, 1877; and by Paul Lacroix, *Récit en prose de la farce des Précieuses,* Paris, 1879. Principal discussions are in Despois, G. Michaut's *Débuts de Molière à Paris,* Paris, 1923, pp. 30 ff., P. Van Vree, *Pamphlets et libelles contre Molière,* Paris, 1934, and Lancaster, *op. cit.,* III (1), 224. Most satisfactory edition is in Despois, where variants from the *Mss. Conrart* appear with the original text.

[2] No trace exists of Luynes' alleged edition. The confusion is made worse by the fact that Molière himself was forced to publish the *Précieuses* with Luynes in January, 1660, when Ribou started to print the work. An edition of the *Récit* by Guillaume Colles, Antwerp, is evidently posterior to that of Barbin. Tallemant's testimony (*op. cit.,* VII, 245) bears out Mlle Desjardins' version. Whether in print or not, the *Récit* was certainly well known in Paris in 1659, before the appearance of the published version of the *Précieuses ridicules.*

edition, contains two rather gross *boufonneries* not found elsewhere: the girls, awaiting Mascarille's entrance, ask the servant not only for the "conseiller des Grâces," but also for a "soucoupe inférieure." In addition, Jodelet in his account of his wounds claims to have sneezed out a bullet received in the head. The *Mss. Conrart* account is specifically dedicated to Mme de Morangis, and is followed by the sonnet "Jouissance," which Tallemant claims appeared with the *Récit* in the Luynes edition.[3]

The alternating prose and verse passages of the *Récit* recount the following action:

> Gorgibus [not, however, referred to by name] angrily summons his niece and daughter, Magdelon and Cathos, from their boudoir occupations to teach them "à vivre." The girls object to their commonplace names and insist on being addressed as Clymène and Philimène [in Molière, "Polyxène" and "Aminte"]. The father, "un vieillard vêtu comme les paladins françois et poli comme un habitant de la Gaule celtique," flies into a rage and leaves the room, after announcing that two suitors are on their way to visit the girls. The honest and simple suitors are yawned out of court by the *précieuses*, and depart "resolus de s'en venger." The father returns to upbraid the girls for their shabby reception of the suitors. They defend themselves with references to the *Grand Cyrus* and recite seven stanzas of "Règles d'amour" based on the love code of the heroic novel. The father storms off the stage. A "nécessaire" announces the visit of the Marquis de Mascarille, who enters with his perruque, his Morocco leather shoes, "ses rubans, ses canons, et sa poudre." [In the *Mss. Conrart* various intercalated *crayons*, now lost, replaced the verbal description of the characters.] The scene with Mascarille ensues, following Molière closely, with the Madrigal and its farcical exegesis, its "tapinois," etc. Jodelet [not named] enters then as a "certain vicomte," cajoles the girls, dances about with Mascarille, etc., until the mistreated lovers, the "maîtres des Précieux," arrive and put a hurried end to the action.[4]

The essential differences between Molière's play and Mlle Desjardins' account of it are as follows: The *Récit* begins with scene III of the *Précieuses*, followed by the first part of Molière's scene IV, and then by a scene which *puts into action* the dialogue of Molière's first scene. The *Récit* then continues with the rest of scene IV, going on through scene

---

[3] Cf. Despois, *op. cit.*, II. Tallemant states that Mme de Morangis, well known for her prudery, was displeased with the dedication (cf. also Van Vree, *op. cit.*, p. 17). Lancaster, *loc. cit.*, points out that the euphemism "soucoupe inférieure" had been used previously with the above meaning in Dorimond's *Amant de sa femme.*

[4] Despois' text has been used. The description of Gorgibus is puzzling, since it clashes with the rôle of *raisonneur* which he plays in Molière and lays him open to charges of preciosity of costume. Jodelet's scene is much briefer in the Conrart version than in the printed account, and some of his military bragging is put into the mouth of Mascarille. The resemblance between the *Précieuses ridicules* and the *Récit* is often almost textual, especially in the scene of Mascarille and the madrigal (IX).

XVII in the approximate order of the original. The father's rôle is more extended in the *Récit* than in the play; nothing is said to indicate that the girls are provincials seeking to ape the *précieuses* of the town; and the preparation of the lovers' revenge, compared with that in Molière, is exceedingly brief. The humor of the original ending is almost completely lost in the hurried termination of the *Récit*.[5]

Both Fournier and Despois put forth the view that the *Récit* represents the first state of Molière's *Précieuses ridicules*, which Mlle Desjardins, despite her denial, must have seen on the stage. The *boufonneries* and other differences in the *Mss. Conrart* version, as compared with the published *Récit*, would correspond with the first changes made by Molière; the large differences between the *Récit* and the *Précieuses* would illustrate the major revisions in Molière's text made after the *Récit* was printed.[6]

Michaut admits the obvious possibility of Molière's having made changes, but denies that the *Récit* either proves that such changes were made, or gives any clue to the changes if they were made. The Fournier-Despois argument, that such an important alteration as putting into action the scene recounted in dialogue by the lovers in scene I of Molière's play could not have been the invention of Mlle Desjardins, is considered by Michaut to be inconclusive in the light of liberties taken throughout the

[5] Cf. Lancaster, *loc. cit.* Michaut, *op. cit.*, p. 32, insists that the girls' reference in the *Récit* to a *Recueil des pièces choisies* marks them as provincials, though he does not explain why, and claims that no inference may be drawn from Mlle Desjardins' failure specifically thus to identify them. If it were possible to prove that Molière later changed the girls to provincials in order to soften his attack on Parisian preciosity, the case against the view that the *Précieuses* was a piece of anti-Rambouillet propaganda would have to be reargued. In this connection Antoine Adam, in "La Genèse des *Précieuses ridicules*," *RHP*, January-March, 1939, pp. 14-16, attacks the view of Roederer, Cousin, Rathery and Boutry, *et al.*, that Molière did not intend to satirize the Parisian *précieuses* of the Hôtel de Rambouillet, and finds in Mlle Desjardins' *Récit* proof of the existence of an *anti-précieux* cabal led by Mme de Chevreuse and Mlle de Montbazon, enemies of the Rambouillet faction. Adam sees Mlle Desjardins as working under the patronage of Mlle de Montbazon and belonging as well to the "coterie aubignacienne," which was also opposed to the Hôtel de Rambouillet. The *Récit* would be conclusive evidence that Molière's first version of the play "visait toutes les Précieuses et les appelait ridicules."

[6] La Grange's *Registre* (Paris, 1876) shows a curious lapse of fourteen days between the first and second performances of the *Précieuses ridicules*, from Nov. 28 to Dec. 12, 1659. A second interval of seventeen days occurred between the sixth and seventh performances (Dec. 9 to 26), after which the play was given almost daily for over a month. Somaize's unreliable *Dictionnaire des précieuses* attributes the first delay to the intervention of an offended "alcoviste de qualité." The second lapse seems more difficult to explain than the first: possible reasons put forth by Lancaster are the preparation of new plays and Jodelet's ill health. Since the *achevé* of the printed version of the *Précieuses* is dated Jan. 29, it cannot be proved that Molière did not make changes during either interval or both.

Récit and because of the authoress' initial warning that "l'ordre que je tiens . . . est un peu différent de celui de cette farce."[7] Moreover, Molière would not, according to Michaut, have written such a "scène froide" as that of the girls ridding themselves of their bourgeois lovers.[8]

The state of the problem from the *moliériste's* point of view is best expressed by Lancaster, who finds Michaut's conclusion "reasonable," but admits that "it remains possible that Molière did make a number of changes in publishing his play." Nothing permits one to say, however, "to what extent his original form corresponded to [Mlle Desjardins'] account of it."[9]

Viewed as a piece of literature, the *Récit* has a charm and excellence which has led Pierre Brun, for one, to place it above Mlle Desjardins' other works.[10] Such a judgment overlooks the fact that it is an imitation of a masterpiece, and that most, if not all, its artistry may be traced to its source, the *Précieuses ridicules*. Only such bits as the descriptions of Mascarille's and Gorgibus' costumes may be directly attributed to Mlle Desjardins. Her transmutation of Cathos' prose lines on love-making *à la Grand Cyrus* into a series of *stances* cannot be called fortunate, for the impression given by these verses is that Mlle Desjardins sympathizes with what Molière contrives so cleverly to mock:

> Premièrement, les grandes passions
> Naissent presque toujours des inclinations:
> Certain charme secret que l'on ne peut comprendre
> Se glisse dans le cœur san qu'on sache comment,
> Par l'ordre du Destin; l'on s'en laisse surprendre,
> Et sans autre raison, l'on s'aime en un moment.[11]

Mlle Desjardins seems to have indulged to some extent the latent preciosity of her own taste by an over-sympathetic handling of Molière's

[7] Despois, *op. cit.*, II, 118. Despois' comment emphasizes the word "farce" as opposed to the "comédie" of the final title—a distinction which Lancaster, *loc. cit.*, shows to be of no importance.

[8] *Op. cit.*, p. 35. Despois on the other hand finds Molière's scene "moins vive" than that of the *Récit*. Michaut scorns Eugène Rigal's conjecture (in *Molière*, Paris, 1908, I, 104) that Molière himself wrote the *Récit*, but suggests that Molière may have "encouraged" the publisher to print it.

[9] Lancaster, *loc. cit.*

[10] *Op. cit.*, p. 378.

[11] Despois, *op. cit.*, II, 125. There are seven stanzas in this vein. The critic Paul du Monceau ("Correspondance," *Moliériste*, I [1880], 352) actually expressed regret that Mlle Desjardins' "Règles de l'amour" were not "conservées dans les *Précieuses ridicules*"!

precious subject matter and by the omission of much of his irony and satire. It would be wrong to suggest that Mlle Desjardins missed the point of the play; but the manner in which she presents it convicts her of sharing a good many of the foibles which it sets out to ridicule.

Recueil de poésies de Mlle Desjardins (1662, édition augmentée, 1664)
Le Carrousel de Monseigneur le Dauphin (1662)
Nouveau recueil de quelques pièces galantes (1669)
Fables (1670)

Mlle Desjardins began her career as a poet, and during the first decade of her fame (1660-1670) produced a great quantity of verse, much of it appearing in her novels and stories as well as in *recueils*. No volume of verse appeared after 1670, however, and the number of poems intercalated in her novels diminished steadily.[12] Her poetry was extremely popular in her time, and continued to appear in *recueils* and anthologies well into the eighteenth century.[13] Corbinelli's alphabetical anthology of *Sentimens d'amour tirez des meilleurs poëtes modernes*, 1671, contained a number of her verses under such headings as *absence, amour réciproque, amour seconde, beauté, colère, crainte, crime*, etc.[14] Some of her *Lettres* in mixed prose and verse appeared in Richelet's *Plus belles lettres françoises*, 1698. Remarks on her poetic merit have been quoted elsewhere from her contemporaries: Loret, Saint-Pavin, Somaize, Pavillon, Pinchesne, Jean de la Forge, and others. Tallemant, who did not like

---

[12] Lachèvre's *Bibliographie des recueils* . . . lists certain pieces by Mlle Desjardins (before 1670) not found in the above works or elsewhere in her *Œuvres*. A single detached poem written after 1670 is found in an appendix to Émile Magne's biography (a 34-line *éloge* on the appointment in 1677 of Le Tellier as chancellor). Some discussion of verses included in novels and stories will be found in the chapters on the latter.

[13] The following list of collections in which poems by Mlle Desjardins appeared was compiled from Lachèvre and other sources: *Les Muses illustres*, 1658; *Recueil de Sercy*, 1659; *Recueil de Sercy*, 1660; *Mss. Conrart, Mss. Tralage, Recueil Barbin*, 1662; *Délices de la poésie galante*, 1663; *Nouveau recueil de pièces galantes de ce tems*, 1665; *Recueil de la Suze*, 1668; *Nouveaux airs de la Cour*, 1670; *Nouveau recueil de pièces curieuses*, 1671; *Les Plaisirs de la poésie galante*, n.d.; *Recueil des plus beaux vers*, n.d.; *Recueil des épigrammes françois*, 1690; *Recueil de la Suze*, 1691; *Recueil Barbin*, 1692; *Recueil de la Suze*, 1725; *Recueil de la Suze*, 1741; *Bibliothèque poétique*, 1745; *Recueil de la Suze*, 1748; *Recueil des plus belles pièces de poëtes françois*, 1752; *Parnasse des Dames*, 1773; *Annales poétiques*, 1783. The last anthology appearance of Mlle Desjardins' poems was in *Les Muses françaises*, ed. A. Séché, Paris, 1908 (reproducing "Jouissance," two "Madrigaux," the "Articles d'une intrigue de galanterie," one "Églogue," and the fable "Le Sansonnet et le Coucou").

[14] See Magne, *op. cit.*, p. 223 for the entire list.

her, quoted a "Madrigal" and a long "Élégie" with apparent approval, and made copies of other poems by her.[15] The presence of her poems in the *Mss. Conrart* and the *Mss. Tralage* shows that such groups as that of Mlle de Scudéry were familiar with her work and esteemed it. A manuscript in the library at La Rochelle contains a "Noël" written at the request of Henriette d'Angleterre.[16] Frequenters of the salons were, according to the testimony of Huygens in 1661, eager to discover "les clefs . . . des vers de Mlle des Jardins."[17] Mlle Desjardins felt sufficiently sure of her position as a poetess to dedicate and address poems and collections to Saint-Aignan, Hugues de Lionne, Mme de Mazarin, Mme de Montausier, the Dauphin, and the King himself.

Her first published poem, included in the *Muses illustres* of 1658, was a sonnet with the maidenly title—of dubious sincerity—"Les plaisirs que l'on n'a point goustez." An "Épigramme sur la mort de M.L.P.P.," extolling the *président* Bellièvre, who died in 1657, is earlier in date of composition, and elicited a "Réponse" from Gilles Boileau.[18] By 1660 she was an established contributor to the *recueils,* the *Recueil de Sercy* of that year offering to its public eleven of her poems.[19] Two years later, Mlle Desjardins published her first *Recueil de poésies* (Barbin, 1662), containing six of the pieces of the *Recueil de Sercy* of 1660, and many new ones. A dedicatory preface to Mme la Duchesse de Mazarin promised the early appearance of "des Ouvrages plus achevez."[20] Barbin published an augmented edition in 1664, and in the same year Quinet issued an edition including not only new poems but also the *Carrousel de Mgr le Dauphin* and the plays *Manlius* and *Nitétis.*[21] The *Nouveau recueil de quelques pièces galantes* (Barbin, 1669), "faites par Mme de Villedieu, autrefois Mlle Desjardins," included chiefly poems from Mlle Desjardins' novels,

[15] *Op. cit.,* VII, 246 and 248 ff. See also Brun, *op. cit.,* "À travers les Mss. de Tallemant."

[16] Magne, *op. cit.,* p. 400, prints this *inédit.*

[17] Brugmans, *loc. cit.*

[18] Both printed in the *Délices de la poésie galante,* 1663, and as an appendix to Mlle Desjardins' *Carrousel,* 1662. Gilles Boileau's reply appears also in *Œuvres posthumes de M.B.,* Paris, n.d., p. 187.

[19] Three portraits in prose, including one of Mlle Desjardins herself, had appeared in the *Recueil de Sercy* of 1659 (cf. Ch. I, above). For other works in collections, cf. n. 13, above; first lines may be found in Lachèvre, *Bibliographie des recueils. . . .*

[20] *Œuvres complètes,* II, 161.

[21] Authority for the rare Quinet edition is Raymond Toinet, *Essai d'une liste raisonnée des auteurs qui ont écrit en vers français de 1600 à 1715,* Tulle, 1911-1913, II, 15. Graesse (*loc. cit.*) lists an edition (highly doubtful) by Barbin in 1663.

published between 1662 and 1669, and from various *recueils* of the same seven-year period.[22]

One of the earliest and best-known of Mlle Desjardins' sonnets, entitled "Jouissance," sets the tone for much of her later verse, and gives evidence of a level of technical skill which she hardly surpassed subsequently. It was written, according to Tallemant, at Dampierre, when Mme de Chevreuse and Mme de Montbazon questioned the young Marie-Catherine concerning her relations with her new lover, Villedieu:

> Aujourd'huy dans tes bras j'ay demeuré pâmée;
> Aujourd'huy, cher Tircis, ton amoureuse ardeur
> Triomphe impunément de toute ma pudeur
> Et je cède aux transports dont mon âme est charmée. . . .
>
> . . . . . .
>
> O vous, foibles esprits, qui ne connoissez pas
> Les plaisirs les plus doux que l'on goûte ici-bas,
> Apprenez les transports dont mon âme est ravie.
>
> Une douce langueur m'oste le sentiment,
> Je meurs entre les bras de mon fidèle amant
> Et c'est dans cette mort que je trouve la vie.[23]

This early, if not innocent, happiness failed to last, and through a stormy emotional career we find changing attitudes and shades of feeling towards love and lovers, reflected in a series of sonnets, madrigals, elegies, *stances*, *vers irréguliers*, and *églogues* in which Mlle Desjardins recounts the amorous fortunes of herself and of certain of her fictional characters who often appear to speak for her. Often the style is carefree and mocking, reminiscent of Hylas in the *Astrée:*

> Pour moy je veux aymer sans soins et sans envie,
> Sans crainte et sans précaution;
> Rien ne peut sur ce point troubler ma fantaisie;
> J'ay mes attraits pour caution.[24]

[22] The *Nouveau recueil* contained one poem from *Alcidamie* (1661), four from the short story *Anaxandre* (1667), and two from *Carmante* (1668), one of which had been given in incomplete form in the novel. The *Recueils* likewise made use of verses intercalated in Mlle Desjardins' prose works, taking some from *Lisandre* (1663?), *Cléonice* (1669), the *Journal amoureux* (1669), the *Annales galantes* (1670), and *Les Exilez* (1672). Even the dedicatory poem to her play *Nitétis* (1663, to Saint-Aignan) was reprinted in the *Nouveau recueil* of 1665.

[23] Not in the *Œuvres complètes*. Reproduced by Tallemant, *op. cit.*, VII. "Tircis," the name applied to Villedieu, was common in the poetry of Racan, Saint-Pavin, and others. This sonnet is found also in the *Mss. Conrart*, Corbinelli, the *Recueil de Sercy* of 1660, the *Recueils de la Suze* of 1668, 1691, 1725, 1741, and 1748, in Brun, and in Magne.

[24] From *Alcidamie*, in *Œuvres complètes*, I, entitled "Règles de service pour Lisicrate." Appears also in the second *Recueil*, as "Articles d'une intrigue de galanterie."

Often, however, she utters a cry of bitterness and anguish over "ce joli jeu d'amour si charmant et si tendre":

> Amour, cruel Amour, barbare inéxorable,
> Tyran, que t'ai-je fait pour être misérable? . . .
> . . . . .
> Pourquoi faut-il aimer? Pourquoi faut-il se rendre? . . .
> . . . . .
> Estes-vous donc absent, cher object de ma flamme? . . .[25]

Much of her later love poetry expresses a disillusioned acceptance of her lover's unfaithfulness, as in "Estrennes":

> Après trois ans de connoissance,
> Tant de longs entretiens, de soins, de complaisances,
> Et même si l'on veut de tant soit peu d'amour. . . .[26]

Nevertheless, other suitors for her favors find her cold to their attentions:

> Car je ne puis donner un cœur que je n'ay plus. . . .[27]

As her regrets multiply she asks herself in regretful retrospect:

> De quels excès d'amour me trouvois-je capable? . . .[28]

When personal feeling, direct or vicarious, is not the subject of her verse, Mlle Desjardins indulges in a kind of *galant* wit, as in "Contre les vieux amans qui entreprennent de plaire à de jeunes dames":

> Quand vieux seigneur entreprend jeune dame,
> Il ne fait qu'applanir les chemins de son âme
> Pour un plus jeune qui le suit.
> Par ses sçavans conseils, ses ruses, son adresse,
> Il va semant les germes de tendresse,
> Dont un autre cueille le fruit.[29]

Sometimes she writes in a gay, precious style similar to that of the eighteenth-century "Bergerettes":

> Mais si pour cette Bergere,
> J'avois de feintes amours,
> Et que mon âme sincere

---

[25] *Œuvres*, II, 200; *Anaxandre* and the *Nouveau recueil; Carmante*. The line beginning "ce joli jeu" is from a poem in the *Journal amoureux* (see Ch. V, below).

[26] In the 1664 edition of the first *Recueil* (quoted from *Œuvres*, II, 243).

[27] "Tircis se plaint de ma rigueur," *Recueil de Sercy*, 1660. In the *Mss. Tallemant* as "Lisis se plaint de ma rigueur." In Brun, *op. cit.*

[28] *Œuvres*, I, 443.

[29] In the *Journal amoureux*, the *Recueil Barbin* of 1692, and the *Recueil des plus belles pièces de poëtes françois*, 1752. The theme is the familiar one of the *École des femmes*.

> Pour vous eût brûlé toujours,
>   Seriez-vous encor cette fidelle Amante,
> De qui je suis si tendrement épris?
>   Et votre cœur feindroit-il pour Timante,
> Si le mien feignoit pour Miris?[30]

Like Segrais, Chaulieu, La Fare, and other poets of her day, Mlle Desjardins wrote a number of pastoral poems, including five fairly long *Églogues*. She was sensitive to the beauties of Nature, even in a semi-cultivated state, and in many moods expressed a preromantic feeling unusual in one so well adapted to the metropolitan atmosphere in which she spent most of her life:

> Dans un charmant Pays éloigné de la Cour,
> Dans un beau lieu planté par les mains de l'Amour,
> Où l'on voit un torrent par sa chûte rapide,
> Applanir des Rochers la verte pyramide,
> Et creuser un chemin pour se précipiter
> Sur un superbe Mont qui veut lui résister,
> Et puis tout glorieus d'une telle dépouille,
> Appaiser sa fureur sur les côteaux qu'il mouille;
> Et laisser écouler ses bouillonnantes eaux,
> Dans un bois de sapins en mille clairs ruisseaux. . . .
> Dans ce bocage épais regne une paix profonde,
> Que ne troubla jamais le tumulte du monde. . . .[31]

At times her invocations have a far-off echo of Ronsard and the almost forgotten Pléiade:

> Solitaires Déserts, et vous, sombres allées. . . .[32]

Of Mlle Desjardins' more than three hundred poems a very small number are *vers de circonstance*. These include the various dedicatory poems (to Mme de Mazarin, Saint-Aignan, *et al.*), verses on the payment of her pension ("Placet au Roy"), sonnets on the activities of notable persons ("Sur le départ de Mlle de Montbazon," etc.), a letter to Séguier on the seizure of her novel *Alcidamie*, letters in mixed prose and verse ("À Monsieur de Lionne, sur les cabinets du Roy," etc.), congratulatory verses ("Sur le mariage de Mlle de Lionne," etc.), *élégies* and *épigrammes*

---

[30] *Œuvres*, I, 447.

[31] *Ibid.*, II, 171. The latter part of the poem recalls Racan's *Stances sur la retraite*, so frequently imitated, but the beginning depicts a more turbulent natural scene than those found in other poets of the time.

[32] *Ibid.*, p. 185. The strain, classical in origin, of course, is that of Ronsard's familiar "Antres, et vous, fontaines."

on the death of well-known figures (Bellièvre, Mazarin, the Comte de Séry), and a description in verse of the *fête* at Versailles on June 13, 1665, when Molière's troupe performed her own play *Le Favory* before the King.[33] She composed one *Récit d'un ballet*, probably based on one of the still unpublished ballets of Benserade, and two original ballets of her own.

The first of these was *Le Carrousel de Mgr le Dauphin*, 1662, dedicated to the Dauphin's *gouvernant*, the Duc de Montausier, and to his daughter Mlle de Montausier.[34] The occasion, as Tallemant points out, was "un petit carrousel que fit le Roy en 1662." Mlle Desjardins must have anticipated the *fête*, given for "les princesses et la reine d'Angleterre," by at least a week, since her piece was praised by Loret in his *Muze historique* of May 27, and Louis' *Carrousel* was not given until June 2. It included races, displays of horsemanship, parades, a Roman *cortège*, arabesques of soldiers, and sham battles between Turks and Moors.[35] Mlle Desjardins in her own *Carrousel* describes how the Dauphin, too young for the larger festival, is carried through a miraculous *prairie* and set upon a mother-of-pearl throne, from which he witnesses a series of *quadrilles* symbolizing the struggle of *Jeunesse*, *Galanterie*, *Beauté*, and *Gloire* for his heart. Through ten pages of mixed prose and verse, against a varied *décor* of balustrades of alabaster, crystal hearts, marine trumpets, coral chariots, "Hercule enchaîné," Grenadine and Italian soldiers, etc., the four god-

---

[33] This account is dedicated to Saint-Aignan, who was in charge of the affair. It begins with a description of Versailles, decorated for the event, the *collation* which preceded the play ("Quatorze grands bassins, remplis confusément, Furent d'un grand Couvert le fertile ornement"), the stage, lighted by "cent flambeaux de cristal dans les airs soûtenus," and the music which rendered "les cœurs . . . bien disposez." At this point Molière "ébaucha le tableau, Et fit sur ce sujet un ouvrage nouveau." Some speculation has occurred as to the nature of this lost introductory *tableau* which Molière gave before presenting *Le Favory* (cf. Ch. IV, below). Modest as to the merits of her own work, Mlle Desjardins pronounced it merely "bien jouée." The rest of the *fête* consisted of a ballet and a "souper," lasting until dawn, when "sur cent petits Chars dorés L'illustre Troupe fut conduite. . . ." (*Œuvres*, I, 406 ff.)

[34] *Le Carrousel de Mgr le Dauphin et autres pièces non encores veues*, Paris, Quinet, 1662. The "autres pièces" were the plays *Manlius* and *Nitétis* (cf. Toinet, *op. cit.*). Other editions of the *Carrousel* were issued by Beaujeu, 1662, and Veuve Blajeart, 1686. Magne, *op. cit.*, p. 225, note, refers to a Ms. version in the Bibliothèque de la Rochelle bearing the notation "À Mlle de Montausier." *Le Carrousel* is not in the *Œuvres complètes*.

[35] Tallemant, *op. cit.*, VII, 250. Cf. Magne, *op. cit.*, pp. 227 ff. There were four *relations* of Louis' *fête* published in 1662, and a final (official) *relation* by Charles Perrault in 1670. J. Cazenave in his article on "Le Roman hispano-mauresque en France," *RLC*, 1925, pp. 596 ff., comments on the evidence of Moorish influence in this *Carrousel*.

desses contend, agreeing at last to a compromise admitting each to a share in the Dauphin's affection. Meanwhile the Dauphin has vanished on a cloud, leaving behind only his heart, which is duly buried on a spot where it will later be covered by a temple built by the four goddesses.

Mlle Desjardins' second ballet, *Le Triomphe de l'amour sur l'enfance,* appeared as an appendix to the *Fables* in 1670. Like the *Carrousel,* it is dedicated to Montausier, and concerns the Dauphin.[36] The theme is almost identical with that of the *Carrousel:* the Dauphin, as *Jeunesse,* is lured away from the Arts, Sciences, and *Gloire* by Love, the Graces, and Virtue. The Arts and Sciences are allowed to guide the Prince's steps, however, until he is old enough to look after himself. Such allegorical flattery was commonplace in the court ballets of writers like Benserade, and Mlle Desjardins' two efforts in this *genre* give no hint of originality. Even Benserade enlivened his ballets with Egyptians, Demons, Furies, Fires, and Icicles, exotic innovations overlooked by the author of the *Carrousel* and the *Triomphe de l'amour* in her precious and stilted mythology.[37]

In 1670, Louis XIV, to whom Mlle Desjardins had addressed one poem in the 1664 edition of her first *Recueil* and two poems in the *Recueil* of 1669, accepted the dedication of her eight *Fables.*[38] These are here summarized briefly:

I. "La Tourterelle et le Ramier." A crafty Ringdove consoles a disconsolate widow Turtledove, winning her by praising her late husband.

II. "Le Singe cupidon." A Monkey with Cupid's bow deceives a nymph until Cupid arrives to expose him. A long moral points out how a pure passion may open one's eyes to unseen defects and ugliness.

III. "La Cigale, le Hanneton, et l'Escarbot." A Beetle advises a June Bug, married to a jealous Cicada, to cure his wife of jealousy by inducing her to take a lover. "Un peu d'intrigue est un mal nécessaire."

IV. "Le Sansonnet et le Coucou." A Starling has its nest robbed by a Cuckoo, who leaves its own eggs. The Starling complains bitterly when its offspring are able only to chirp "Cou-Cou."

V. "Le Papillon, le Freslon, et la Chenille." While a Butterfly and a Hornet argue

[36] In *Œuvres,* I, 365 ff. The dedicatory epistle mentions how "Mme la Duchesse de Montausier reçut autrefois si favorablement la vision du Carrousel de Mgr le Dauphin."

[37] Cf. Charles Silin, *Benserade and his Ballets de Cour,* Baltimore, 1940.

[38] *Œuvres,* II, 241 ("Placet au Roy") and I, 392 and 395 ("Sur ce que le Roy se baignoit dans sa Chambre, au lieu de se baigner dans la Rivière" and "Au Roy, le jour de la fête de S. Louis"). The *Fables ou histoires allégoriques dédiées au Roy,* Paris, Barbin, 1670, began with a dedicatory *éloge* in the usual style: "Grand Roy, des vrais Roys le modelle, Qui du sommet de l'univers, Daigne souvent jetter l'œil sur mes vers," etc.

over a tuberose, one bragging of ancestry and the other of youth and charm, a quiet Caterpillar eats the prize.

VI. "Le Chat et le Grillon." The Cat and the Cricket discuss the inferiority of Man to the Animals, the Cat using as evidence what he has seen on his nightly prowls, the Cricket his observations from the hearth. The voice of the master of the house sends them both scampering.

VII. "L'Agneau et ses frères." A selfish Lamb monopolizes the milk supply, grow-ing fat while his brothers starve. A merchant inspecting the flock finds only the fat Lamb ready for slaughter, carrying him off.

VIII. "L'Hirondelle et l'Oiseau de Paradis." A Swallow flying to Carthage for the winter falls in love with a Bird of Paradise, who never descends to earth for food. The Swallow, unable to continue without food, is forced to abandon its new love. "Sur un peu de prudence appuyez votre amour."[39]

The debt of Mlle Desjardins to La Fontaine is all too obvious. Although each fable is about seventy-five lines in length, somewhat longer than the average in La Fontaine, the verse forms, the themes, the language, and the spirit show plainly the influence of Books I-VI of the master's *Fables* (1668). Nearly all the insects and animals mentioned above appear here: *Cigale, Hirondelle, Agneau, Freslon, Guêpe, Singe, Escarbot, Chat.* The moral of "La Tourterelle et le Ramier" is that of La Fontaine's "Jeune veuve" (VI, 21): the consolation theme of the Matron of Ephesus. "Le Singe cupidon" recalls "Le Corbeau voulant imiter l'aigle" (II, 16), "Le Loup devenu berger" (III, 3), "Le Geai paré des plumes de Paon" (IV, 9), and "Le Singe et le Dauphin" (IV, 7). The fable of the cater-pillar who devours the morsel over which others are quarreling states the same moral as "Les Voleurs et l'Âne" (I, 13).

Mlle Desjardins employs not only the same verse forms as La Fontaine (principally a mixture of 8- and 12-syllable lines, with rhymes arranged variously), but also many of the same phrases, epithets, and *tournures.* She refers to "Maître Magon," "Dame Cigale," "Frère le Rossignol," "Père Freslon," "Compère Hanneton," etc.[40] There is the same use of

---

[39] *Œuvres*, I, 337-374. The calligraph Ms. of the *Fables*, perhaps in Mlle Desjardins' own hand, is in the Bib. Nat. Seven of the pieces were reprinted in the *Nouveau recueil de pièces curieuses*, 1671. *Fable I* appeared in the *Recueil Barbin* of 1692 and in Le Fort de la Morinière's *Bibliothèque poétique*, 1745. Séché and Bertaut republished "Le Sansonnet" in their article "Une Aventurière de lettres au XVIIe siècle, Mme de Villedieu," *Mercure de France*, Feb. 15, 1900. All eight *Fables* were reproduced as an appendix in Auguste-Louis Ménard's *La Fontaine et Mme de Villedieu*, Paris, 1882 (cf. below).

[40] Cf. La Fontaine's "Maître Aliboron," "Dame Fourmi," "Sire Rat," "Messer Lion," "Compère le Renard," etc.

archaism in terms like "jadis," "certain," etc.[41] Such phrases as Mlle Desjardins' "gente Escarbote" recall the famous "gent trottemenu" and "gent marécageuse" of La Fontaine (III, 18; III, 4). Her phrase "un Escarbot du voisinage" resembles La Fontaine's "un fier Lion, seigneur du voisinage" (I, 6), as does her "une Guêpe sa voisine" his "la Fourmi sa voisine" (I, 1). Mlle Desjardins calls the cricket "notre Grillon," after La Fontaine's "notre Lièvre" (II, 14). She places the adjective before the noun in a manner characteristic of La Fontaine: "en féminin courroux" (cf. La Fontaine's "mélancholique animal," "moutonnière créature," "malin vouloir" II, 14; II, 16; VI, 5). There is the same reference to the follies of "le genre humain." A few verses of "Le Papillon, le Freslon, et la Chenille" will show the derivative style of Mlle Desjardins' *Fables:*

> Un vieux Freslon depuis long-tems
> Avoit fait des desseins sur une Tubéreuse;
> Un Papillon, nouveau fils du Printems,
> Traversoit en secret, sa fortune amoureuse.
> D'un grand murmure, et d'un sanglant combat,
>   Se vit alors sa prochaine apparence,
>   C'est toujours de la concurrence,
>   Que naissent et le bruit et l'éclat.
> À maintenir leurs droits, les Rivaus s'apprêterent.
>   Pere Freslon de bourdonner,
>   Papillon de papillonner,
>   Tant volerent, tant bourdonnerent,
>   Qu'enfin l'Amour ils obligerent,
>   À juger de leur differend. . . .
>
>   . . . . .
>   Malgré le Royal Parentage,
>   Le Papillon auroit eu l'avantage,
>   Si la Fleur eût reglé son sort:
>   Il étoit jeune, il étoit agréable;
> Mais pendant que tous deux redoubloient leur effort,
>   Pour obtenir un Arrêt favorable,
>   Une Chenille impitoyable
> Achevoit sourdement de les mettre d'accord.[42]

A certain preciosity, apparent also in the above, infects the "Tourterelle" and the "Singe cupidon." On the other hand, *terre-à-terre* realism makes both "Le Chat et le Grillon" and "L'Hirondelle" amusing minor examples

[41] Cf. La Fontaine, *Fables*, VI, 4. Mlle Desjardins: "Certain Grillon." La Fontaine: "Certaine Guêpe," "Certain Renard" (I, 21; III, 11).
[42] *Œuvres*, I, 351-355.

of the *genre*. When the Swallow tries to follow the Bird of Paradise as it rises into the sky, the poor bird is torn cruelly from its airy ideal by the pangs of earthly hunger:

> Tant d'amour qu'on voudra, tant de charmans appas,
> Il faut toujours manger et boire,
> Et c'est un incident nécessaire à l'histoire,
> Que de prendre un léger repas . . .[43]

—verses remembered by Brueys and quoted in his *Le Muet* (1691). Once again, as in the case of the *Récit de la farce des Précieuses*, Mlle Desjardins in imitating a superior artist has achieved a result which approaches excellence as it approaches its model.

Two rather curious events occurred in the literary fortune of the *Fables*. In 1858, an edition of the *Nouveau recueil de pièces curieuses* fell into the hands of Albert de La Fizelière, a collaborator of the *Bulletin du bibliophile*. The contents of the *Recueil*, as well as its apparently false *lieu* of Cologne, led the critic to assume that Mlle Desjardins' *Fables* (included in the *Recueil* without name of author) were written as a criticism of the régime of Louis XIV, thus reflecting the "audacious" freedom of the press at the time:

> Le livre finit par six fables. . . . Ici notre recueil revient bien vite à son caractère satirique, et il n'est pas difficile de saisir, sous la transparence des images, le sens secret de ces fables. "La Cigale et le Hanneton" . . . est une allusion assez audacieuse aux froideurs du monarque vis-à-vis de la reine et à ses infidélités; on reconnoît sous l'allégorie du "Singe et de Cupidon" [*sic*] certaine anecdote de cour dont parle Saint-Simon, d'une belle Dame qui prit au bal masqué quelque épais écuyer pour le roi qu'elle attendoit.[44]

It hardly seems necessary to defend the *Fables* against the charge of

---

[43] *Ibid.*, p. 363. La Fontaine also writes of "une Hirondelle en ses voyages" (I, 8). For Brueys, cf. Ch. I, above.

[44] Albert de La Fizelière, "De la liberté de la presse sous Louis XIV," *Bulletin du bibliophile*, 1858, pp. 1207 ff. The *Nouveau recueil* appeared in 1671, but the edition used by de La Fizelière bore the date 1681, and the *lieu* "Cologne," which was contradicted by the presence of the *fleurons* of a Rouen printer. Some of the pieces in the *Recueil* have, it is true, a certain satirical ring, and some criticize social and political situations: the contents include various "Stances" of Protestant apology, a letter on the marriage question, a "Requeste des Dames de la Cour contre les bourgeoises," directed at the luxury displayed by the *bourgeoises* of Paris, a "Réponse aux griefs susmentionnés," some sonnets on the war of 1668, and a letter against the suppression of saints' days and against the attack on Port-Royal. There are also several non-polemic pieces: a number of "Stances irrégulières" on love, a "Satire contre un Jaloux," La Fontaine's *conte* in verse "La Coupe enchantée," and Mlle Desjardins' *Fables*. I have been unable to identify what episode in Saint-Simon is referred to in the text cited above.

boldness or indiscretion. Mlle Desjardins was not a rebel, but a conformist; she was not one to ruin her chances of advancement in society by even a veiled reference to matters unpleasant to the King, above all in a set of verses dedicated to him. Her *Fables* must be accepted for what they are, innocent imitations of La Fontaine, no more disguised pieces of social criticism than are the works of her model.

The almost too-evident similarity between Mlle Desjardins' *Fables* and those of La Fontaine led to another and more serious error in their appraisal. In 1882, Auguste-Louis Ménard undertook to "restore" her *Fables* to La Fontaine himself, putting forth the theory that La Fontaine was Mlle Desjardins' lover, and that the autograph manuscript of the Bib. Nat. bears corrections "attribuables à La Fontaine." The attitude of what Magne terms Ménard's "grossier pamphlet" towards Mlle Desjardins is one of exaggerated hostility:

> Cette restitution . . . une étude approfondie m'ordonne de la poursuivre. . . . Mais avant d'étaler toutes les raisons qui forcent à retirer du milieu choquant de poésies alambiquées, triviales et libertines un chef-d'œuvre de fin badinage, de grace galante, et de nudité chaste, il faut faire connaître le monstre féminin qui l'a publié sous son nom en 1670 . . . la courtisane de lettres, Demoiselle Catherine Desjardins, qui se faisait si crânement apeller Mme de Villedieu. . . .
>
> La logique, la critique, l'histoire, tout plaide l'authenticité [des *Fables*]. Si je perds une si bonne cause, la faute n'en sera imputable qu'à mon faible talent. . . .[45]

Ménard's "cause," needless to say, has been completely lost. Not a shred of evidence exists to connect Mlle Desjardins with La Fontaine, nor is there any indication whatever, logical, critical, or historical, that her *Fables,* openly published under her name and recognized to be hers by all contemporaries, were written, or even read, by La Fontaine.

A general estimate of Mlle Desjardins' verse shows it to be neither better nor worse than what passed generally for "poetry" at the time. Verse had become largely a vehicle for wit, rhetorically stylized, full of clichés and empty abstractions. Feeling, although not wholly absent, is never presented in a personalized, lyrical fashion, as for example in the sonnets of Louise Labbé in the preceding century. Images occur seldom, mostly in the form of commonplace mythological comparisons. From the precious artistry of a Voiture to the insipid doggerel of a Robinet, runs a strain of versifying for its own sake, alien to modern conceptions of poetry. Mlle Desjardins herself expresses aptly the general theory of

[45] Cf. Ménard, *op. cit., passim.* Cf. Magne, *op. cit.,* p. 368.

"Poësie" of the period. Two characters of *Alcidamie*, discussing the aesthetic of verse, sum up her ideas:

> J'ai une si grande passion pour la Poësie en général, que pourvu que je voye des sillabes arrangées dans un certain ordre, et qui fassent une cadence à mon oreille, je trouve toujours cela le plus beau du monde. . . .
> Comme il y a des pensées vives auxquelles l'espression Poetique convient mieux que celle de la Prose, il arrive insensiblement qu'on fait des Vers sans dessein d'en faire.[46]

This conception of the "pensée vive" is fundamental to the understanding of the *raison d'être* of much of seventeenth-century French poetry. It bears witness to the presence in the best works of the period of something beyond mere versification, a certain emotionalized thought content, which, feeble as it is, lifts from mediocrity a handful of the poems of such writers as Segrais, Chaulieu, La Fare, Saint-Pavin, de Cailly, Charleval, Benserade, Mme Deshoulières, and Mlle Desjardins.

Recueil de quelques lettres ou relations galantes (1668)

Mlle Desjardins' publisher Barbin assembled in book form in the late spring of 1668 the letters written by her during her trip to Flanders, issuing them with an *Avis au lecteur* in which he presented the collection to Mlle de Sévigné, alleging as his reason for the dedication the "estime particulière" in which the daughter of the famous letter writer was held by the author of the *relations galantes*.[47] The *privilège*, accorded to Barbin, bears out the story that it was he and not Mlle Desjardins who arranged the publication.[48] Further evidence is provided by one of the letters themselves, discouraging the suggestions of publication:

---

[46] *Œuvres*, IV, 344, 350. A remark of Montaigne at the beginning of *De l'institution des enfants* refers to the "plus vifve secousse" made on the reader by "la sentence pressée aux pieds nombreux de la poësie."

[47] *Recueil de quelques lettres ou relations galantes, dédié à Mlle de Sévigné*, par Mlle Desjardins, Paris, Barbin, 1668. A second edition (used here) appeared in 1669. The *achevé* is dated July 20, 1668. Barbin's introductory epistle is highly laudatory, speaks of the "favorable recueil" always given to Mlle Desjardins' works, the fame of Madame de Sévigné as an inspiration to feminine writers, etc. "Ces lettres," he writes, "m'ont été mises entre les mains, par des gens qui n'avoient pas receu cette commission de sa part [*i. e.*, from Mlle Desjardins]. . . . Je les fais imprimer sans sa permission." This assertion was, as already stated, probably a publisher's stratagem.

[48] "Notre bien aimé CLAUDE BARBIN, Marchand Libraire de notre ville de Paris, nous a fait remontrer que la satisfaction que le Public a témoigné en la lecture des Ouvrages de la Damoiselle DESJARDINS, l'a obligé de prendre le soin de recouvre [*sic*] les Lettres en forme de Relations, qu'elle a faites depuis peu, lesquelles il desireroit faire imprimer" (*Recueil de lettres*, ed. 1669, p. 178).

À la Haye, le 15 May 1667

Vous en voulez à mes jours, mon cher Monsieur, puis que vous me conseillez de faire imprimer mes Lettres. . . . Quoy, bon Dieu, rendre mes Lettres publiques, moy, qui pour l'ordinaire ne prens pas la peine de les relire avant que de les cacheter, moy, qui ne sçay aucune Langue estrangere, qui n'ay jamais lû d'Autheur plus ancien que Mr d'Vrfé, et Mr de Gomberville. . . . Le tour de mes Lettres n'est pas assez desagreable pour donner la migraine aux personnes qui les reçoivent. Mais, Monsieur, est-ce là dequoy soûtenir l'impression? . . .[49]

The itinerary of the letters, whose dates extend from April until some-time after October, 1667, has been traced in the account of Mlle Des-jardins' biography. We are concerned here only with the literary and descriptive aspects of the letters, which constitute a sort of sentimental journal, ornamented with word pictures of Flanders and interspersed with miniature essays. The majority of the letters do not refer to personal matters (most names are given only in initials), but seem rather designed to entertain the recipient and his circle.

The volume opens with a letter which sets the bantering, *galant* tone of most of the collection: the observations of a sophisticated Parisian woman among the prudes of Brussels and the merchants of Holland:

Ie suis enfin venuë jusques en cette Ville, Monseigneur. . . . I'examine l'esprit qui regne parmi les Dames de Bruxelles. . . . Iamais la pruderie n'a eu de si belles esclaves qu'elle en a dans ce lieu icy. Ie n'ay entendu prononcer le mot d'amour, que par des Predicateurs; c'est un crime capital que d'avoir un homme dans son Carosse; et si la passion du jeu ne faisoit juger que les Dames ne sont pas absolument im-passibles, ie croirois estre à l'ecole de Seneque, plustost qu'à la Cour de Bruxelles. . . .[50]

---

[49] *Ibid.*, pp. 67-77. The continuation of the above passage throws some light on Mlle Desjardins' conception of epistolary art: "Vous me direz peut-estre que je n'ay pas toujours esté si circonspecte, et que le nombre des Livres qu'on voit imprimez sous mon nom, doivent avoir surmonté cette premiere pudeur. . . . il y a une grande difference (selon moy) entre le stile des Romans et des Nouvelles, et celuy des Lettres. Quand on fait un Livre . . . on tasche d'y traiter de matieres generales, dont le public puisse estre satisfait. Mais lorsqu'on écrit à ses amis . . . on leur parle dans des termes qui ne sçauroit convenir à nul autre. . . . Il faut donc s'attendre à se brouiller, ou avec le general ou avec le particulier, quand on trahit les secrets de son Cabinet. . . . Vous me verriez aussi effrayée aux noms de Perse et de Juvenal, que le Capitant des Visionnaires le fut à la veuë des Rooles du poëte extravagant. Je n'eus jamais d'autres reigles pour écrire, que les Lettres mesmes, ausquelles je fais réponse, et les authorivez, et les citations, sont des terres inconnuës pour un esprit comme le mien. . . ." Cf. the letter quoted in Ch. VII, below, from the *Œuvres* of René Le Pays. The *Visionnaires* is, of course, the play by Desmaretz de Saint-Sorlin. The style of Mlle Desjardins is in fact much less formal and "literary" than that of her novels. The elaborateness of her descriptions, however, raises the suspicion that she at least intended her letters to circulate in Ms. form. Her list of admitted works in 1671 contains the *Recueil de lettres*. Her disparage-ment of her own erudition may be exaggerated (cf. below).

[50] *Recueil de lettres*, pp. 1-5.

Prudish criticism was apparently directed at Mlle Desjardins in Liége as well, for she writes from that city:

> Peu s'en est fallu que je n'aye esté regardée comme une perturbatrice du repos public, parce que j'ay fait imprimer des Vers et de la Prose. Il m'a fallu des attestations de Mr de L. . . . sur l'intégrité de mes sentimens, pour dissiper le nuage que la vivacité de mon esprit evoit élevé.[51]

Further measures to insure the good will of the Belgian ladies included the publication of the *nouvelle, Anaxandre,* dedicated "Aux Dames de la Cour de Bruxelles":

> Je ne puis souffrir, Mesdames, que vous murmuriez contre moy plus longtems; l'honneur de votre bienveillance est trop précieux pour ne pas estre acheté par tout ce qui dépend de mon Génie; et puis qu'il ne faut qu'une Histoire de ma façon pour obtenir ma grace de Vous, ie vais satisfaire à la curiosité obligeante que vous témoignez pour mes Ouvrages.[52]

Mlle Desjardins' descriptions of the cities through which she passed, especially Antwerp and Amsterdam, are remarkably colorful and full of lively detail. Here is part of the picture of Amsterdam:

> Du reste Amsterdam est une grande Ville bastie sur pilotis à l'imitation de Venise. Ie suis si peu sçavante en Chronologie que j'ignore si c'est Venise qui est bastie à l'imitation d'Amsterdam, ou Amsterdam à l'imitation de Venise, mais ce que je sçay, c'est qu'elles sont sur pilotis toutes deux, avec cette difference toutefois, que Venise est arrosée des eaües de la Mer, et qu'Amsterdam ne l'est que par un de ses bras. Que les Canaux de Venise sont couverts de Gondoles peintes et dorées, et que ceux d'Amsterdam ne le sont que de barques fumantes de Bitume. Que les rües de Venise sont remplis de nobles Venitiens, et que celles-cy sont pleines d'un nombre presque infini de Bourgeois mal civilisez. . . . Cependant Amsterdam a ses beautez, comme elle a ses deffauts, les rües y sont larges et nettes, et arrosées de Canaux bordés de grands et de beaux arbres, elle est habitée par une affluance de Peuples de tous Païs, dont la confusion et la difference forment une idée de l'ancienne Babylone qui ne déplaist point aux Voyageurs. . . . On pendit un Estranger, il y a quelque tems, pour avoir porté des Pistolets aprés neuf heures sonnées. . . . On prolonge aisément la Justice en cette Ville.[53]

Such extended descriptions soon became to the author irksome and impossible; she complains to her correspondent that "chacune des villes de Hollande me coûtera une Lettre de six feuillets, si je veux satisfaire vostre humeur curieuse." Nevertheless we pick up throughout constant

---

[51] *Ibid.*, pp. 119-120. "Mr de L. . ." is the minister Hugues de Lionne.

[52] *Anaxandre*, 1667, unpaginated dedicatory letter. Cf. Ch. VI, below. The story was carefully provided with a moral and exemplary *dénouement.*

[53] *Recueil de lettres*, pp. 83-88. The last sentence appears to be a reference to the *procès* which Mlle Desjardins alleged as the motive of her trip. Cf. Ch. I, above.

references to details: the cleanliness and neatness of the uniform brick houses (p. 92), the omnipresence of commerce among these "peuples amoureux de l'argent" (p. 92), the University of Leiden, the tombs of the Princes of Orange at Delft, the horrible "vapeur du charbon souffré, dont on se chauffe en ce Païs icy" (p. 116), the "fossez . . . contrescarpes . . . et bastions" of Breda (p. 124), the Marcins' estate at Modave, with its gardens and romantic rocky landscape (pp. 130-139), the gay crowd at Spa (pp. 140-147), etc. The Hague is accorded a full description, with its beautiful streets, its "Maisons de plaisance," the canals and quais, the famous "douze allées d'arbres à double rang, à qui le Canal sert comme de Perspectives naturelles, qui sont toutes si droites et si couvertes, que rien ne peut surpasser leur beauté," the Mall, the Dowager Princess' palace, with its museum containing ". . . non seulement des Rubens, et des Wendix [*sic*] . . . mais des Peintres les plus renommez de l'Italie . . . des Animaux de Mer inconnus . . . une Bibliothèque de Livres choisis . . . la plus rare et la plus curieuse . . ." and its other wonders (pp. 94-101). With unfailing instinct, Mlle Desjardins selects significant details, the picturesque, the unusual, the elegant, often the beautiful. Her prose is more colorful here than in any of the "descriptions" found in her novels and stories. Left to her own imagination, Mlle Desjardins invents abstract, traditional scenes, insipid terraces, gardens, and all-too-familiar "splendid" apartments. Pinned down to reality, her style becomes direct and familiar, precise and vivid; her comparisons and contrasts throw genuine light and shadow. Often a certain preromantic taste for wild natural beauty, or an imitation of such, comes to light, as in this description of the estate at Modave:

Ne vous attendez pas à voir . . . un bastiment superbe . . . un nombre de lambriz dorez . . . une terasse avancée, des Statues de Marbres. M * * * n'est encore rien de tout cela. . . . La maison est bastie sur la pointe d'un Rocher, si élevé, que le vallon dont il sort, paroist un precipice, à le regarder des fenestres du premier appartement. . . . De la mesme Chambre, on découvre une Campagne, et une solitude; on jouït d'une veuë estendue, et d'une veuë bornée; on voit la maison sur une hauteur, et dans un fons. . . . Le jardin est planté sur un Rocher de mesme hauteur . . . il est escarpé tout autour. . . . Une petite riviere claire et bruyante qui serpentant entre les Rochers qui la bordent, va se rendre dans les fossez du Château.[54]

The *Lettres* contain references to a great number of well-known people,

---

[54] *Ibid.*, pp. 130 ff. A romantic flair for direct and unrestrained expression of feeling also appears in the *Recueil de lettres:* "Il y a de certaines fautes dans les Lettres d'Amour qui font leurs plus grandes beautez, et l'irregularité des periodes est un effet des desordres du cœur, qui est beaucoup plus agréable aux gens amoureux, que le sens froid d'une Lettre raisonnée" (p. 81).

but the only word portrait of any length is that of the old Sieur de Zuy-lichem, father of the famous Huygens. The "Alexandre de mon idée" is depicted as a handsome, elderly man, gifted musically, with the soul of a philosopher, so busy with his varied interests that "à moins d'estre un Livre rare, ou un Medecin Arabe, on ne peut luy dérober qu'un quart d'heure de ses journées."[55] Mentions are made of Gourville, the Marcins, du Buisson, the Baron d'Ysola, the Prince d'Aremberg, the Duc d'Arschot, M. de la Nogerette, the Marquis de Castel-Rodrigo, the minister Hugues de Lionne, and others. Many unnamed persons also appear: an anony-mous abbé, a woman who has asked Mlle Desjardins to "apprendre à son fils de soupirer," several unidentified correspondents, and numerous per-sonages sketched in to add piquancy to such scenes as the one at Spa, etc. Of her own family Mlle Desjardins writes little. She refers to her father's death as an event on the same level as her recent financial losses, and sends her mother as a messenger to solicit a favor from "M. le P.D.R." in Paris.[56]

Several literary opinions and discussions of interest may be culled from the *Recueil de lettres*. Despite Mlle Desjardins' assertion, quoted earlier, that she was lacking in all matters of erudition, having read no authors "plus anciens que Mr d'Vrfé et Mr de Gomberville," and that she was "effrayée aux noms de Perse et de Juvenal," we find her stating with great authority that

les Anciens n'ont pû joindre la beauté de la Diction, auec la subtilité des Pensées; la Rapidité de leur Imagination les a entrainez. . . . Monsieur D* * * [Despréaux] au contraire a trouvé le secret de faire cet assemblage. . . .[57]

This letter on Boileau, addressed to Gourville, is concerned with the current attacks on the *Satires*. Pointing out that only "les ouvrages les plus achevez" provoke such quantities of criticism, Mlle Desjardins pro-ceeds to defend Boileau against charges which, though she does not name

[55] *Ibid.*, pp. 105 ff. Cf. Ch. I, above. Magne, *op. cit.*, at several points mistakes Christian Huygens' father for the son.

[56] Since Mlle Desjardins had risen above her social station, it was natural that she should refrain from boring her distinguished audience with the domestic problems of the family of a lady's maid. (Cf. Tallemant, *op. cit.*, VII, 244. Mlle Desjardins' mother, Catherine Ferrand, was "une femme qui a esté à feue Mme de Montbazon.")

[57] *Recueil de lettres*, pp. 44-45. It is unlikely that, whatever its precise meaning, this opinion represents Mlle Desjardins' own thought. The most obvious source would be Boileau's own *Discours sur la satire*, but the *Lettres* are dated from April to October, 1667, and the *Discours* did not appear until sometime in 1668 (cf. the Gidel edition of Boileau's *Œuvres*, I, 45).

their author, are obviously those of the abbé Cotin in his *Critique désintéressée sur les satires du temps*.[58] Cotin had charged that Boileau had been heard

. . . dans la ville capitale d'un royaume chrétien, à la barbe du magistrat et de la police, dire que
> Souvent de tous nos maux la raison est le pire.

Et pourquoi? Parce que
> C'est elle qui, farouche, au milieu des plaisirs,
> D'un remords importun vient brider nos désirs.

Je vous laisse à penser, après une si belle morale, combien la vie humaine, la vie civile, la vie des honnêtes gens est obligée à un si raisonnable censeur.

The author then blames Boileau for mentioning the preacher Joly by name, and accuses the poet of the *Satires* of willfully enfeebling his religious views so as not to displease his friends, the *esprits forts*.[59] Mlle Desjardins comments on the argument over the morality of Boileau's verses on reason in this fashion:

Un homme qui entreprend de faire la Satyre des vices, ne doit pas détruire l'Empire de la raison, comme on prétend que notre Amy l'a détruit, lorsqu'il dit:
> C'est elle qui, farouche, au milieu des plaisirs,
> D'un remords importun vient brider nos désirs.

Vous semble-t-il, Monsieur, que ce Tableau fait une grande injure à la Raison [?]. . . . On nous la represente . . . comme une gouvernante severe . . . qui ouvre les yeux sur nos égaremens. . . . N'est-elle pas bien défigurée dans cette peinture [?]. . . .

She dismisses the accusation of libertinage thus:

On . . . traite [Boileau] avec autant de rigueur, comme s'il avoit renversé la Loy des Prophetes, on se rescrie contre luy, comme contre un Athée convaincu, et le fondement unique de cette calomnie, c'est qu'il a nommé Monsieur Joly par son nom.[60]

She then speaks of Boileau's personal merits, and of "l'estime que je fais de toute la famille de Messieurs B* * *," closing her defense by begging Gourville to believe

. . . que ceux qui font de si meschans portraits de Monsieur D* * *, ne l'ont jamais envisagé qu'une plume à la main, pour crayonner leurs deffaut[s], il leur paroistroit

---

[58] Brossette gives the publication date of Cotin's pamphlet as 1666, Niceron, as 1667; cf. Gidel, *op. cit.*, p. CCXXI, for a discussion of this and other "libelles diffamatoires" directed against Boileau. Gidel was not acquainted with Mlle Desjardins' defense of the poet.

[59] The passage is reproduced in Gidel, *op. cit.*, pp. CCXXI ff. Boileau's remarks on reason are from *Satire IV*, where he had also said of Joly that "[il] perd son temps à prêcher."

[60] *Recueil de lettres*, pp. 46 ff.

plus agreable . . . s'ils le representoient sous une autre forme, aussi bien que l'un de
ses freres, que d'un des plus honnestes homme[s] du monde, ils erigent en franc
Taupin.[61]

Mlle Desjardins refers once to Voiture, quoting some lines of his on
the vanity of life and adding to these several of her own invention. Of her
melancholy state of mind at Spa in July, 1667, she writes:

Je commence à comprendre que les honneurs qui suivent le trépas, sont très peu
dignes de la convoitise des vivans.

> Du moment que la fiere Parque
> Nous a fait entrer dans la Barque,
> Où l'on ne reçoit pas les corps;
> Et la Gloire et la Renomée,
> Ne sont que songe et fumée,
> Et ne vont point jusques aux morts.

J'aurois pû me passer de faire un larcin de ces Vers à Mr de Voiture, et ajouter
encore à sa pensée.

> Quand une funeste avanture,
> Nous fait payer à la Nature,
> Ce tribut general que doivent les Humains,
> Les Charges, les Tresors, les honneurs Souverains,
> Ne sont que des fantosmes vains;
> Qui loin de nous servir pour la gloire future,
> Sont autant de pesans fardeaux,
> Qui causent nos terreurs, et redoublent nos maux.[62]

This feeling, expressed many times in the *Recueil de lettres*, shows most
plainly in the undated *Lettre XXII*. The death of her father, the financial
losses suffered by the family, the death of her lover Villedieu, all affected
her usually cheerful disposition:

J'ay perdue des personnes depuis quelques mois . . . pour lesquelles j'aurois donné
sans peine, tout ce que la mauvaise foy d'autruy vient de m'arracher, et la mélancholie
qui me devore presentement, me donne une si grande indifference pour la vie. . . .
Quand on fait une reflection solide sur les biens, et sur les maux que le fortune

[61] *Ibid.*, pp. 53-54. "Un de ses frères" was doubtless Gilles Boileau, a special friend
(cf. Ch. 1, above). The construction of the last sentence of the quotation is weak;
its sense is obviously "plutôt que d'ériger en franc Taupin un des plus honnêtes
hommes du monde." Mlle Desjardins says that the term "franc Taupin" is new to
her, and that she had at first mistaken it for one of praise rather than blame (p. 54).
The *francs Taupins* formed the first infantry corps under Charles VII, but the insub-
ordination and cowardice of these troops soon caused the term to become an epithet
of abuse (cf. Gallier, *op. cit.*, p. 41).

[62] *Ibid.*, pp. 144-145. Voiture's lines appear in his *Épitre à Monsieur le Prince sur
son retour d'Allemagne*, written in 1645 (*Œuvres*, ed. Ubicini, II, 395). It was
Voiture who, seeing Mlle Desjardins as a child, "predit que cette petite fille auroit
beaucoup d'esprit, mais qu'elle seroit folle" (Tallemant, *op. cit.*, VII, 244).

peut nous départir, on les trouve les uns et les autres si peu considerables. . . .
Peut-elle prolonger nos jours d'un moment? Peut-elle arracher nos Amis de la mort?
Nous rendre une santé perduë, restablir un esprit alteré, ou délivrer une ame de ses
vices? Rien moins que cela: au contraire, nous voyons tous qu'elle est une source
feconde de déreglemens, qu'elle nourrit nos passions . . . qu'elle avance la fin de
nostre vie . . . etc.[63]

This tendency to philosophize is further exemplified by a letter on religious questions, in which Mlle Desjardins attempts to answer two problems
raised by a correspondent: one, why we believe "qu'il y aura un Iugement
final, puis que nous tombons d'accord que les Ames sont jugées au
moment qu'elles se séparent de nos corps," and another, "pourquoy la
Providence a permis que Saint Augustin soit tombé dans tant d'erreurs
differentes, puis que Dieu sçavoit qu'il devoit devenir un vase d'election
et un exemple d'Amour divin" (p. 196). Her explanation of the first
problem is that it is not enough for the elect of Heaven to recognize that
they have been saved and that those who are absent have been damned,—
God must hold a final judgment in order to "faire éclater la cause de ses
jugemens differens, à la veuë de tous les mortels" (p. 200). Mlle Desjardins feels that it would be unsatisfactory merely to know that a certain
"Hypocrite" of one's acquaintance has been sent to Hell; one really
desires the malicious pleasure of seeing him confronted with his sins and
condemned before one's very eyes. In the case of Saint Augustine, the argument has a familiar ring: "je trouve, que ce que nos libertins regardent
comme des abandonnemens de la Providence, sont des marques de son
soin Paternel pour ce grand Saint" (p. 203). Hence, God led Saint
Augustine into a series of temptations only in order to "luy fournir des
raisonnemens plus forts pour les refuser." Such obvious rationalizations
force one to assign to Mlle Desjardins the theologian a somewhat mediocre rank.

Another province outside her scope is politics, but, like most travelers,
Mlle Desjardins is unable to resist the temptation to play the rôle of
foreign correspondent. Aware of her shortcomings, she warns her reader
that she is not at all "femme d'Estat," and that he will laugh when he
sees "que je me ruë sur la Politique." Nevertheless, she formulates a few
superficial ideas concerning the political and military situation of the
day, recommending rather naïvely that France's enemies give themselves
over to France and thus enjoy the benefits of French control.[64]

[63] *Recueil de lettres*, p. 209.
[64] *Ibid.*, pp. 215 ff.

Taken as a whole, the *Lettres* are a varied and engaging revelation of the personality, outlook, and world view of a woman who, forced to live by her wits and charm, so successfully sounded out the tastes and ideas of her time that she was able not only to flatter her public's desires in her verse and fiction, but also able to discuss and debate contemporary problems with clarity and grace, and furnish amusing descriptive *reportage* from a foreign land. With their unaffected style, their picturesque descriptions, and their sympathetic expression of sentiments, the *Lettres* retain a certain value as human documents, and as evocations of historical *milieux*. They appeal more to modern taste than Mlle Desjardins' large production of poor verse, which, without images, color, or lyrical feeling, is at best a kind of witty versifying with an occasional flash of real emotion to lift it above the lowest level. As a poet, Mlle Desjardins may be ranked with such writers as Charleval, de Cailly, and the like, just below Segrais, Saint-Pavin, and Mme Deshoulières, and barely above a writer of doggerel like Robinet; but as a letter writer she may still hold her own against any of her contemporaries, with the inevitable exception of Mme de Sévigné herself.

CHAPTER III

ALCIDAMIE (1661) : THE HEROIC NOVEL AND BEGINNINGS OF THE NOUVELLE GALANTE

Alcidamie, Mlle Desjardins' first novel, was published and on sale by February 23, 1661.[1] The work comprises several different stories held together by a cadre reminiscent of Gomberville's Polexandre (1629-1637). The main plot is left unfinished, and the words "Fin . . . de la première partie," which occur on the last page, suggest that a sequel was intended.

Prince Haly Joseph of Morocco and his servant Muly arrive at the Isle Délicieuse, where Haly heroically saves Queen Alcidamie from the attack of a wild boar. In the apartments of her palace, Plaisance, Muly relates his master's story. Before the Queen, Haly's mother, had yet given birth to him, her husband the King had died, and she herself had been captured by her brother-in-law Almansor, who had seized the throne. Fearing that her son, if discovered, would be put to death, the Queen concealed the fact of his birth and had him secretly transported to an island where the sage Oraste and another disguised prince, Amador, were living and studying in idyllic peace. Young Haly (now called by the name of one of the Queen's officers, Théocrite) is reported dead, and the Queen's daughter Zélide plans to occupy the throne. News that Haly still lives reaches Zélide and she conspires to have her brother murdered. Through a suivante Lindarache she sends Rustan to kill the Prince, but Rustan, conscience-stricken, hides Haly on Samos. Zélide, believing him murdered, prepares to ascend the throne. She then discovers that Lindarache has allowed Rustan to believe that his love for her [Zélide] is returned, and has even encouraged him in his belief. When she orders Lindarache to tell him the truth, the suivante lies and allows Rustan to believe that the Princess is betraying him. Zélide meanwhile plans to marry Gomelle. Rustan attempts to fight with Gomelle, accuses Zélide of infidelity, and is banished from the city. (End of Book I.)

Rustan goes to the Queen Mother and reveals the existence of Haly. The Queen now opposes Zélide's marriage to Gomelle, who is beneath her in rank, and sends a party to bring back the Prince. Zélide hears of this and sends her own men to prevent Haly's return. Meanwhile she marries Gomelle. The Queen's party is victorious and the return of Haly is announced by the Queen to the Council. Zélide declares him an impostor and orders him banished. Haly secretly joins Zélide's army and fights beside Gomelle against the once more insurgent Almansor. Then the Prince, unwilling to contest his sister's occupancy of the throne, causes his death to

[1] Cf. Brugmans, op. cit., p. 155, for evidence from Huygens' journal that a copy was purchased from a shop near the Palais-Royal on that date. Barbin issued the work in 2 volumes, the only edition before the appearance of the Œuvres complètes at Toulouse in 1703. Unlike most of Mlle Desjardins' later novels, it was not translated into English.

be announced. He sends another messenger to his mother to reassure her that the rumor is false, but this messenger falls into a river and drowns. Convinced that Haly no longer threatens their position, Zélide and Gomelle, having defeated Almansor, are enjoying their usurped throne. In self-imposed exile, Haly and his servant Muly wander from place to place, thus coming upon Alcidamie's Isle Délicieuse.

After Haly's story is told, members of Alcidamie's court engage in "conversations galantes" and *questioni d'amore* debates concerning "l'Amour d'Inclination," "l'Amour Interéssé," "l'Amour Galand," and "l'Amour Solitaire." A "Cabinet d'Amour" and a "Cabinet des tristes avantures" containing statues of the famous lovers of history are visited. The story of Célie, one of the women represented in the second *Cabinet*, is told by Philimène.

Histoire de Célie. Célimedon, son of the Governor of Athens, falls in love with Climène, Princess of Cyprus. Climène's *suivante* Célie also loves Célimedon, who is unable to win Climène's affection. Falling ill of an unknown sickness, Célie calls Célimedon to her, reveals to him her love, which she pretends to have overcome, and promises to aid his suit with Climène. When the latter at last shows an interest in Célimedon, he, remembering Célie's plight, gives up the Princess to save Célie's failing spirit. Célie refuses this sacrifice, unites the lovers, and dies. But Célimedon retires to another country and Climène finishes her days alone. (End of Book II.)

Histoire de Cinthie et d'Iphile. This story is told by Lisicrate to illustrate another group of statues. Iphile, long in love with Princess Cinthie of Milo, at last persuades her to accompany him to the country, where for a while they enjoy solitary happiness. Iphile, however, soon grows bored and finds an excuse to leave her and return to Milo, where he joins his old friends in revelry. Testing his love with an indifferent letter, Cinthie receives from him a more indifferent one breaking with her entirely. After several unsuccessful attempts to win him back, Cinthie retires to a convent, from which she writes him a final letter. He, affected at last, asks her to return to him. She refuses and Iphile, now desperate with love for the woman whom he has scorned, kills himself.

During further conversations at Alcidamie's court two beautiful ladies arrive, having just been rescued from a shipwreck. They are Almanzaïde, Queen of the Canary Islands, and her sister Zélinde. The Queen promises to tell her story as soon as she has changed clothes, rested, and eaten. (End of Book III.)

Histoire d'Almanzaïde et d'Artambert. Almanzaïde, widowed Queen of the Canaries, whose laws transmit the throne through girl children only, and forbid them to marry more than once, is the object of the pressing attentions of Artambert, Prince of Thule. Her efforts to avoid him are unsuccessful, and Almanzaïde at last recognizes that she loves him. She consents to a secret marriage. They retire to a country place where after a brief interlude of happiness Artambert becomes bored and sulky. He demands that Almanzaïde find some way for him to share the throne openly with her. This is impossible. After many cruelties, Artambert finally abandons Almanzaïde, whose boy baby, born soon after, dies. Soon Amador [the prince whose acquaintance was made in the story of Haly Joseph] informs Almanzaïde that Artambert is planning to marry the Princess of Greenland. Artambert sends word that as a prince he does not consider himself bound by his secret marriage. Almanzaïde sails to Greenland, arrives in time for the marriage ceremony, and hides behind the ceremonial altar.

The Princess of Greenland, who has learned of Artambert's infidelity to Almanzaïde, stabs herself before the guests. Artambert's arrest is ordered, but Almanzaïde saves him by drawing him in behind her arras and showing him a door to the sea. Almanzaïde and Zélinde set out to return to the Canaries. Attacked by pirates, they lose Amador, who seizes the pirate chief and leaps with him into the sea. Rescued by a member of Alcidamie's court, they land upon the Isle Délicieuse. (End of Book IV.)

It was the *cadre* story of Haly Joseph, which forms roughly the first third of *Alcidamie's* 450 pages, that was interpreted by certain contemporaries to constitute a thinly disguised version of "l'histoire de Mme de Rohan, de Ruvigny, et de Chabot," a well-known scandal.[2] The historical facts are that the Duc Henri de Rohan, desiring to buy the island of Cyprus in order to convert it into a Protestant refuge, had sent Mme de Rohan, their daughter Marguerite, and a certain M. Candalle from Venice to Paris in order to effect the purchase. There Mme de Rohan gave birth to a son (attributed by Tallemant to Candalle) whom she named Tancrède, after a valet in her suite. The Duc de Rohan ordered the birth of Tancrède to be kept secret in order to protect the child from the possible anti-Protestant machinations of Richelieu. While negotiations for the purchase of Cyprus proceeded, Tancrède was sent to Normandy for safety. An officer, Ruvigny, became Marguerite's lover. Fearing Tancrède's position as heir of the family, Marguerite persuaded Ruvigny to attempt to get rid of her brother by having him sent to the Indies. Tancrède was taken as far as Holland, and his death announced to Mme de Rohan. Marguerite, believing herself to be left sole inheritor, discarded her lover Ruvigny in favor of Chabot, who later became a duke. Ruvigny, furious, attempted to fight a duel with Chabot. Marguerite made two abjurations of faith and married Chabot, offending the Protestants. Mme de Rohan decided to bring Tancrède, who was now known to be alive, back to Paris, and set him up as heir, thus ruining Marguerite. Both Mme de Rohan and Marguerite, who learned of the scheme, sent envoys to secure Tancrède's person; those of Mme de Rohan arrived first and the boy was brought back. A *procès* was instituted to establish his "qualité de Rohan." Mme de Rohan's unsavory reputation and the fact that the Protestants backed Tancrède alienated the court, which decided the case against him. Tancrède, denied the use of the Rohan name, perished shortly afterward in the troubles of the Fronde.[3]

[2] Tallemant, *op. cit.*, VII, 247. Cf. also Magne, *op. cit.*, pp. 39 ff. The first modern critic to deal with this problem was Gallier (*op. cit.*, pp. 23-24).

[3] Cf. Giffret, *Histoire de Tancrède de Rohan*, Paris, 1767. Most of the above details

The identifications in *Alcidamie* made by readers familiar with this episode in the annals of the Rohans were:

Haly Joseph (the elder)	The dead Duc de Rohan
Haly (Théocrite)	Tancrède de Rohan
Queen Mother	Mme de Rohan
Zélide	Marguerite de Rohan
Rustan	Ruvigny
Gomelle	Chabot[4]

The Duchesse Marguerite de Rohan-Chabot, who, before the publication of the novel, had heard that her questionable behavior of more than a decade before was about to be brought to light, attempted to dissuade Mlle Desjardins from printing *Alcidamie*. To this end the Duchesse asked the Marquis de Langey, a ridiculous character who had been publicly proved impotent during a *Congrès* demanded by his wife, to intercede with the authoress. Tallemant states that Mlle Desjardins replied to Langey by proposing a private *Congrès* of her own, which the Marquis refused. Hearing that Ruvigny, another personage of the Tancrède affair, was also angry at the forthcoming publication, Mlle Desjardins wrote to Langey a denial that the book was based on Rohan family history. Her denial served ingeniously to whitewash Ruvigny's character and further to blacken that of Marguerite de Rohan. She wrote:

Vous m'avez causé une douleur très-sensible, mon cher Monsieur, en m'apprenant les sentiments de M. de R[uvigny] . . . sur mon *Alcidamie*. J'avois abandonné cet Ouvrage à sa destinée, sans précaution et sans inquiétude, et l'extrême jeunesse où j'estois lors que je l'ay entrepris, me répondant en quelque sorte de l'indulgeance du Public; je croyois que pour le mériter, il suffisoit de dire que je n'avois que seize ans, lors que ce Livre a esté composé. Mais, puis qu'on prétend estendre les bornes de mon imagination, jusques à une allégorie, dont elle estoit entièrement incapable en ce temps-là . . . on me force encore à défendre la vérité qu'on attribue, comme la fixion que j'avois inventée. Je vais vous faire l'Apologie de Rustan en général, et je prétends vous faire voir, que non seulement il n'est le Portrait que de luy mesme,

are found also in the works of Tallemant, in the *Mémoires* of Mme de Rohan (in the *Mss. Conrart*), in Balzac, Saint-Simon, and Gui Patin.

[4] Magne, *op. cit.*, p. 39, goes so far as to suggest Almansor as Richelieu. Mlle Desjardins' names throughout *Alcidamie* are reminiscent of earlier fiction: "Rustan" appears in Mlle de Scudéry's *Ibrahim*, Mairet's *Solyman*, etc., and is a standard villain's name; "Lindarache" appears in Lisdan's *Avantures de Lyndarache* and as a perfidious character in Quinault's play *La Généreuse Ingratitude*, which also has a "Fatime" (the Queen's maid in *Alcidamie*) and an "Almansor," as well as a "Zélinde." *Polexandre* also has an "Almansor" (for evidences of direct imitation of *Polexandre*, see below), a name whose decline from the sublime in Gomberville to the ridiculous in the *Précieuses ridicules* throws a side light on the fall of the heroic novel.

mais, que quand il le seroit d'un autre, il ne fait rien dans mon Livre qu'un tres-honneste homme ne puisse avouer sans honte. Toute l'intrigue d'*Alcidamie* a un fondement solide dans l'Histoire d'Affrique, dont je l'ay tirée presque mot à mot.[5]

The letter proceeds to defend Rustan (Ruvigny) and praise his conduct when he finds himself "abandonné de ses Amis, trahy de sa Maistresse, et insulté de son Rival."

Such specious reasoning may have flattered Ruvigny, but it did not appease the Rohans. The Duchesse sent for Mlle Desjardins, read the manuscript (still following Tallemant's account), and insisted on certain changes. Mlle Desjardins suddenly decided to publish the novel as it stood. A lackey of Langey secured a *huissier* to seize the presses. Mlle Desjardins threatened to include in *Alcidamie* the story of Langey's *Congrès*. The affair was taken before the chancellor Séguier, to whom Mlle Desjardins quickly addressed a sonnet entitled "À Monsieur le Chancelier, pour lui demander son Roman qu'il avoit fait saisir," begging this "Ministre magnanime,"

> De ne pas étouffer un Ouvrage naissant,
> Dont les seuls ennemies ont causé tout le crime.[6]

Séguier found nothing libelous in the book and released it. Tallemant, of the same opinion, writes:

J'ay leu l'ouvrage; il n'y a pas grand chose et Mme de Rohan est bien au-dessous en toute chose celle sous le nom de laquelle on a mis quelques endroits de son histoire. Ce livre est meilleur qu'on n'avoit lieu de l'espérer d'une telle cervelle; il n'y a encore qu'un volume.

According to Somaize, Mlle de Montbazon, a Rohan on her father's side, also took offense at the novel.[7] Yet Mlle Desjardins did not hesitate to include in her *Recueil de poésies* of the following year (1662) several poems addressed to the reigning member of the family with which her mother had been connected as lady's maid.

The public does not seem to have accorded to *Alcidamie* the *succès de scandale* which the foregoing account might have led one to expect. This

---

[5] *Recueil de lettres*, pp. 259 ff. Mlle Desjardins claimed to have been born in 1640, which would have put "seize ans" at 1656 according to her own reckoning. She was probably sixteen in 1648. Though Magne does not seem to doubt her word about the date of composition of *Alcidamie* (while rejecting her denial that it is an "allégorie"), there is no reason to accept such an allegation of youthful authorship. Moreover, the "fondement solide" in African history seems no more solid than that of Gerzan's romanesque *Histoire afriquaine* (cf. Maurice Magendie, *Le Roman français au XVIIe siècle de l'Astrée au Grand Cyrus*, Paris, 1932, p. 42).

[6] *Œuvres*, II, 207.

[7] Tallemant, *op. cit.*, VII, 247. Cf. Somaize, *loc. cit.*

fact is not difficult to explain. Readers seeking esoteric information or new revelations concerning the amours of the Duchesse de Rohan-Chabot in its pages must have been disappointed.[8] Instead of setting down the facts, Mlle Desjardins so changed the details of the affair as to render the elder Mme de Rohan a long-suffering martyr, Ruvigny a pure-minded idealist loving Marguerite de Rohan from afar, Tancrède (in reality a wretched, pathetic creature) a model prince, and the infamous Marguerite herself no more reprehensible than an ambitious princess in the Racinian pattern, most of whose sins could be blamed on the treacherous Lindarache, a character with no counterpart in reality. The picture given by Magne of *Alcidamie* as filled with secrets of the Rohans, written by one "remarquablement instruite des machinations les plus obscures," is much exaggerated. What seems clear is that the author's intentions were not to write an exposé of a family scandal, but to compose an heroic novel, and that her use of the Rohan affair as a plot was a matter of secondary importance. What interested her was the dressed-up, much-altered version with its *faux exotique* Morocco, its melodramatic complications, and the "conversations galantes" of its "Isle Délicieuse."

Alcidamie abounds in resemblances to the heroic novel of the period preceding 1660. Into this work of her youth Marie-Catherine poured her imitative and derivative fancy, writing in the style of her favorite authors, Gomberville, d'Urfé, Mlle de Scudéry and La Calprenède. Any author "plus ancien" than these she claimed not to have read; the statement might well be true as far as *Alcidamie* is concerned.[9] The landing of Haly Joseph on the "Isle Délicieuse, . . . un des plus beaux endroits du

---

[8] There existed, moreover, a novel in which those interested in the Rohan affair could find it narrated without Mlle Desjardins' Moorish heroic apparatus. Magendie, *op. cit.*, pp. 259-261, analyzes this novel, which he calls Lamotte du Broquart's *Florigénie, ou l'illustre victorieuse*, published in 1647 and dedicated to Marguerite de Rohan. Magendie affirms it to be a revision of the same author's *Bellaure triomphante*, 1630-1633, with the inclusion of Mme de Rohan's return to Paris, the birth of Tancrède, his sequestration, reappearance, the dispute over his identity, etc. There is a mystery here, for the copies of both *Florigénie* and *Bellaure triomphante* which I consulted in the Arsenal contain nothing which could be interpreted as a reference to the Rohan affair. Moreover, the analysis of *Florigénie* in the *BUR* (1786, II [2], 112-144) likewise contains none of the incidents mentioned by Magendie. The author of the résumé in the *BUR* does mention a preface by Broquart (not in the copies I have seen) identifying Florigénie with Marguerite de Rohan, but is forced, as I have been, to state that he can see no resemblance between the novel and its alleged subject. I can only conclude that Magendie's analysis is in error, or that (as seems probable in view of the preface referred to in the *BUR*) there exists an entirely different version of *Florigénie*, utterly unlike the heroic-pastoral work consulted by the critic of the *BUR* and myself.

[9] *Recueil de lettres*, p. 67.

monde, et que le Ciel semble avoir choisi pour y verser ses meilleures influences . . ." (p. 3) is a repetition of the hero's arrival on the "Isle Inaccessible" of Gomberville's *Polexandre*. Haly, like Polexandre, saves the Queen of the island from the attack of a wild animal. Alcidamie, in the fashion of Alcidiane, her counterpart in the earlier novel, takes her rescuer to court and there requests him to tell his story. Alcidamie's costume, which, like the costumes of Gomberville's characters, is minutely described, resembles her predecessor's no less than her name suggests that of Alcidiane.[10] The "sage Oraste" who protects Haly and Amador is a descendant of the "sage Osmin" of Gomberville.[11] Almanzaïde, in one of the minor stories, seems modeled after *Polexandre's* Almanzaïre. The "courses et tournois" on the Canary Islands resemble those in Gomberville. Polexandre's trip to Denmark probably suggested Artambert's excursion to Greenland. Specific elements from the novels of Mlle de Scudéry and La Calprenède are not numerous; her debt to those authors is a general one of style and technique. The device of the concealed prince (cf. Sesotris in *Le Grand Cyrus*) was a commonplace in fiction. The whole story of Tancrède de Rohan, in fact, stripped of its contemporary trappings, must have appealed to Mlle Desjardins because of its inherently romanesque character. By taking her *cadre* from Gomberville, adding such tricks as the substitution of children (cf. *Cassandre,* etc.), the treachery of *suivantes,* disguises, messengers dying before the delivery of their all-important messages, shipwrecks, pirates, and the like, and by mixing with these the battle scenes, sieges, personal combats, and holding of hostages, devices familiar to readers of the *Grand Cyrus, Cléopâtre,* etc., she turned out a product which should, by all contemporary standards, have enjoyed a large public. But the heroic novel, with its interminable central story cut by *histoires intercalées,* was by 1661 a dying *genre* (of the many-volumed heroic novels only *Faramond* ap-

[10] Cf. *Alcidamie* in the 1741 edition of Mlle Desjardins' *Œuvres,* IV, 7 ff. and the description of Alcidiane's costume in the passage from *Polexandre* reproduced in the *BUR,* 1776, VI (1), 114. Mlle Desjardins, of course, adds a *galant* touch: "Sa robe étoit d'une étoffe blanche . . . retroussée à l'endroit du genouil par une agraffe de pierres, et laissoit voir une jambe . . . dont la perfection étoit achevée. . . ." For the similarity in names, cf. Bayle's article "Jardins" in the *Dictionnaire.* Writing in 1699 or later, and recounting how "une grande Dame" (Mme de Rohan) had forced Mlle Desjardins to stop "à moitié chemin" this novel in which her family was represented, Bayle is unable to recall whether the work was entitled *Alcidamie* or *Alcidiane.*

[11] These wise tutors and their charges were a commonplace of the heroic novel: cf. La Calprenède's *Cassandre,* etc. The "sages" later became the Mentors of such works as Fénelon's *Télémaque* and the *porte-paroles* of the political Utopia novels of the late seventeenth and early eighteenth century.

peared later). The public, as we have seen, was not interested in a
héroïne à clef whose "qualité de Rohan" was obscured by the machinations of a *suivante* and by a false Moorish atmosphere. Mlle Desjardins
probably sensed that her own talents hardly appeared at their best in
such an imitative work. Magne suggests that the labor of writing ten
volumes only to arrive at a foreseen conclusion "l'énerve et l'exaspère,"
causing her to leave the novel unfinished.[12] What seems more likely is
that she was feeling her way toward the forms best suited to her temper-
ament. The story of Haly was abandoned for the minor stories, which,
while still more or less "heroic" in form, suggest the novelist's later
galant method.

In her first novel, Mlle Desjardins' debt to Honoré d'Urfé is quite
apparent. The rôle played by the *Astrée* in the development of the novel
in the seventeenth century in France is a dual one. It exerted a general
influence, through the gradual accumulation of imitations and modifica-
tions of its style and content, and it had in most cases a specific influence
on each author directly as he read (and doubtless re-read) the original.[13]
Alcidamie is full of direct imitations of the *Astrée*. The gallant gentlemen
and ladies at the court of Alcidamie all descend from characters of the
Lignon valley. Céladon and Galatée are, however, less in evidence than
certain minor figures who appealed to later readers for other reasons. The
chief survivor is Hylas.[14] As the Lisicrate of *Alcidamie*, he draws up
for his Diane (here Philimène) a list of "règles de service" which are
hardly more than a copy of Hylas' marriage contract:

> Quand on voudra changer d'amant ou de maîtresse,
> Pendant un mois on le dira,

[12] *Op. cit.*, p. 48. Magne describes the main story of *Alcidamie* as "coupé . . .
d'aventures collatérales." This is not true; Haly's story is narrated without a break.
When it ends, it has been brought up to the "present" moment, that is, with Haly's
arrival on the island. This is also true of the minor stories. To have carried any one
story beyond the point which is reached in the novel would have required a complete
change in the *cadre* device used to excuse the telling of the stories. This may be one
reason why *Alcidamie* remained "unfinished." Mlle Desjardins had become caught
in her own time-scheme; she had, so to speak, like the amateur she then was,
"painted herself into a corner" with her novel. That she thought of the possibility
of a "suite d'*Alcidamie*" is suggested by the preface of *Anaxandre*. As far as the
story of Tancrède is concerned, it is difficult to imagine what she could have included
in it; Haly had only to die to complete his resemblance to his alleged prototype!

[13] There is no need here to mention the "Astrée" games and other evidences of the
popular influence of the novel; cf. Magendie, *op. cit.*

[14] Cf. Magendie and Lancaster for novels and plays concerning this lastingly popular figure. Mlle Desjardins here, as elsewhere, consistently flatters contemporary taste.

> Et après on changera,
> Sans qu'on soit accusé d'erreur ou de foiblesse;
> Mais on conservera toujours la tendresse. . . .[15]

The *badinage* about life and love found in d'Urfé continues unabated in *Alcidamie*. Lisicrate, taking his cue from one of the "Cabinets" of statues which themselves derive from the portrait-gallery of the *Astrée* (borrowed in turn by d'Urfé from Montemayor's *Diana*), exclaims:

> Quoi! Seigneur, vous traitez l'Amour Galand de fiction, lui qui est la source de tous les plaisirs et de tous les divertissements qu'on peut goûter dans le monde; sans l'amour galand cette belle saison de nos jours, qu'on appelle le Printems, ne produiroit que des soucis au lieu de roses; le bal, les promenades, et les festins qui rendent l'Amour si enjoué, et si plaisant, seroient absoluement bannis de la société civile, et l'on seroit réduit à passer dans une chambre, tout le tems qu'on passe aux lieux que la Nature ne semble avoir produits que pour nostre divertissement.[16]

The characters in the stories address to each other letters headed "Le Trop Heureux Rustan, à son Adorable Princesse," "La Trop Constante Cinthie, à l'Infidèle Iphile," etc., all titles modeled on those of the *Astrée*. There is no direct reference to the famous work, but interior evidence proves Mlle Desjardins' acquaintance with it.[17]

Alcidamie owes to the endless volumes of *Cassandre, Cléopâtre, Clélie,* and the like, not only the heroic apparatus of battles, escapes, disguises, concealments, etc., but also stylistic clichés and mannerisms. Haly's mother is "la vertueuse Reine," Célimedon's mistress "la charmante Célie," and the "sage Oraste" a "vénérable Vieillard," or an "officieux Inconnu," full of "sages discours." Periodically, a "tempête furieuse" shipwrecks one or another character, leading to further "Milesian" adventures. Haly is "transporté de joie" at the sight of the men sent to bring him to Fez, and returns there with "un équipage proportionné à sa naissance." The ambitious Zélide is full of "horreur" and "dédain" for the "conseils abominables" of the "perfide Lindarache":

---

[15] *Alcidamie,* p. 331. There is much more; the entire poem was reproduced in Mlle Desjardins' *Nouveau recueil* as "Articles d'une Intrigue de Galanterie."

[16] *Ibid.,* pp. 179-180. A remarkable coincidence may be noted in the conjunction of the word "divertissement" and the phrase "l'on seroit réduit à passer dans une chambre. . . ." Pascal's famous attack on *divertissements* attributes all the evils of the world, in his notable phrase, to "une seule chose, qui est ne savoir pas se tenir en repos dans une chambre." Although the first edition of the *Pensées* (1670) appeared nine years after *Alcidamie,* and Pascal himself died one year after the publication of Mlle Desjardins' work, there seems little likelihood that the passage cited above bears more than an accidental relation to Pascal's well-known line.

[17] She refers to the *Astrée* by name only once in her works (in the *Mémoires de Henriette-Sylvie de Molière*). See Ch. VII, below.

Je veux régner, mais, Lindarache, je veux que ce soit, s'il se peut, sans attirer le Courroux du Ciel sur ma tête, et c'est assez que je me dépouille des sentiments de sœur de Théocrite, sans prendre ceux de sa meurtrière.[18]

The amorous outbursts of Rustan are couched in a similar formalized phraseology:

Ah! Madame . . . je vous jure par Zélide, qui est ma Divinité visible, que quand je sçaurois d'une certitude infaillible, qu'elle auroit assez de bonté pour recevoir la déclaration de mon amour sans me bannir, je ne la lui ferois pas (p. 58).

Even the shock of disillusionment is not enough to disrupt such high-flown rhetoric:

De cette même bouche adorable qui prononce à présent l'Arrest de mon banisse-ment, ne revoquez pas les glorieuses assurances que vous m'avez données de ma félicité. . . . Je sçai, Madame, que cet honneur est tel qu'il n'y a point de mortel qui en soit digne . . . (p. 123).

The characters described in these phrases and who use these words are scarcely more individualized. Alcidamie is given no qualities of personality beyond those suitable to the reigning queen of an heroic novel. Haly is a "généreux Prince" of surpassing virtue but little interest. Rustan is an amorous simpleton; Gomelle feeble and lifeless. Lindarache's cunning and deceit are not elaborated upon, and her own motives are left almost wholly unexplained. The people at Alcidamie's court comprise such "types" as Arpalice ("elle avoit l'âme tendre, et les inclinations douces"), Philimène (whose "rares qualités d'esprit et . . . mérite particulier" make her a favorite), the neo-Hylas Lisicrate ("un des hommes du monde le plus agréable; il étoit bien fait de sa personne, et il avoit un air par-ticulier de dire les choses, qui rendoit sa conversation incomparable"), and Osomar, another conversationalist, "qui avoit un mérite extraordinaire" (pp. 171-174). There is little attempt to depict the physical features of the characters. Alcidamie is described as having

. . . le tour du visage ovale, le nez aquilin, la bouche petite et incarnate, et d'une forme si particulière, qu'elle sembloit toujours sourire. . . . Ses yeux étoient bleus, grands et bien fendus (p. 9).

We may assume that the other characters fit some such abstract pattern of appearance.[19] Indeed, Mlle Desjardins accords far more space to feminine

---

[18] *Alcidamie*, p. 53. The foregoing phrases are found on pp. 26, 37, 39, 40, 41, 43, and *passim*.

[19] Cf. the description of Artambert (p. 360): "Il étoit grand et de bonne mine, ses cheveux étoient châtains-clairs, ses yeux noirs, vifs et pleins de feu, il avoit le nez aquilain, le tour du visage ovale, et un air de grandeur dans sa phisionomie. . . ." Aquiline noses and oval faces appear to be *de rigueur* for both sexes.

clothes than to the feminine soul. When Cinthie consents to see the
repentant Iphile for one last time (her lover, as it turns out, kills himself
after the interview), she is depicted in this emotional crisis, as far as
her features are concerned, with only the two adjectives "pâle et lan-
guissante." Her costume, however, is detailed minutely:

Elle étoit vêtue d'une grande robe blanche qui lui trainoit jusqu'à terre. Les manches
qui en étoient larges et longues, étoient rattachées sur le bras d'une boutonnière de
soye noire. Une ceinture de même couleur la seignoit par dessus les hanches, et
laissant voir la forme de sa taille, retomboit à terre terminé par deux grosses houpes
de soye (p. 304).

The same procedure is followed in other instances. To this propensity
to write seventeenth-century fashion copy should doubtless be connected
Mlle Desjardins' attempts to evoke in words the architecture, *paysages*
and *décors* which surround her characters. The "Isle Délicieuse" is

. . . un des plus beaux endroits du monde, que le Ciel semble avoir choisi pour y
verser ses meilleures influences. . . . Elle est située dans un endroit de la Méditerranée,
qui semble former un Canal exprès pour servir de Port à Plaisance, qui est la
capitale de ses Villes (p. 3).

Yet there is little if any leaning toward the exotic; escape in space serves
only to bring the reader again to the customary delights and elegancies
of contemporary mundane luxury. Alcidamie's Nepenthe has no volcanic
cliffs, no olive trees growing on wind-swept promontories, no Blue
Grotto.[20] Instead, Le Nôtre-like scenes of idealized Italian architecture
and landscaping, more elaborate even than Versailles, form the background against which the characters move:

Ils se trouvèrent dans un petit bois de cyprès, divisé par plusieurs routes longues et
droites, qui se terminoient toutes à un tapis de gazons qu'un agréable ruisseau
traversoit par le milieu . . . (p. 5).
On y abordoit [au "Château d'Alcidamie"] du côté de Plaisance par une grande
terrasse balustrée, élevée de douze marches, et ornée de niches remplies de plusieurs
figures de Neptune et autres Dieux marins. . . . Une cour tapissée de gazon, et ornée
d'une grande fontaine. . . . Ils passèrent sur un pontlevis qui traversoit de larges
fossés . . . et entrèrent dans une seconde cour. . . . Elle étoit entournée de superbes
bâtiments, que leur antiquité n'empêchoit pas d'être fort beaux. . . . Un parterre
entouré de quatre larges canaux, au bout de chacun desquels sont douze cascades. . . .

[20] The "Isle Délicieuse's" only grotto, far from being picturesque or romantic, is a
reductio ad absurdum of geometrical classicism: "[La Grotte] . . . pour tout lambris
n'avoit que de grandes plaques de glaces de Venise, séparées les unes des autres en
forme de chassis, qui représentoient autant de grottes qu'il y avoit de quarrées, et qui
multiploient si agréablement les objets, qu'on voyoit ce soir-là mille Alcidamies dans
ce lieu" (p. 340).

Au milieu de ce parterre il y a un jet d'eau d'une hauteur prodigeuse . . . (pp. 320-322).

La principale Cour du Palais . . . étoit entourée de balustrades de marbre, sur laquelle il y avoit plusieurs statues de Jaspe et de Porphyre . . . un perron de marbre à deux rampes. . . . Dans la masse de pierre qui séparoit ces deux rampes, il y avoit une niche de marbre noir, dans laquelle étoit la figure d'un petit Amour de marbre blanc. . . . Une salle bâtie à l'Italienne, de la voute de laquelle pendoient quantité de lampes de cristal. . . . La chambre de la Princesse . . . étoit d'un argent très-poli, tout semé de Topazes et d'Amatistes, et le platfonds étoit de bois de Cèdre. . . . Une longue galerie de tableaux, qui conduisoit à une terrasse qui regnoit tout le long du derrière de cette maison. . . . Les quatre avenues par lesquelles on avoit communication du quartier Royal aux quatres autres, étoient bordées d'Orangers, et avoient chacune une fontaine qui jettoit de l'eau jusqu'aux nues.[21]

The extent to which this reproduction of contemporary reality expresses an affirmation of the taste of the day may be read in Alcidamie's concern, upon first meeting Haly, "qu'il ne fût d'un pays, où les bâtiments superbes ne fussent pas approuvés." This fear she excuses with a somewhat surprising scrap of relativistic philosophy:

Vous sçavez que la bizarrerie de certains peuples est telle que ce qui fait la laideur de tous les autres lieux du monde, compose la beauté de celui qu'ils habitent. De là vient que toutes les productions de la Nature sont toujours utiles à quelque chose, quelques difformes qu'elles nous paroissent . . . (p. 19).

The *Cabinets d'Amour* which stand on the terrace of Alcidamie's palace are precious and baroque indeed. "Quatre petits amours désolés qui brisoient leurs fleches, qui éteignoient leur flambeaux," oppose, standing before the *Cabinet des tristes avantures,* the four joyous Cupids of the true *Cabinet d'Amour.* Beneath a mighty painting of Jupiter ravishing Europa are represented: *l'Amour d'Inclination* (a young Cupid sharpening his arrows), *l'Amour Intéressé* ("si laid, qu'il en faisoit peur, et cependant il étoit assis sur un Trône d'or"), *l'Amour Galand* (surrounded by demolished arrows and broken chains), and *l'Amour Solitaire* (leaning over a river bank, receiving from the Graces hearts crowned with myrtle). A two-line motto accompanies each tableau.[22]

If the imitative nature of the heroic material and style of most of *Alcidamie* is all too evident, and if the *cadre* in which its stories are

---

[21] *Alcidamie*, pp. 15-17. These descriptive passages may be compared with those from earlier novels quoted by Magendie, *op. cit.*, pp. 262 ff. The advance in technique (such as it is) in depicting "le monde extérieur" is evident.

[22] *Alcidamie*, pp. 176-177. An example of the mottoes (for *l'Amour Solitaire*): "Belles, cet Amour seul mérite vos désirs, Puisque seul il promet de tranquilles plaisirs."

placed varies only slightly from that of the *Astrée,* there are nevertheless in the novel certain evidences of a tendency in a new direction. It is the trend toward a more subtle analysis of the psychology of love, which will become Mlle Desjardins' *forte* and which will give rise to a whole *genre* of fiction of which the *Princesse de Clèves* is the finest example. The preparation for such a movement had long existed.[23] *Alcidamie* contributes little to it, but we may detect already in the work the young authoress' dissatisfaction with the *Polexandre-Grand Cyrus* type of fiction, and her inclination to write of the more engrossing psychological problems of love.

This new manner, which replaces the heroic technique employed in the story of Haly Joseph, may be seen best in the *histoires intercalées* of *Alcidamie.* The break between the two styles is never complete, but it is evident enough. First, the subject matter of Haly's story is, in the main, the ambitious effort of a princess to usurp her brother's throne. The theme of the three later episodes is, however, *les désordres de l'amour.* War and intrigues of state are left behind; so too, for the most part, are disguises, concealments, false letters, and the rest of the apparatus of the *roman d'aventures.* In their place appear rudimentary studies of *âmes sensibles,* quasi-romantic personal relations, passions, cruelties, sacrifices, amorous melancholy, and other emotional states. The principle of *honnêteté* which dominates the lovers in the *Histoire de Célie,* in which the heroine confesses her love to a man who does not love her but who through respect for her feelings gives up his real mistress, foreshadows the code of behavior which was later to touch readers of the time in Mlle Desjardins' own *Désordres de l'amour,* and in the *aveu* and chaste widowhood of the Princesse de Clèves. The characters grow introspective and self-analytical, in the manner of an incipient Proust:

> . . . D'où vient que je suis rêveuse, quand Célimedon est rêveur? que je sens de la joie toutes les fois que je lui en vois témoigner, et que j'ai une inquiétude effroyable lorsqu'il n'est pas auprès de moi? . . . Toutes les fois que je le vois mélancholique, je sens une certaine tristesse qui me saisit insensiblement, sans que j'en puisse dire la cause, qui me rend aussi consternée que lui, et lorsque je suis dans un lieu où il n'est pas, je change mille fois de place dans un moment, et je tourne incessament la tête du côté qu'il doit entrer. . . . Ah! ma chère sœur. . . . Les inquiétudes que je ressens, sont d'une espèce dont je n'en avois jamais ressentie. . . (pp. 195-196).

[23] Cf. G. Reynier, *Le Roman sentimental avant l'Astrée,* Paris, 1908, and Ch. V, below.

To a great extent the verbal tags and clichés so noticeable before have here disappeared. Passion, which in the heroic novel is largely absent, or, if present, seems stilted and unreal, is occasionally depicted in *Alcidamie* in specific terms of its physical manifestations, anticipating the realistic descriptions which invaded the novel after the theory of sensationalism gave to the outward effects of emotion a new importance. When Célie discovers Célimedon's love for her rival Climène,

> . . . elle sentit comme un glaçon courir dans ses veines, à cette connoissance qui la pensa priver du sentiment. . . . Je la trouvai dans son cabinet, couchée sur un lit de repos, les yeux mouillés de larmes, et le visage si changé, qu'à peine en étoit-elle connoissable.[24]

When Cinthie's letter reaches Iphile, who has abandoned her, and awakens in him "un reste de la passion qu'il avoit eûe dans l'âme,"

> [il] changea plusieurs fois de couleur pendant la lecture de cette lettre, et lorsqu'elle fut finie, il me la présenta en me regardant languissament, et se laissa tomber sur un siège qui étoit proche de lui, où il demeura sur une de ses mains sans prononcer un seule parole (p. 300).

Lovers may be attracted to each other, we find in *Alcidamie* (which is in certain passages almost a handbook for the amorous) in many ways and degrees, by "l'Amour solitaire," "l'Amour tranquille," "l'Amour galand," and the like. But the love which "seul se peut proprement nommer Amour," and which "fait qu'on s'aime sans s'être vus, et qu'on s'adore quand on se voit" (p. 180), is the "Amour d'inclination," which the Romantics were later to call Fatal Passion. One character defines it in a rather surprisingly naturalistic fashion:

> L'on aime, parce qu'on ne peut s'empêcher d'aimer, et tel est passionnément amoureux, qui n'en sçauroit d'autre raison que celle qui porte un animal à choisir les bêtes de son espèce (p. 181).

It is this obsession which grips the lovers Iphile and Cinthie, Almanzaïde and Artambert. Paul and Virginie will not surpass their early ecstasies:

> [Iphile] passa des journées entières au bord de quelque ruisseau, avec son aimable Maîtresse, sans craindre que rien ne pût interrompre leur conversation, que la chûte inopinée de quelque pluye d'Été, ou le désir de changer de promenade. . . . Il fut deux mois entiers sans partir d'auprès de Cinthie. . . . Il goutoit des plaisirs si grands, qu'ils avoient jusques alors surpassé son imagination. . . (p. 275).

The women Célie and Cinthie both have "une fièvre violente" of love. It

---

[24] *Alcidamie*, p. 205. We are at the beginning of the path leading to the *Nouvelle Héloïse* and its characters who burst into tears on every page.

is brought about, however, by the indifference of their lovers. The minor stories of *Alcidamie* are all studies of a woman's persistent love for a man who has either ignored or betrayed her.[25] Iphile and Artambert are the chief betrayers; each has the same pattern of behavior. Both are descendants of Hylas, but lack that character's gay, cynical, openly mocking and yet sincere frankness. Instead they are serious, brooding, full of exaggerated self-importance. No sooner has Iphile enjoyed his few months' happiness with Cinthie than

> . . . il se lassa de sa félicité. La vue de Cinthie ne lui sembla plus prétieuse. . . . Son séjour [avec elle] lui devint si insupportable, qu'il fut obligé de venir faire un voyage à Milo pour se divertir. . . (p. 277).

Almanzaïde relates the same difficulty experienced with Artambert:

> Les Dieux semblèrent se lasser de ma félicité: Car tout d'un coup Artambert devint si rêveur et si mélancholique, qu'il n'en étoit plus connoissable. . . . J'eus une extrême inquiétude de ce changement. . . . Je le priai de me dire le sujet de la mélancholie que je remarquais sur son visage. Il me répondit avec assez de froideur que c'étoit un effet de son tempérament. . . (p. 398).

Contemporaries must have felt about this new type of lover a mixture of disapproval and self-recognition; such at least seems to have been the reaction of one of them, Boursault:

> C'est au commencement du Roman d'*Alcidamie* que vous trouverez l'Histoire de Cinthie et d'Iphile; vous aurez beaucoup de plaisir à la lire, parce que Cinthie qui est de votre sexe, y fait le plus beau personnage du monde. . . . Je haïs autant ce coquin d'Iphile, à cause de son inconstance, que j'aime Cinthie à cause de sa fidélité; et malgré tout le remors qu'il a, s'il n'avoit pû mourir, et qu'on m'eût fait arbitre de sa vie, je l'aurois condamné à être pendu. Ne vous lassez point de conserver le caractère de Cinthie, belle Philis: Et quand même vos bontés devroient faire un Iphile, songez que vous ne perdriez rien de votre gloire, et que votre mémoire seroit autant respectée de tous les honnêtes gens, que la mienne leur seroit odieuse.[26]

Iphile in one passage defends himself against his friend's charge of will-

---

[25] Of the heroes, only one (Artambert) is legally married to his "Maîtresse." It is impossible to say just what sexual relations, if any, existed, for example, between Iphile and Cinthie. A convention of silence surrounds all similar situations in most fiction of the period, although later Mlle Desjardins becomes, upon occasion, more explicit. To a modern eye, Cinthie's reactions to Iphile's desertion would seem absurdly disproportionate unless the word "mistress" had its full meaning. There is evidence that readers of the period made their own interpretations; Bayle in the *Nouvelles de la république des lettres* of October, 1684 (*Œuvres*, I, 157) wrote: "On est persuadé en lisant les Histoires amoureuses, que le Héros va beaucoup plus loin que le Livre ne dit."

[26] *Op. cit.*, III, 59. The story of Cinthie is not "au commencement"; it is in Book III.

ful indifference, blaming it on a sort of "je ne sais quoi" change of
emotional state for which he does not feel responsible. His self-analysis is
of some interest because it forms a strong contrast to the fully integrated
"classical" personality usually associated with the seventeenth century,
in which motives, passions, and actions follow a constant and almost
determinable pattern. Iphile is the victim of psychological processes
which take place within him without his knowledge; he is vacillating and
uncertain, both of the present and of the future, not because of any
Hamlet-like problem confronting him, but on account of the sheer un-
predictability of his psyche:

> . . . je ne quitte point Cinthie, et je ne crois pas que vous puissiez me reprocher
> que je sois un infidèle. . . . Je sens bien que je ne l'aime pas avec autant d'empresse-
> ment que je faisois il y a quelque mois, mais je n'aime pourtant aucune autre personne
> plus qu'elle; et quoique mon cœur soit un peu plus à moi qu'il n'étoit autrefois . . .
> je l'aime tendrement, je l'estime autant qu'on la peut estimer; je donnerois ma vie
> pour son service, si j'en trouvois l'occasion. . . . Mais par l'effet d'une tiédeur dont
> je ne sçaurois dire la cause, je sens bien que je la dois nommer ma première amie
> plutôt que ma maîtresse. . . . Comment devineroit-elle mon changement? . . . Peut-être
> même avant qu'elle le sache, elle sera entièrement rétablie [dans mon âme]: car
> enfin comme ma tiédeur n'a point de cause légitime, elle ne peut pas long-tems
> durer. . . (pp. 280-281).

He underestimates the permanence of his irrational change of heart, as
it becomes apparent when Cinthie writes him a seemingly indifferent
letter, giving him an excuse to break off their relationship entirely. When
he later learns the truth, he refuses to return to her and "l'abuser par
un feint empressement" (p. 293). Artambert's situation is a different
one, for he is a prince; and he confesses to Almanzaïde that "la tristesse
que vous remarquez dans [son] esprit" comes from his enforced idleness
and his desire to occupy a throne (p. 399). Nevertheless, it seems
obvious that what ails both melancholy heroes is fundamentally that
same sort of *ennui*, dissatisfaction, and desire for escape from over-
familiar surroundings which will reappear to afflict the Byronic heroes
of Romanticism—René, *l'homme fatal,* and later, Emma Bovary.

The indirect criticism of contemporary fashions in love, which may
be sensed in *Alcidamie's* minor stories, finds outright expression in the
conversations galantes of the figures in the *cadre* of the novel. Philimène,
for example, seeks "un Amour tout nouveau," pronouncing "celui du siècle
présent, terrible pour une personne de mon humeur." She continues:

L'Amour à la mode est indiscret, emporté et inconstant; on ne voit plus ni probité ni tendresse dans le monde. . . . Sans pénétrer dans toutes les distinctions qu'on fait à présent de l'amour, je le considère tel qu'il étoit dans les premiers siècles. . . .[27]

Unfortunately, we are given no description of this "primitivist" love "du bon vieulx temps." Philimène proceeds only to another denunciation, this time of "l'Amour intéressé, dont je ne voulusse rien prendre pour faire une manière d'aimer à mon usage" (p. 186).

A curious passage in the *Histoire de Cinthie* depicts a rite in honor of Neptune on the island of Milo, "renommée par la naissance de Socrate," and which appeared out of the sea, according to the author, "toute entière tout d'un coup, comme par un miracle de la nature." The *décor* of the ceremony is an odd mixture of the classical baroque and sombre trappings of romantic aspect:

Pendant huit jours tout le peuple fait des danses et des festins; les Ouvriers quittent leurs ouvrages, les Dames sont superbement parées. . . . Un homme chez lequel nous logeâmes nous mena dans un Temple consacré à Neptune. . . . Le Temple où nous entrâmes, nous parut d'abord en quelque façon affreux, car il étoit grand et si obscur, qu'on n'y voyoit pour lumière qu'une petite lampe, dont la sombre lueur rendoit l'obscurité encore plus horrible. . . . Nous entendîmes une Musique lugubre, qui quoiqu'elle fût assez triste, ne laissoit pas pourtant d'être fort charmante. . . . Une femme chanta une ôde, par laquelle on demandoit à Neptune de tirer Milo de l'obscurité . . . [Cette prière] ne fut pas plutôt finie que par l'effet d'une machine qui nous parut un enchantement, cent lampes de cristal à plusieurs branches, sortirent d'une fausse voûte. . . . Nous remarquâmes donc que le Temple étoit d'une forme ovale, que l'architecture en étoit magnifique, qu'il étoit orné de quantité de festons de coquilles de diverses couleurs, et qu'à chaque côté de l'Autel il y avoit six femmes couvertes d'un voile noir qui leur traînoit jusques à la terre, qui tenoient une trompe marine dans la main, dont elles jouèrent quelque tems. Lorsqu'elles eurent cessé leur concert, nous vîmes un petit char suspendu en l'air, où il y avoit un jeune enfant. . . . Toutes ces femmes jettèrent le voile noir qui les couvroit, et nous firent voir la plus agréable métamorphose. . . . Dessous ce voile elles avoient des habits d'une étoffe verte tissue d'or et d'argent, qui parroissoit de la couleur des ondes de la Mer lorsque le Soleil se couche dans son sein . . . (pp. 226-230).

Though all the "sombre," "lugubre," and "horrible" elements of this tableau are dissipated by the appearance of colored shells, "trompes marines," crystal chandeliers, and a "char suspendu" (doubtless a reminiscence of the machine play of the period, in which such devices were employed), one feels nevertheless that, as in the case of the sad music,

---

[27] *Alcidamie,* p. 186. Thomas Corneille's play *L'Amour à la mode,* performed about 1652, had as its *marotique* theme the same superficial love as that denounced in the passage above (cf. Lancaster, *op. cit.,* II [II], 758). The various Hylas plays are examples of the same trend.

"qui ne laissoit pas pourtant d'être fort charmante," the obscure and "affreux" aspects of the scene were calculated to arouse in the reader a certain thrilling and unfamiliar pleasure. The ballet of the period, which the above scene in many ways recalls, must have appealed to the same preromantic desire for something other than the bare, rational elegance of the usual classical scene.[28]

Mixed with *questioni d'amore* conversations of gallantry and love engaged in by the characters at Alcidamie's court are several brief arguments of literary interest. One concerns the pleasure aroused in the reader by poetry. It is a matter of common agreement that nearly all of what was in seventeenth-century France considered lyric poetry seems to modern taste not poetry at all, but only rhymed prose, or a sort of light versification. Poetry as we know it disappeared largely, to be replaced by vast quantities of verse, most of which now seems hardly above the level of a popular song. If the public shared the views of Alcidamie, this view is not surprising; certainly her standards have little to do with pure, or any other poetry:

> J'ai une si grande passion pour la Poësie en général, que pourvû que je voye des sillabes arrangées dans un certain ordre, et qui fassent une cadance à mon oreille, je trouve toujours cela le plus beau du monde (p. 344).

It is difficult not to suspect that Alcidamie is something of a *porte-parole* here for Mlle Desjardins, who turned out rapidly an enormous production of precisely this kind of "Poësie." When another character remarks that "les qualités les plus essentiellement nécessaires à des beaux Vers, c'est la pureté du language, et la netteté de l'expression" (p. 345), she is told in answer that "ce n'est d'ordinaire que dans les grands ouvrages que cette délicatesse de langue est à observer." The conversation centers then on short improvisations, in which one looks only for "un sens agréable, du feu et des rimes justes," hardly taking care to examine "s'il y a des mots impropres dedans, ou non" (p. 345). After some discussion of whether the writing of poetry is a suitable occupation anyway for a "galant homme,"[29] we are given in one sentence the fundamental principle of contemporary verse:

---

[28] Cf. especially the ballets of Benserade (Silin, *op. cit., passim*).

[29] "Cette sort de petits vers libres et faits sans préparation, sont presque les seuls qu'un galant homme . . . peut impunément faire. . . . Il ne seroit pas bienséant à un homme d'une grande qualité d'entreprendre un Poëme Épique. . . . Je voudrois qu'on considérât [la Poësie] comme un divertissement plutôt que comme occupation," etc. (pp. 347-348). This attitude was widespread; both La Calprenède and Georges

Il y a des *pensées vives* auxquelles l'expression poëtique convient mieux que celle de la Prose (p. 350).

Pensées vives is indeed an apt phrase to describe the ideas, sentiments, and wit with which most of the poetry of the period was concerned, and the pseudo-poetic, pseudo-emotional *badinage* of Mlle Desjardins' own verse.[30]

To sum up, Mlle Desjardins' first novel, *Alcidamie,* begins as an heroic *roman d'aventures* in the style of Gomberville, La Calprenède, and Scudéry, to change midway into a group of love stories or *nouvelles galantes* recounted in a *cadre* recalling both the *Astrée* and *Polexandre.* The style and the technique of character delineation of *Alcidamie* improve noticeably once the subject matter unsympathetic to her talent (political intrigue, sequestrated princes, melodramatic shipwrecks, etc.) is left behind, and the description of the "disorders of love," which came to be her literary *forte,* replaces straight narration of action. *Alcidamie* is spoiled in part by a preciosity which never entirely disappeared from the work of Mlle Desjardins, who remained one of the chief devotees and lawgivers of the realm of *galanterie.* The novel proved to be for her a valuable *coup d'essai.* From it she undoubtedly learned that heroic fiction was not to be her province, and that she could better portray the anguish of a betrayed woman than an ambitious princess' intrigues to gain the throne. Her first reaction to the lack of success of *Alcidamie* was to abandon the novel form entirely. During the next seven years she turned almost exclusively to plays, verse, and letters, attaining a wide reputation in those *genres.* Yet she did return to prose fiction, with a firmer and more expert grasp of its technique, and, avoiding many of the defects apparent in *Alcidamie,* acquired as a novelist even greater popularity and recognition than that granted her as a poet and a dramatist.

de Scudéry apologized for being writers, deeming it beneath a man of quality. The familiar anecdote of Voltaire and Congreve illustrates the same social prejudice in England in the eighteenth century.

[30] Cf. Ch. II, above. To Mlle Desjardins' credit it should be stated that she in one passage recognizes the existence of "other" poems written by poets with "de la passion dans l'âme" (p. 350).

CHAPTER IV

THEATRE: TRAGI-COMEDY, TRAGEDY, AND COMEDY

By 1662 Mlle Desjardins had laid the foundations of her literary career with her *Récit de la farce des Précieuses* (1659), the various poems in *recueils* which she was soon to collect with many unpublished ones in her first *Recueil de poésies* (1662), and her novel *Alcidamie* (1661). Encouraged by the success of these ventures, she decided to test her talents by trying the theatre, a *genre* unfamiliar to her pen.[1] With the exception of the *Carrousel* for the Dauphin, a short composition in verse written sometime in the spring of 1662, and of *Lisandre, nouvelle,* which belongs probably to the year 1663, the drama remained her sole field of literary activity until the time of her trip to the Low Countries and the publication of her *Lettres* and *Anaxandre* (1667-1668). She then turned once more to fiction, and never again wrote a play.

Manlius (1662)

Manlius, like Corneille's *Sertorius,* which had enjoyed great success earlier in the same year (1662), was a play based on Roman history. The consul Torquatus orders his son Manlius killed, presumably because he has disobeyed orders and defeated the Latins, but in reality because the father loves his son's betrothed Omphale. When a revolt of the soldiers frees Manlius, he returns to his father and offers to submit to his sentence; the consul, conscience-stricken, pardons him and allows his marriage with Omphale to take place, consoling himself with Camille, the widow of Decius.[2]

The tragi-comedy was acted at the Hôtel de Bourgogne sometime early in May, 1662.[3] Tallemant writes, contrary to the opinion expressed by Loret later in the same month, that "cette pièce réussit médiocrement."[4]

---

[1] For the legend that Mlle Desjardins had acted with Molière in the provinces, cf. Ch. I, above. Whatever her associations with the stage had been, she had certainly not yet written a play.

[2] *Manlius* is in the *Œuvres,* ed. of 1741, II. It is discussed by Lancaster, *op. cit.,* III (II), 560, Chatenet, *op. cit.,* pp. 44 ff., Hauréau, *loc. cit.,* and the frères Parfaict, *op. cit.,* IX, 118 ff.

[3] Loret, *Gazette,* May 6, 1662, gives a *compte rendu* of the *première* and an *éloge.* The issue of May 13 contains a second reference to the play, and that of May 27 states that it was enjoying a "grand succès."

[4] *Op. cit.,* VII, 251. Tallemant was probably writing some while afterwards, when the play was no longer being performed and was almost forgotten. The critics, from

When it was published, Mlle de Montpensier accepted the dedication, as she later accepted that of *Lisandre*.[5] The first edition was printed by Barbin and Quinet in October of 1662; there were others—further evidence of the popularity of the work—printed in Holland in 1662, 1718, and 1741, and one at Paris in 1718. A Dutch translation appeared in 1669. All of the eighteenth-century editions of the *Œuvres* contain Mlle Desjardins' three plays.

If it were not for the quarrel over Corneille's *Sophonisbe* of the following year, little would remain to be said of *Manlius*, with the exception of a few remarks on its source and structure. But Mlle Desjardins' work became one of the counters in a drawn-out critical *partie* involving the abbé d'Aubignac, Donneau de Visé, an anonymous author, and the great Corneille himself. Tallemant writes that "Corneille dit quelque chose contre *Manlius*, qui chocqua cet abbé [d'Aubignac] qui prit feu sur-le-champ, car il est tout de souffre. Il critique aussitôt les ouvrages de Corneille; on imprime de part et d'autre" (VII, 251).

The real facts, however, differ slightly from this brief account, and may be summarized as follows: After the appearance of Corneille's *Sophonisbe* in January, 1663, almost a year after *Manlius*, Donneau de Visé, then young and anxious to attract attention, inserted into one of his *Nouvelles nouvelles*, entitled *Le Jaloux par force* (which Magne erroneously lists as a work of Mlle Desjardins—p. 354), an acrid account of *Sophonisbe*, in which he mentioned what must have been a current criticism of *Manlius*—since Tallemant makes the same objection—namely, that Mlle Desjardins had changed the well-known historical event related by Livy, and caused Torquatus to forgive his son instead of killing him. The *Nouvelles nouvelles* appeared early in February. Shortly afterward, the abbé d'Aubignac added to de Visé's criticisms of Corneille's play, but sought to excuse Mlle Desjardins from the journalist's attacks:

Si l'on a blâmé injustement Mlle D. d'avoir sauvé la vie à Manlius, qui par les raisons de la nature et de l'humanité ne devoit point périr. . . .[6]

Yet d'Aubignac himself in his *Pratique du Théâtre* (1657) had laid

Hauréau to Mélèse, have stated one point of view or the other without any real evidence as to the play's success or failure. If anything may be said, it appears unlikely that Loret could have written publicly of a "grand succès" unless *Manlius* was at least well received.

[5] She is mentioned by name in the latter work, but called only "Mademoiselle" in the dedication of *Manlius*.

[6] The abbé d'Aubignac, *Remarques sur la Sophonisbe de M. Corneille* (1ère dissertation), February, 1663. For citations, see n. 9, below.

down as a principle the retention of well-known historical facts. In March, de Visé made an abrupt *volte-face* and published a *Défense de Sophonisbe*, in which he retracted his attacks on Corneille, saying that he had had time to reconsider his hasty judgments, but renewed his criticism of *Manlius*, uncovering the abbé d'Aubignac's probable motive in defending it, as well as his own excuse for using the play as a weapon against the would-be legislator of the drama: for, it appeared now, d'Aubignac had supplied Mlle Desjardins with the plot, and had not disapproved of her changing a well-known event. De Visé takes pains to praise what he considers to be Mlle Desjardins' sole contribution to *Manlius*, namely, its verses, and addresses d'Aubignac thus:

> Vous devriez confesser que le sujet de cette pièce est aussi ennuyeux, qu'il est mal conduit, et que vous êtes obligé à Mlle D. de l'avoir soûtenu par de si beaux vers.

Later in March appeared an anonymous *Lettre sur les Remarques . . . sur la Sophonisbe*, in which the author defended Corneille, and wrote of Mlle Desjardins' work:

> J'ai ouï dire à plusieurs personnes, que si elle n'avoit pas déféré trop aveuglement aux sentimens d'un Savant, qui s'est mêlé de conduire sa pièce, elle eût fait mourir Manlius. . . .

Public opinion, as we see it exemplified in Tallemant, had decided definitely that d'Aubignac was her "précepteur."[7] The abbé failed to comment on this charge in his *Dissertation sur Sertorius*, a further attack on Corneille published in March, 1663. But in his third and fourth *Dissertations*, published in July (after Corneille himself had bribed one printer not to accept them), d'Aubignac wrote:

> Vous pourriez attribuer cette même pièce *Manlius* à M. le chevalier du Buisson qui l'a veue tout entière aussi bien que moy et n'a pas refusé de donner son avis.

He thus placed the blame partly at least on another's shoulders.[8] After this, the quarrel ceased, and d'Aubignac turned his efforts to the completion of his "roman allégorique de la philosophie des Stoiciens," the *Macarise* (1664). Mlle Desjardins herself had had the intelligence and good taste not to intervene in the affair, as well as the wisdom to write her second play, *Nitétis*, without help from the "sulphuric" abbé.[9]

---

[7] *Op. cit.*, VII, 251.

[8] The *Mémoires de Henriette-Sylvie de Molière* and the *Recueil de lettres* both mention du Buisson, a fact which would lend some plausibility to the abbé's statement.

[9] All the foregoing citations are from the pamphlets and *dissertations* collected and printed together in 1739 by Granet, *Recueil de dissertations . . . sur Sertorius*, Paris,

The source of *Manlius* has already been mentioned: Livy.[10] There had been two earlier plays on the same subject, but there is no evidence that Mlle Desjardins knew of them.[11] Despite her efforts to force her material into the mould of the classical drama, she could not make it fit perfectly. De Visé in his *Défense de Sophonisbe* criticized Camille's rôle as superfluous, and found Torquatus' irresolute repetitions of his decision to have his son put to death out of keeping with the true nature of the consul. His vacillations and those of other characters violate the unity of action. Decius' widow, thought the critic, behaves in an inconsistent manner, turning from Torquatus and back to him, although it is never made clear whether she really loves him. D'Aubignac answered the main criticism of Mlle Desjardins' change in well-known history by saying that Corneille had been guilty of the same thing, and that the change occurred only in a few lines at the end, which might easily be altered to permit Manlius to die.[12]

De Visé's comment on the "beaux vers" of *Manlius* has been quoted; even Tallemant admits that sometimes "elle rencontre heureusement" (VII, 251). The tributes of Loret in his *Muze historique* are extravagant, both concerning the "sujet grave, sujet romain," and "les plus charmants vers dont Paris sur un beau théâtre ait été jamais idolâtre" (May 6 and May 13, 1662). René Le Pays wrote to Marie-Catherine that "ce poète C. . . . doit vous avoir fourni les plus beaux vers de Manlius et de Nitétis,"[13]

1739. The best account of the criticisms leveled against Mlle Desjardins is in Lancaster, *loc. cit.* Chatenet and Magne both relate the affair. Pierre Mélèse's *Répertoire analytique*, Paris, 1934, pp. 119-120, cites most of the brief passages reproduced above. His *Théâtre et le public sous Louis XIV*, Paris, 1934, and his *Donneau de Visé*, Paris, 1936, contain the same account of the quarrel over *Sophonisbe*, with brief mention of Mlle Desjardins. René Bray in *La Tragédie cornélienne devant la critique classique*, Dijon, 1927, mentions her once (p. 5). Martino, in his edition of d'Aubignac's *Pratique du théâtre*, Paris, 1927, p. 409, assigns the *Macarise* to the year 1642, although Tallemant dates it after the *Manlius* affair, and the catalogue of the Bib. Nat. lists no edition earlier than 1664. The frères Parfaict (*op. cit.*, IX, 118-120) quote from the various pamphlets most of the passages relative to *Manlius*.

[10] The source was generally recognized by contemporaries. The anonymous author of the *Lettre . . . sur la Sophonisbe*, for example, writes: "Mlle Des Jardins ne devoit point donner à Torquatus un caractère tout contraire à celui qu'il a dans Tite-Live" (quoted by the frères Parfaict, *op. cit.*, IX, 121).

[11] De Noguères' *Mort de Manlie* (1659), and Faure's *Manlius Torquatus* (1661). Cf. Lancaster, *loc. cit.*

[12] Lancaster, *loc. cit.*; Chatenet, *op. cit.*; Granet, *op. cit.* Mlle Desjardins preserves the unity of time by beginning her play in the Roman camp after Manlius' defeat of the Latins.

[13] Quoted by Magne, *op. cit.*, p. 251, from *Les Nouvelles œuvres de M. Le Pays*.

a remark which, though intended as a compliment, may have been provoked by one or two servile imitations of Corneille, such as:

> Tendresse, tes efforts sont ici superflus:
> Mon fils est mon rival, je ne le connois plus.[14]

The frères Parfaict, however, state that the versification "en général est non-seulement très-foible, mais très-prosaique, et mêlée d'expressions basses, et quelquefois ridicules," giving an example.[15] Hauréau, in the nineteenth century, summed up the matter in these words:

> Si l'on rencontre plus d'une tirade précieuse dans les longs discours que tiennent les personnages de cette tragédie [sic], ils récitent quelquefois des vers de la bonne fabrique.[16]

From the standpoint of both structure and versification, *Manlius* gains and loses at the same time from Mlle Desjardins' imitative talents, already so clearly displayed in the *Récit de la farce des Précieuses*, and later to appear in the *Fables*, for example, and throughout her fiction. She seems to have set out to write a play as nearly like those of Corneille as possible, with the result that her best lines affect the reader merely as Cornelian, and second-rate Cornelian at that. One wonders constantly if most of her phrases are not modeled after lines from Corneille which one cannot quite remember; her rhythms and vocabulary seem to belong not to her but to the master:

> Dans un tel embarras, un peu de solitude
> Est un puissant remede à notre inquiétude.
> Mais songez bien sur-tout, que le repos du cœur
> Est ce qu'on peut nommer le suprème bonheur (IV, 4).
> Tu l'as dit, ç'en est fait, qu'on le moine au trépas (V, 3).
> Manlius n'est pas mort? hé quel bras téméraire
> A pu le dérober à ma juste colere (V, 6)?

All the familiar commonplaces of "l'objet de ma flamme," "son cour-

---

[14] Act IV, scene 1. Cf. *Horace*, vv. 501-502: "Et pour trancher enfin ces discours superflus, Albe vous a nommé, je ne vous connois plus." Cf. Lancaster, *loc. cit.*, who mentions also the resemblance of one line to a line in *Sertorius*, and the Cornelian "moral earnestness" of a minor character, Junius.

[15] *Op. cit.*, IX, 117. The lines which they find ridiculous occur in Act IV, scene 4:
Dieux! l'horrible tourment qu'un pareil entretien!
Sa raison est sujette à certaines allarmes,
Dont les noires vapeurs ternissent bien ses charmes:
Et je veux désormais éviter son courroux.

[16] *Op. cit.*, p. 16. He quotes lengthy passages from the play, as does É. Neveu, in Baratte's *Poètes normands*, Paris, 1846, p. 7, the latter praising extravagantly Omphale's ". . . Va, va, c'est assez dit," and the "Adieu, barbare . . ." of Act III, scene 4. Chatenet (*op. cit.*) comments on the merits of many passages.

roux," "belle inhumaine," "grands Dieux," "Hé quoi!," etc. of the
dramatic style of the day abound in *Manlius;* Mlle Desjardins makes no
attempt to keep such phrases down to a minimum, but seems to feel that
they must be thrown in as often as possible to give the right "tone."
Rather curious—and contrary to Cornelian doctrine—is the sentimental
episode of Torquatus' change of heart at the end of the play. The change
is attributed to a kind of romantic natural or inner man, who, with what
resembles the goodness of a *bon sauvage,* rises in the consul, like a
prophetic spectre:

> TORQUATUS: Le cœur pressé, je sens . . .
> OMPHALE: O Dieux! il s'attendrit.
> TORQUATUS: Je sens que dans mon âme il se forme un murmure . . .
> JUNIUS: Gardez-vous d'étouffer la voix de la nature,
>   Elle presse, elle parle, écoutez-la, Seigneur (V, 7).

Nitétis (1663)

The fair success which may at least be attributed to *Manlius* in the
spring of 1662 doubtless encouraged Mlle Desjardins to compose another
play. This time she wisely refrained from asking the assistance of
d'Aubignac; it is probable that before she had done more than begin
her new work the quarrel over *Sophonisbe* broke out in print (February,
1663), adding to her disinclination to seek the abbé's help. According to
Loret, *Nitétis, tragédie* was first played at the Hôtel de Bourgogne on
April 27, 1663, after having been "depuis plus de six mois promise"
(*Lettre* of April 28).[17] The author of the *Muze historique* praises it
highly; it is "*Nitétis,* Tragédie exquise . . ." and:

> On y voit de l'esprit galant,
> Du doux, du fort, et du brillant . . .
> Enfin, icelle *Nitétis,*
> Plaît, dit-on, à de grands esprits,
> Et des quidams, m'ont fait entendre,
> Qu'elle a des endroits à surprendre.

Tallemant, however, writes that "*Nitétis* réussit encore moins que *Manlius*"
(VII, 251). The play was not published until December, 1663.[18] It was

[17] Jean de la Forge, *op. cit.,* mentions Mlle Desjardins' "*pièces* de théâtre," which
would argue that *Nitétis* was completed before La Forge published his work (1663).
In March, 1663, d'Aubignac in his *Dissertation sur Sertorius,* insisted that *Nitétis*
would defend Mlle Desjardins against the attacks of de Visé on *Manlius.* Cf. Granet,
op. cit.

[18] By Barbin and Quinet; the *privilège* is of Sept. 7, the *achevé,* Dec. 19; cf. Lancaster, *op. cit.,* III (II), 457. There were no further editions until the *Œuvres
complètes* of the eighteenth century.

dedicated to Saint-Aignan, through whom Mlle Desjardins hoped to gain the favor of Louis XIV, and who indeed was later responsible in part for the performance of her play *Le Favory* at Versailles in 1665.[19] The dedication followed a brief correspondence, which may be reconstructed thus: In October or early November of 1663, Marie-Catherine wrote to Saint-Aignan a letter in which she wittily turned ordinary epistolary form upside down, putting the ending at the beginning:

Monseigneur, je suis,

                         Votre très-humble et très-

obéissante Servante

         DESJARDINS

À ce nom poursuivez de grace,

Ce n'est ni Placet pour le Roi,

Ni Vers nouveaux, ni Dédicace,

Ni rien de ce qui peut regarder votre emploi:

Il me semble déjà voir quelqu'un de Messieurs les Sçavans,

    (Car on sçait que chez vous on voit incessament

Tous les Illustres de notre age)

Se révolter à ce commencement,

Et dire avec emportement,

Quelle faute contre l'usage!

Juste ciel quel déréglement!

Quoi, renverser ainsi la belle œconomie,

Dont Voiture et Balzac ont tracé leurs écrits;

Et que dira l'Académie?

Que diront tous les beaux esprits?

Pour moi je ne m'en sçaurois taire,

Et pour en parler franc et net:

Dedans le genre épistolaire,

C'est un monstre qu'un tel Billet.

J'en conviens avec Messire le Docte; il est vrai, brave et généreux Duc, en bonne police, le République des Lettres devoit me condamner à l'amende; mais j'ai cru qu'il étoit moins périlleux pour moi d'en courir les risques, que de vous laisser prendre ce Poulet pour un oiseau de mauvais augure; vous êtes **exposé à tant de** prières importunes,

Que pour mieux éviter cette punition,

J'ai d'abord mis mon nom en tête;

Car on sçait que sur la requête,

DESJARDINS n'est pas trop sujette à caution;

Bien que ma fortune soit basse,

---

[19] Cf. Chapters I and II, above, for Mlle Desjardins' relations with the "Illustre Saint-Aignan, qui déjà tant de fois, / As daigné de ma Muse être le digne choix" (*Nouveau recueil, Œuvres*, I, 403).

> Et qu'on croit rarement un Poëte sur sa foi,
> Si-tôt qu'en quelque lieu vous lirez que c'est moi,
> À ce nom poursuivez de grace.

En effet, Monsieur, ceci n'est qu'un très-humble remerciement des bontez que vous me témoignâtes à Versailles, et une protestation sincere que j'en ai une reconnoissance infinie, et que je ferai tous mes efforts pour m'en rendre digne; je sçai que l'entreprise n'est pas petite, et votre estime étant très-glorieuse pour ceux qui la possèdent, elle est difficile à obtenir; mais, Monseigneur, je crois pouvoir tout oser, quand je songe à quel point je suis,

> Ce que j'ai pris la liberté de vous protester au commencement de cette Lettre.[20]

Evidently her device was successful, for Saint-Aignan, recognizing her name at the beginning of the letter, read it through sympathetically. In November, 1663, he replied as follows:

> Je ne m'estonneray jamais qu'une personne dont le mérite est au-dessus du commun et qui fait des ouvrages qui n'ont point de prix, escrive des billets singuliers et extraordinaires, et qu'avant toute la galanterie qui peut compâtir avec une haute vertu, elle surprenne par les plus agréables choses du monde. . . . Je . . . ne souhaite ma guerison d'un mal dont on me persuade que la cause c'est assez pour moy, qu'afin de vous aller rendre grâce très humble chez vous d'un souvenir si obligeant et d'une lettre si spirituelle que le plus délicat de tous les hommes et le plus grand de tous les roys la verra un jour aparemment à son coucher. . . .[21]

Whether Saint-Aignan actually showed the King Marie-Catherine's letter is not known; but the authoress thought it sufficiently worth while to continue her cultivation of the Duke's favor, and dedicated *Nitétis* to him:

> Monseigneur, la lettre que vous m'avez fait l'honneur de m'écrire m'a paru si obligeante que j'ay creu ne pouvoir y répondre que par un poeme tout entier. . . . Ce n'est que pour m'acquitter envers vous que *Nitétis* prend la liberté de vous rendre une visite. . . . Vous êtes mieux connu par vos actions que vous ne pourriez l'être par les louanges d'une Epistre dédicatoire et je trouverois *Nitétis* trop audacieuse si elle entreprenoit d'ajouter quelque chose à la gloire que vous possédez, etc. . . .[22]

[20] *Œuvres*, II, 326-328. Saint-Aignan was Louis' public-relations counsel, handling, among other things, literary requests. The letter was also published in the *Nouveau recueil de plusieurs et diverses pièces galantes de ce temps*, 1665, II, 183 (cf. Lachèvre's *Bibliographie des recueils* . . .) and is found in the *Mss. Conrart*.

[21] Reproduced by Magne, *op. cit.*, p. 242, from the *Mss. Conrart*. The phrase "recevoir un poulet, comme elle dit, en oiseau de mauvais augure," which appears in a part of its text not quoted above, proves its connection with Mlle Desjardins' letter beyond a doubt. Saint-Aignan's letter also appeared in the 1665 *Recueil* mentioned above.

[22] In front of *Nitétis*, *Œuvres*, II, 324. Mlle Desjardins' letter would be of December, 1663, shortly before the *achevé* of the play.

Nor was she mistaken in thus dedicating her play to the man who was practically Louis' confidential secretary. For, next to Hugues de Lionne, Saint-Aignan became the most helpful of her protectors.

The source and structure of *Nitétis*, as well as the literary influences apparent in it, have been discussed by Lancaster with completeness and finality.[23] The subject of the tragedy was taken from Herodotus' account of Amasis' revolt, Apriez' death, Apriez' earlier sending of his daughter to Cambyses the Persian king, the latter's invasion of Egypt, his marriage with his sister, ordering of his brother's death, and his own accidental death after a revolt of his subjects. Mlle Desjardins was doubtless influenced in her choice of subject by the success of the novel *Le Grand Cyrus* and Boyer's play *Oropaste* (1662), both of which, derived largely from Herodotus, had dealt with certain aspects of the story of Nitetis (cf. Lancaster's discussion). Mlle Desjardins uses her material freely, bringing into her play Amasis' son, Apriez' daughter, Cambyses' brother Smerdis and his sister Mandanne; inventing a love affair between Amasis' son, Phameine, and Apriez' daughter, Nitétis; and changing, among other details, Cambyses' accidental death into suicide:

Nitétis. The Persian king Cambyses is married to Apriez' daughter Nitétis, but wishes to get rid of her in order to marry his sister Mandanne. Mandanne objects; among other reasons, she loves Prasitte, friend of Cambyses' brother Smiris [Smerdis]. Smiris adds his protests, and Cambyses has him killed. Nitétis' former lover Phameine escapes from prison, comes to her, and they are discovered together by Cambyses, who orders Phameine held to be tortured to death. Prasitte arouses the people to avenge Smiris' death; Nitétis frees Phameine in order that he may take the guards to defend Cambyses, but the latter mistakes the Egyptian and his men for his enemies, and kills himself. Mandanne succeeds to the throne and becomes the wife of Prasitte, but Nitétis sacrifices herself to her peculiar standard of honor and refuses to marry Phameine.[24]

"Cambyse, roi de Perse et Nitétis, reine de Perse, sont des précieux," writes Chatenet (*op. cit.*, p. 56). Mlle Desjardins indeed, as Lancaster points out, left out all the picturesque details of Herodotus' account of the sadistic Cambyses, referring only in passing to his indifference to

---

[23] *Op. cit.*, III (II), 457-459. The author gives an analysis. Chatenet devotes one page to *Nitétis*.

[24] Lancaster, *loc. cit.*, points out that the name Prasitte probably came from a combination of Herodotus' Patisithis and Prexaspes, and that the love between Phameine and Nitétis was doubtless suggested by *Le Grand Cyrus*. The abbé de la Porte in his *Dictionnaire dramatique*, Paris, 1776, calls Nitétis a character "fait à l'imitation d'Hermione dans *Andromaque*." *Andromaque*, however, appeared in 1667, four years after *Nitétis*.

religion, and making him a tyrant of unusual but not surpassing cruelty. At times he vacillates as Torquatus had done in *Manlius:* compare the following passage, spoken as he is trying to make up his mind to have Smiris put to death:

> Mais quel trouble secret s'empare de mon ame!
> Je ne sçai quel effroi se saisit de mon cœur;
> Je sens mon front couvert d'une morne sueur:
> Certain frisson mortel se glisse dans mes veines.
> Allez, je ne veux rien. . . . Mais d'où naissent ces peines?
> Je tremble en ordonnant une si juste mort;
> Quoi, punir un rebelle, est-ce un si grand effort?
> Il est vrai, je sçai, ce rebelle est mon frere;
> Même sang nous forma . . . (II, 7).

Nitétis, in a conflict between love and duty like that of Pauline in *Polyeucte,* rejects her former lover because of a husband whom she does not love, but without the excuse of religion or admiration for Cambyses, that Pauline had felt for Polyeucte. Her conduct is motivated solely by "la gloire," honor:

> Une ame à qui la gloire est fortement connue,
> Sur tous ses mouvemens est toujours absolue;
> C'est l'honneur qui la regle et non ses passions (III, 2).

Mandanne likewise attempts to follow "une vertu si pure, Que l'ombre d'un forfait est . . . une injure" (V, 1), but she realistically consents in the end to marry a man who, without such hesitations, revolted against his sovereign.

Though, from the standpoint of the ordinary classical principles and unities, *Nitétis* is well constructed, the frères Parfaict find the play poorly built:

> Il suffit d'ajouter par forme de correctif au passage de Loret, que le plan de Nitétis est mal construit, que les personnages de la Pièce sont foibles ou manqués, et que la versification en est si médiocre, qu'elle pourroit passer pour de la prose rimée (*op. cit.,* IX, 198).

The critics have, on the whole, agreed with this judgment; despite Loret's praise of the work of the only woman then writing for the Parisian stage, René Le Pays' opinion of the "beaux vers" of *Nitétis,* and d'Aubignac's retort to de Visé that "sa seconde pièce la justifie assez contre votre calomnie," it appears to be generally conceded that *Nitétis,* compared with *Manlius,* was a dramatic failure, though not a sufficiently bad one to cause Mlle Desjardins to despair completely of succeeding in the theatre.[25]

Le Favory (1665)

If Tallemant's chronology is correct, Mlle Desjardins had composed and given to Molière's troupe for presentation her third and last play, *La Coquette ou Le Favory*—subsequently known simply as *Le Favory*— by July, 1664, the date of the campaign of Gigery, when Mlle Desjardins probably saw Villedieu for the last time. Tallemant writes:

> Pour revenir à Mlle des Jardins au temps de l'entreprise de Gigery, sçachant que Villedieu devait passer à Avignon pour y aller, elle se fit donner trente pistolles par avance sur une troisième pièce de theatre, appellée *le Favory, ou la Coquette*, qu'elle avoit donnée à la troupe de Molière. Avec cette somme elle s'en va en poste à Avignon. . . . Elle revint ici vers Pasques; il fut question de jouer sa pièce. . . .[26]

There are two possible explanations of Mlle Desjardins' leaving the Hôtel de Bourgogne, where *Manlius* and *Nitétis* had been performed, and going to Molière with her new play: the fact that Molière's theatre, the Palais-Royal, was gradually becoming the favorite stage for the presentation of comedies (while the Hôtel de Bourgogne was given over largely to tragedy), and Mlle Desjardins' hypothetical earlier acquaintance with the playwright.[27] The delay in the presentation of *Le Favory* may perhaps be explained by the play's having been given to Molière before it was complete; almost a year passed before its first performance took place, a year during which Mlle Desjardins had parted from Villedieu, and consoled herself near Avignon with the *homme de lettres* from Grenoble, René Le Pays, to whom she read "parts" of *Le Favory* and the beginnings of the *Mémoires de Henriette-Sylvie de Molière*.[28]

---

[25] Loret and de Visé are quoted by the frères Parfaict, *op. cit.*, Le Pays by Magne. Cf. Tallemant, *op. cit.*, VII, 251; Hauréau, *op. cit.*; Chatenet, *op. cit.*, p. 58; Mélèse *Répertoire analytique*. Hauréau attributes to the failure of *Nitétis* the fact that Mlle Desjardins abandoned writing tragedy. Cf. also É. Thierry's article, "Le *Favory*," *Moliériste*, III (1882), 9.

[26] *Op. cit.*, VII, 255. Cf. Ch. I, above. Mlle Desjardins returned to Paris in the spring of 1665.

[27] Cf. Ch. I, above, and Tallemant, *op. cit.*, VII, 256.

[28] Cf. Ch. I, above, and Ch. VII, below. Le Pays wrote to Mlle Desjardins in June, 1665, asking for a printed copy of *Le Favory*, or, if it were not printed, "du moins la copie des fragments que vous me recitâtes icy et que je trouvay si beaux" (quoted by Magne, *op. cit.*, p. 269). Molière could hardly have been delayed in presenting *Le Favory* because of too many new plays on hand, for between July, 1664, and the performance of *Le Favory* in April, 1665, only two new plays (*La Princesse d'Élide* and *Le Festin de pierre*) were given. He may, however, have been busy working on *Tartuffe* or *Le Misanthrope*.

Mlle Desjardins seems to have returned to Paris in a quarrelsome mood, for, while *Le Favory* was being rehearsed, "une comedienne et elle se pensèrent descoiffer," and, worse yet,

> . . . elle querella Molière de ce qu'il mettoit dans ses affiches, *Le Favory de Mademoiselle des Jardins*, et . . . qu'elle s'appelloit *Madame de Villedieu*. . . . Molière luy respondit doucement qu'il avoit annoncé sa pièce sous le nom de Mademoiselle des Jardins; que de l'annoncer sous le nom de Madame de Villedieu, cela feroit du galimatias; qu'il la prioit pour cette fois de trouver bon qu'il l'appellast Madame de Villedieu partout, hormis sur le theatre et dans ses affiches.[29]

Mlle Desjardins doubtless granted this reasonable request, and on Friday, April 24, La Grange notes the first performance of *Le Favory*.[30] During its first thirteen performances in Paris (given between April 24 and May 22) it enjoyed only mild success from the standpoint of the box-office; its "take" ranged from 123 francs to 418 francs, as compared with the average of well over 1000 francs for the newest play previous to it, *Le Festin de pierre*.

At this point Saint-Aignan, who had charge of the festivals of Louis XIV at Versailles, and to whom Mlle Desjardins had dedicated *Nitétis*, saw an opportunity of repaying the attentions of the authoress, and requested, for the *fête* of the thirteenth of June, 1665, that Molière bring his troupe to Versailles and there perform before the King her new play, *Le Favory*. She expressly attributes her fortune to Saint-Aignan:

> O toi! dont l'ordre exprès, m'inspire cette audace;
> Illustre Saint-Aignan, qui déjà tant de fois,
> As daigné de ma Muse être le digne choix,
> Accorde à mes desirs, de nouveau cette grace.
> Sois le vivant Echo, de ma timide voix;
> Et puisque c'est par toi que je rompts le silence,
> Que par toi cet essai de mon obeissance,
> Vole jusques aux pieds du plus puissant des Rois.[31]

---

[29] Tallemant, *loc. cit.* The author goes on to relate the incident mentioned in Ch. I, above, when Molière is said to have called on Mlle Desjardins and failed to recognize her, provoking her ambiguous remark, "Allez, vous êtes un ingrat; quand vous jouiez à Narbonne, on n'alloit à vostre theatre que pour me voir." See also Louis de La Sicotière, "Mme Desjardins de Villedieu et ses relations avec Molière," in the *Bulletin de la Soc. hist. de l'Orne*, 1883.

[30] *Registre*, p. 73. The theatre was, of course, the Palais-Royal.

[31] *Description d'une des Fêtes que le Roi a faites à Versailles*, in the *Nouveau recueil* of 1669. Magne (*op. cit.*, pp. 258-259) states that Marie-Catherine's elegy on the death of Saint-Aignan's son the Comte de Séry "resserra leur amitié" and influenced Saint-Aignan in his choice of her play for the *fête*. This is an impossibility, for although Mlle Desjardins did indeed write an "Élégie" on Séry's death, Séry did not die until October, 1666, a year and a half after the performance of *Le Favory* at Versailles (see Loret, *Lettre du 6 Octobre 1666*).

La Grange recounts the episode thus:

> Le Vendredy 12 Juin, la Troupe est allée a Versailles par ordre du Roy, où on a joué le Fauory dans le jardin, sur un theastre tout garni d'orangers. Mr de Molière fist un prologue en marquis ridiculle qui uouloit estre sur le theastre malgré les gardes, et eust vne conuersation risible auec vne actrice qui fist la marquise ridiculle, placée au milieu de l'assemblée. La Troupe est reuenue le Dimanche 14me.[32]

The *Gazette de France* relates:

> Le 13 . . . la Troupe du Roy représenta le Favory, comédie entremeslée d'intermèdes et d'entrées de ballet . . . avec concerts de voix et d'instruments. . . . Vigarani, ingenieur du Roy, avoit préparé la scène destinée à ce divertissement.[33]

Robinet wrote:

> Passons dans cette Isle Enchantée [Versailles] . . . .
> La nuit du treize au quatorzième . . . .
>
> La Troupe plaisante et comique,
> Qu'on peut nommer *Moliérique,*
> Dont le Théatre est si chéri,
> Représenta *le Favory,*
> Pièce divertissante et belle,
> D'une fameuse Demoiselle. . . .
>
> Après, sur le Théatre même,
> Notre Cour en liesse extrême,
> Ayant pris la collation. . . .
> . . . notre rare et digne Sire
> Voulut aussi donner la bal,
> Pour augmenter ce beau régal.[34]

Mlle Desjardins' own account of the evening, with her modest reference to the performance of her work, and her praise of "ce Terence du tems," Molière, has been quoted and discussed elsewhere (Chapter II, above). It was a gala night, one of the great moments of Mlle Desjardins' active and varied career.

It was not until some time after the troupe's return to Paris that *Le Favory* was again performed (August 7). It continued to be played, off and on, to a total of twenty-six performances in 1665-1666, being paired once with the *École des maris,* several times with *L'Amour médecin,*

---

[32] *Registre,* p. 74. This lost prologue of Molière's has caused speculation among the critics. Cf. Paul Lacroix, "Le Prologue du *Favory," Moliériste,* III (1881), 3, and Ch. II, above, where Mlle Desjardins' description of Molière's appearance is quoted.

[33] June 20, 1665; see Mélèse, *Le Théâtre et le public sous Louis XIV.*

[34] *Lettre du 21 juin 1665,* also quoted by the frères Parfaict, *op. cit.,* IX, 357-358.

and thrice with the *Médecin malgré lui* (August, 1666).[35] Mlle Desjardins finally published her play in October, 1665, dedicating it to Hugues de Lionne, the minister, who became her staunch protector until his sudden death in 1671.[36]

The scene of *Le Favory, tragi-comédie,* is the favorite Moncade's "maison de Campagne" near Barcelona. Moncade is a sensitive, sincere man who mistrusts the attentions and flatteries of those about him, feeling that they are addressed not to him, but to his station of favorite. He carries his suspicions so far as to doubt the love expressed for him by Lindamire, whom he loves, thinking it may arise only from ambition. Chief among Moncade's flatterers are Prince Clotaire, whose life he has saved, and Elvire, a woman who delights to boast in private of the system of tricks and deceptions which she practices on men. The King, perceiving Moncade uncertain of his mistress and besieged by flatterers, pretends to become angry with him and has him banished to an estate, and later arrested. Clotaire and Elvire immediately abandon him, but Lindamire wishes to be allowed to follow him into exile, asking, like Emilie in *Cinna,* to share the fate of her lover. The King then reveals his ruse,[37] banishes Clotaire, and promises to marry Moncade to Lindamire. Elvire remains completely indifferent to the entire episode, announcing,

> Tout cela ne vaut pas la peine d'en parler,
> Et Dom Lope m'attend qui m'en va consoler.[38]

The frères Parfaict attributed the invention of the plot of *Le Favory* to Mlle Desjardins: "Rien de plus petit que le sujet de cette Tragi-Comédie, qui paroit être imaginée par Mademoiselle Des Jardins."[39] Édouard Thierry, in 1882, put forth the hypothesis that the subject of the play was the disgrace of Fouquet, and found Mlle Desjardins' use of such a theme an "hardiesse." He writes:

> Mais quel pouvait être le danger du *Favori,* à la Cour? Celui d'une pièce de circonstance d'abord. . . . L'ouvrage devait avoir été conçu pendant le procès de l'ex-Surintendant—l'idée vient de là, la disgrâce d'un illustre favori. . . . L'allusion à la disgrâce de Fouquet ne se dissimule pas un seul instant.[40]

---

[35] La Grange, *Registre.* Cf. also the frères Parfaict, Chappuzeau's *Théâtre françois,* p. 109, the abbé de Pure's *Idée des spectacles,* p. 165, and Sorel's *Bibliothèque françoise,* p. 210, for mention of *Le Favory* and evidence of its popularity.

[36] *Achevé* of Oct. 10, 1665. Published at Paris by Billaine and Quinet. Magne (*op. cit.,* p. 413) lists an edition of Amsterdam, 1666, which I have also seen listed by a bookseller. All the eighteenth-century collected editions contain the play. For Lionne, cf. Ch. I, above, and Ch. VII, below.

[37] Thierry, "Le *Favory,*" *Moliériste,* III, 17, writes "le roi de Barcelonne renouvelle le 'soyons amis' d'Auguste." The parallel is hardly a good one.

[38] *Œuvres,* II, 574. Other summaries of *Le Favory* are found in the frères Parfaict, Hauréau, Chatenet, and Lancaster.

[39] *Op. cit.,* IX, 350. There is extant one reference (in 1637) to an earlier religious play entitled *Le Favory solitaire;* cf. Lancaster, *op. cit.,* III (II), 893.

[40] "Le *Favory,*" in the *Moliériste,* III, 14. Fouquet's trial lasted roughly from 1661 to 1664.

Magne accepted Thierry's hypothesis at as late a date as 1907; he speaks of

> ... les allusions dangereuses de la thèse. Car dans ce favori tout d'abord comblé d'honneurs, puis disgrâcié, arrêté, emprisonné, toute la cour reconnaît le surintendant Fouquet.[41]

But it seems hardly necessary to say that it is absurd to imagine Mlle Desjardins, anxious to make her way in the world with a literary career, touching upon a subject which would certainly have aroused Louis' intense displeasure, especially in a play presented before him at Versailles. The real source of *Le Favory*, as Martinenche pointed out (in 1900), is Tirso de Molina's *El amor y la amistad.*

Martinenche's comment on the differences in style and atmosphere between the Spanish work and Mlle Desjardins' imitation of it is somewhat harsh towards the latter:

> Son *Favory* traite la même matière qu'*el Amor y la Amistad* de Tirso de Molina. Mais que tout y devient froidement doucereux! Il y avait chez l'Espagnol de la force et de la grâce. Le Comte de Barcelone montrait sa reconnaissance envers don Guillen de Moncade avec une noblesse émouvante. Ses cousines d. Gracia et d. Victoria se disputaient d'abord avec esprit un favori que sa feinte disgrâce leur faisait fuir ensuite avec le comique empressement. Don Grao enfin et doña Estela se faisaient un admirable point d'honneur de leur amitié et de leur amour. La sentimentale demoiselle Des Jardins ne donne à sa Lindamire qu'une pudeur ridicule. . . . Tout l'intérêt de la comédie s'envole, et il ne reste que la romanesque situation d'un favori qui se fait mettre en disgrâce par son roi pour éprouver sa maîtresse et son ami.[42]

Lancaster, allowing a slight advantage to Mlle Desjardins on the score of dramatic structure, summarizes the differences as follows:

> Mlle Desjardins assigns the invention of the trick [Moncade's false disgrace] to the ruler in order that both the hero and the audience may believe until the last part of the play that the disgrace is real. She thus creates suspense that is not in the original. She omits the peasants, reduces the false friends to one woman and to one man who tries to win the heroine. In her play the real friend is not in love with Moncade's sweetheart. What she owes to Tirso is chiefly the main incidents of the plot, the moral, the setting, and references to the beauties of Nature. She does not follow him in detail. . . . The tragi-comedy, with its simple and unified plot, free from disguises, exchanged children, abductions, etc., is pleasingly written and compares advantageously with the author's other plays.[43]

---

[41] *Op. cit.*, p. 266.

[42] Erneste Martinenche, *La Comedia espagnole en France*, Paris, 1900, pp. 399-400. The last sentence in the passage would seem to indicate that M. Martinenche read *Le Favory* only superficially, if at all, for Moncade in Mlle Desjardins' play is unaware of the reason for his disgrace.

[43] *Op. cit.*, III (II), 545-546.

The passages in which Mlle Desjardins refers to the beauties of Nature are indeed unusual in her dramatic work, though they are not dissimilar to certain of her pastoral verses:

> Cette diversité de côteaux et de plaines,
> Ces superbes jardins, ces marbres, ces fontaines,
> Ces refuges sacrez de l'ombre et de l'effroi,
> Ces fertiles déserts . . . (I, 1).

> Je prends tous les matins un plaisir sans pareil,
> À voir dans ce beau lieu le lever du Soleil:
> Il embellit alors, se mêlant à l'Aurore,
> D'un émail naturel tous les endroits qu'il dore . . . (I, 4).[44]

Certain lines in *Le Favory* appear to be imitations, and some even bear a slight resemblance to lines in the *Misanthrope*, commonly thought to have been written after Mlle Desjardins' play. The following line,

> Vous changez d'un amant comme on fait d'un mouchoir,

of Act IV, scene 1, resembles, as Lancaster points out, the line,

> À changer de mari comme on fait de chemise,

of *Sganarelle* (v. 138). Malherbe's famous "Et rose elle a vécu ce que vivent les roses, L'espace d'un matin," appears to find a feeble echo in Mlle Desjardins'

> Passe comme une fleur dans le cours d'un matin (III, 6).

The following lines have partial parallels in the *Misanthrope:*

> Me confondoit souvent avec tout l'Universe (III, 6).
> Quand on n'a plus d'appas pour paroître agréable,
> Il est bon de tâcher à se rendre estimable. . . .
> Que chacun croit toujours ce qu'il aime parfait;
> Plaisons donc dans le tems d'une belle jeunesse,
> Et laissons sans regret l'estime à la vieillesse.
> Se pique qui voudra de grande probité,
> Pour moi je ne veux point de cette qualité,
> Et comme par le tems elle m'est destinée,
> J'attens pour l'obtenir ma cinquantiéme année (II, 1).[45]

---

[44] These imitations occur especially at the beginning of the play. Cf. the pastoral verses cited in Ch. II, above.

[45] Pointed out by Lancaster, *loc. cit.* Cf. the following lines of Molière's play:
> Dès qu'on voit qu'on nous mêle avec tout l'univers . . . (v. 56).
> Quand de nos jeunes ans l'éclat est amorti . . . (v. 980).
> Et l'on voit des amants vanter toujours leur choix (v. 712).
> L'âge amènera tout, et ce n'est pas le temps,
> Madame, comme on sait, d'être prude à vingt ans (vv. 983-984).

Indeed, a certain similarity between Moncade, the sensitive courtier who mistrusts flattery, and Alceste, obsessed with *la franchise,* the presence of a few rather outspoken passages in *Le Favory,* and our uncertainty as to the exact date of composition of the *Misanthrope,* have given rise to a theory that, as Magne phrases it,

> . . . le Favory aurait été pour Molière une pièce d'expérience. En le jouant il aurait appris quelles vérités la Cour accepte sans murmures. Ensuite il aurait écrit le *Misanthrope.* Il est certain que plusieurs passages du *Favory* marquent une extrême témérité.[46]

This view was first expressed by Thierry, who wrote, in 1883:

> Suivant l'apparence, la pensée du *Misanthrope* . . . commença vers les représentations du *Favori.* . . . Il n'y a donc rien de trop hasardé à compter le *Favori* parmi les origines du *Misanthrope,* si l'on songe surtout que Molière avait naturellement mis la main à la pièce. . . . Avait-il joué le rôle de Moncade, le Favori? . . . Ce rôle devait lui plaire. . . .[47]

The single bold passage which Thierry points out is that in which Moncade speaks of the discomforts and dangers of being a favorite:

> Envers les Souverains il est de certains crimes,
> Qui bien qu'ils ne soient pas défendus par nos loix,
> Blessent jusqu'au cœur la personne des Rois.
> Un Prince tient du ciel la suprême puissance,
> Le droit de commander est un bien de naissance;
> Mais cet esprit du monde, et ce tendre talent
> Qui tiennent moins du Roi que de l'homme galant,
> Comme un Prince ne peut les devoir qu'à lui même,
> Il en est plus jaloux que du pouvoir suprême,
> Et c'est sur un tel point qu'un Favori prudent
> Doit surtout éviter d'être son concurrent (I, 1).

The critic adds:

> Que dut penser Louis XIV? . . . Que dut penser la Cour à voir le maître aussi directement mis en cause? Le regard indiscret jeté par Mlle Des Jardins dans la conscience du prince courait grand risque de déplaire. . . .[48]

Chatenet considers bold statements Moncade's further complaint that all favorites

> Doivent incessament rêver à leur disgrace;
> Regarder le present comme un moment qui fuit,
> Et qu'on voit effacer par celui qui le suit . . . (II, 2).

—and Lindamire's

---

[46] *Op. cit.,* p. 266.
[47] "Le *Misanthrope* avant la représentation," *Moliériste,* IV (1883), 137-138.
[48] *Ibid.* Chatenet (*op. cit.,* p. 71) mentions Thierry's hypothesis favorably.

Cette erreur se dissipe, et je commence à voir
Qu'un Roi peut ce qu'il veut, et n'a qu'à tout vouloir (III, 1).

Such evidence is hardly sufficient to convince one either that Molière took the idea of the *Misanthrope* from *Le Favory*, or that the latter was for him a sort of gauge by which to determine to what extent criticism of Louis or of the Court could be expressed. If there were bolder passages in *Le Favory*, a case might be made out for the second view; the first cannot be held in the light of the evidence that before the publication of Boileau's second *Satire*, in July, 1664, that is, before Mlle Desjardins had presented her play to Molière's troupe (if we may accept Tallemant's chronology), Molière had already read aloud the first act of the *Misanthrope*.[49]

The success of *Le Favory*, as we have seen, was not great.[50] Mlle Desjardins, having written a Roman tragi-comedy, a Persian tragedy, and a Spanish tragi-comedy, apparently began work on a Spartan tragedy in June, 1667, for in a letter written at that time from Liége she refers to "le travail de mon *Agis*," and tells her correspondent that "je vous aurois envoyé le premier Acte de cette Tragédie par nostre amy V."[51] Whatever *Agis* may have been, it does not seem ever to have been published or performed.[52]

Disillusioned with, or weary of, the theatre, Mlle Desjardins, on her return from the Low Countries (spring, 1668), turned to the novel, the story, the letter form, and verse. The decade which follows witnesses the best of her literary production, the growth of her fictional technique in a variety of *genres*, and the spread of her fame. The three brief years which she devoted to the drama seem to have faded from her memory without leaving the faintest nostalgia for the stage.

[49] Cf. Lancaster, *op. cit.*, III (II), 654.

[50] Hauréau writes that "le succes du *Favori* compensa l'echec de *Nitétis*" (*op. cit.*, p. 38). La Grange's statistics do not permit us to call *Le Favory* a commercial success, though it did have the honor to be presented before Louis XIV, and had a total of twenty-six performances within a year's time.

[51] *Lettre* of June 12, 1667, *Recueil de lettres*, p. 120. She refers to a friend who has given her "une idée de Lacedemone."

[52] For the misunderstanding of both Baron Rothschild and Magne concerning *Agis* see Ch. I, above, and Ch. VI, below. Magne mistakenly identified it with *Anaxandre, nouvelle* (1667).

CHAPTER V

HISTORICAL NOVELS AND *NOUVELLES:* REALISM AND PSYCHOLOGICAL ANALYSIS

The most important contributions made by Mlle Desjardins to the development of the seventeenth-century novel are found in three works which take their subjects from European history. These display the trend toward a shorter form, the concern with realistic psychology and action, and the interest in historical *milieu* which made possible such works as Mme de La Fayette's *Princesse de Clèves* and Saint-Réal's *Dom Carlos,* and thus laid down to a large extent the pattern of the modern historical and psychological novel. These two fictional types, now so distinct, were at the beginning a mixed form, leaning now in the direction of psychological analysis, as in Mme de La Fayette, and now toward historical reconstruction, or invention, as in Saint-Réal. Both aspects are present in the historical stories of Mlle Desjardins, who, departing from the technique and formulae of earlier writers, anticipated, if not actually provided models for, later practitioners of the *genre.*

The historical novel of the seventeenth century emerged gradually from the heroic and pastoral novels which followed the *Astrée.* D'Urfé, in that work, had placed in a *milieu* which he thought to be more or less historically accurate a group of imaginary characters involved in a fictitious plot. Desmaretz followed the same procedure in *Ariane,* adding a few details taken from historical documents. La Calprenède chose famous characters from antiquity (or from legend, as in *Faramond*) and involved them in a plot of his own invention. Mlle de Scudéry represented her own acquaintances in a false *cadre* of antiquity, using historical names which were merely masks designed to conceal the identity of her contemporaries. Segrais and Mme de La Fayette, the earliest of whose efforts in the field precede those of Mlle Desjardins, introduced "bon sens" into the historical novel, and reduced it almost to the dimensions of the *nouvelle.*[1]

The short novel and the *nouvelle* existed, of course, even at the beginning of the seventeenth century: Camus wrote short novels, and Sorel

---

[1] Cf. Gustave Dulong, *L'Abbé de Saint-Réal, étude sur les rapports de l'histoire et du roman au XVIIe siècle,* Paris, 1921, for an outstanding scholarly treatment of this background of development.

published his *Nouvelles françoises* in 1623. The *histoires intercalées* of the *Astrée*, of the heroic novels, and even of the "realistic" novels like the *Roman comique*, were no more than *nouvelles*, frequently taken from Spanish *novelas*, and sometimes containing historical subject matter. The *nouvelle* did not materialize out of thin air, nor did it begin, as is sometimes stated, with Segrais' *Nouvelles françoises ou divertissements de la Princesse Aurélie* of 1656.

The method used by Mlle Desjardins in her first historical work (the *Journal amoureux*) is substantially that set forth in the preface to the *Princesse de Montpensier* by Segrais' disciple Mme de La Fayette. The work appeared in 1662:

> [Cette histoire] n'a esté tirée d'aucun manuscrit qui nous soit demeuré du temps des personnes dont elle parle. L'auteur ayant voulu . . . escrire des avantures inventées à plaisir, a jugé plus à propos de prendre des noms connus dans nos histoires que de se servir de ceux que l'on trouve dans des romans, croyant bien que la réputation de Mme de Montpensier ne seroit pas blessée par un récit effectivement fabuleux.[2]

The theory expressed here is similar to that of La Calprenède; but the historical *milieu* differs by reason of its proximity to the author's period, and the action is scaled to a more realistic pattern, more appropriate to a narrative of events supposedly drawn from the recent past. Mlle Desjardins' conceptions will be traced from this point of departure to their culmination in the theory of historical fiction put forth and exemplified in her later works, in which the fundamental plot, drawn from history, is adorned with suitable inventions of action and psychology, the whole forming an amalgamation of fiction and history designed to appear to the reader as a vivid and moving reconstruction of the past.

Le Journal amoureux (1669)

The *Journal amoureux* appeared in 1669, and was admitted by Mlle Desjardins as an authentic work in her list of 1671.[3] The word *amoureux, amoureuse* had already appeared in the titles of several novels and of many plays.[4] The vogue of *mémoires* at the time may have suggested the

---

[2] Cf. comments by Dulong, *ibid.*, p. 74.

[3] Magne, *op. cit.*, p. 415, lists the rare first edition published *chez* Barbin. The list referred to repudiates certain *Parties* of the *Journal*; cf. below. Editions appeared by Barbin in 1671, in Lyons in 1680 and 1696, in Paris in 1701, in Toulouse in 1702, and in the half-dozen sets of *Œuvres complètes* of the eighteenth century.

[4] Cf. Bussy-Rabutin's *Histoire amoureuse des Gaules* (1665), the anonymous *Lupanie, histoire amoureuse de ce temps* (1668), etc. Titles of plays were *Les Travaux amoureux du Marquis de la Rotonde* (Vesaci, 1660), *Les Barbons amoureux* (Chevalier, 1662), *Les Intrigues amoureuses* (Gilbert, 1663), *Le Vieillard amoureux* (Françoise Pascal, 1664), *Le Pédagogue amoureux* (Chevalier, 1665).

idea of a *journal;* the word had appeared (in a somewhat different sense) in the *Journal des sçavans,* founded in 1665. The *Journal amoureux* is not, as its title suggests, a novel in diary form written in the first person; although the action is broken up into sections numbered as *journées,* it is simply a series of stories related in what purports to be a day-by-day fashion. There are six distinct *Parties,* the first four comprising the reigns of Henri II and Charles IX, with *journées* running consecutively from I to LXVIII, and the last two recounting events taking place under the earlier reign of François I, with a new series of *journées* from I to XX:

Partie I. Octave Farnèse, son of the Duke of Parma, seeks aid from Henri II against the Emperor Charles V, murderer of his father. Octave, at first a cold, aloof young man, takes part in a series of hunts, concerts, festivals with fireworks, and the like. Diane de Poitiers, the King's mistress, causes Octave to fall in love with her. She tells Henri that the Prince d'Écosse, Comte Stuart, is making efforts to court her, and the King innocently appoints Octave to shield Diane. Octave's indiscreet comments on a painting of Actaeon and Diana are satirized by Marot at the request of Catherine de' Medici, who plots with Stuart to expose the lovers. Diane, fearing treachery, goes to Anet, where each night Octave swims a river to join her. Stuart has him detained and swims the river in his stead, but Henri II has learned of these happenings, and his guards fish Stuart out of the river. Stuart leaves for Scotland. Diane forgets herself in Henri's arms and addresses him as "Octave," confirming the King's suspicions. Octave is constrained to depart.

Partie II. Charles IX and his court leave Paris in May, 1564, for a trip to Lyons, Arles, Avignon, and Marseilles. The Duc d'Aumale undertakes to usurp the place which the Amiral de Chastillon has in the affections of Marguerite de Valois. The Cardinal d'Armagnac, envoy of the Pope, also falls in love with Marguerite, and profits by a temporary exile of Aumale to pay court to her. He arranges to meet her during a pilgrimage, which he will attend dressed as a monk. Chastillon appears dressed as a merchant; the two rivals meet and declare a truce. At a celebration of the marriage of Nevers with Mlle de Clèves, a "jeu sur la mer en forme de combat naval," Armagnac, Aumale, and Chastillon set out to keep a rendezvous with Marguerite in a grotto. Aumale and Chastillon find there the Duc de Guise, Marguerite's latest suitor, and withdraw in his favor. Armagnac mistakes the grotto and goes into that of Henri, the King's brother, who is disguised as a seagod. Monsieur lets the Cardinal kiss his hand and make declarations of love, then reveals his identity. Armagnac in shame returns to Rome to seek forgiveness for "ses désirs criminels."

Partie III. Henri, the Duc d'Anjou, falls in love with Mme d'Urfé and she with him. After attempts to arouse each other's jealousy with false letters, etc., they admit their passion. Several attempts to enjoy a nocturnal rendezvous fail; once Anjou is forced to hide in the *ruelle* of Mme d'Urfé's bed. Anjou's friend Tournon loves Mme d'Annebault, but she loves Anjou and seeks to ruin his affair with Mme d'Urfé. The Prince de la Roche-sur-Yon, a rival for Mme d'Urfé's esteem, tries to win her by magic, employing the magician Turgietan, in league with Anjou. The Prince is left naked in the woods, where M. d'Urfé finds him and takes him home, placing him in

Mme d'Urfé's bed. The next morning Anjou sees him leave the house and thinks himself betrayed. He rushes into Mme d'Urfé's boudoir. She explains all and they at last enjoy a private rendezvous. Anjou flaunts his success before Mme d'Annebault, who goes to the Queen to ask that Mme d'Urfé be exiled. The Queen sends for Mme d'Urfé; a carriage is waiting; all imagine she is to be sent away. Instead, the Queen gives her blessing and exiles Mme d'Annebault.

Partie IV. When Tournon fails to mourn the exile of Mme d'Annebault, Anjou and Mme d'Urfé criticize his faithlessness. He tells the story of his love for her, her betrayal, and his change of heart in favor of Mme de l'Archaut. Later, however, he discovers that Madame herself looks upon him favorably, and he turns his attentions to her. The Duc de Guise, furious, allies himself with Mme de l'Archaut to ruin the new affair. Tournon rides in a tournament with a scarf of Mme de l'Archaut's which he believes to be one belonging to Madame, and a misunderstanding results. Guise persuades the King to exile Tournon, but before he is sent away the lovers are reconciled and enjoy several days of happiness together.

Partie V. Dom Carlos, illegitimate son of the Emperor Charles V, comes to the court of François I. Accused by the ladies of loving Elvira of Cordova, he tells the story of her love for his father's minister Guast, Guast's banishment, and of the meeting of himself with Elvira, in a special room which was suddenly lifted by machinery into the Emperor's quarters, throwing Elvira into his arms, and thus giving rise to the legend that he loved her. Dom Carlos and Madame (the Dauphin's sister) fall in love. Jacques V of Scotland, who is at court, is believed to love Mlle de Vendôme, but secretly loves Madame. The Amiral de Brion tells of his love for Mlle de Pisseleu, who was taken from him by François and made the Duchesse d'Estampes. Madame and Mlle de Vendôme together find a portrait of Mlle de Saint-Vallier; each imagines it is evidence of her lover's unfaithfulness. Jacques relates to Monsieur (the future Henri II) how he spied on Madame in her bath through a secret mirror arranged by François in the sumptuous bath-grotto of the palace. Dom Carlos and Madame settle the matter of the portrait, and Dom Carlos hopes for a successful suit for Madame's hand. The Duchesse d'Estampes falls from a horse and is put to bed. Her visitors are entertained by Marot's account of his love for Mlle de Telligny, who pretended an interest in him only to secure love verses which she passes on to her real lover, thus inspiring Marot, when he discovered the truth, to write the sonnet "Au bon vieulx tems."

Partie VI. Brion visits the Duchesse d'Estampes, and is discovered with her by François while the two are reading a translation of an Italian *novella* about a Roman lady who pretended to drown herself, remained away a year in the company of certain hermits, and then reappeared in the river, to return to her husband as resuscitated. The Amiral is imprisoned, but the Duchesse wins his release. Mlle de Vendôme learns of Jacques' love for Madame, and reproaches the latter for allowing Jacques to fall in love with her. It transpires that the portrait of Mlle de Saint-Vallier (see Part V, above) belongs to the Emperor Charles V himself. The Dauphin loves her, and sends Marot to her to make a rendezvous in the Emperor's name. The Dauphin meets her disguised as Charles V, but Mlle de Saint-Vallier recognizes him and is able to persuade him of her fidelity. François and Charles both oppose the marriage between Dom Carlos and Madame; Dom Juan is sent away to Flanders.

Madame is given to Jacques as his bride, but shortly dies. Dom Juan hears the news and mourns.

An *Au lecteur* which appeared before the first *Partie* of the 1680 edition of the *Journal amoureux* stated the purpose of the author in inventing these historical fantasies. The passage recalls the manifesto cited earlier from the *Princesse de Montpensier:*

> Encore qu'il y ait beaucoup de noms Illustres dans cette Histoire, qui la font croire véritable, il ne faut pas toutefois la regarder de cette manière. C'est un petit roman fait sous le Regne de Henri II, comme nous avons vû sous celuy d'Alexandre et d'Auguste. L'on n'y a inseré des noms connus, que pour flatter plus agréablement vostre imagination.[5]

A similar disclaimer precedes the second *Partie:*

> L'Avertissement que je vous ay fait sur la premiere Partie du Iournal sembleroit devoir suffire pour celle-cy. La protestation sincere qu'on y fait, que les noms connus ne sont qu'une couleur affectée, pour rendre la fable plus agréable, convient encore mieux à Madame Marguerite qu'à Madame la Duchesse de Valentinois . . . mais comme il se trouve des censeurs qui aiment mieux dementir leur propre connoissance, que de renoncer à la censure, je me suis crû obligeé d'avertir de nouveau les lecteurs qu'il n'y a rien de vray dans cet Ouvrage que la protestation que je luy fais qu'il est un mensonge.[6]

Mlle Desjardins added that Marguerite was only nine or ten years old at the time the action is presumed to have occurred, and that Aumale and Chastillon, characters in the plot, were in Paris "en ce temps-là," and not with the court in the provinces.[7] We are frankly within the limits of the La Calprenède system, as modified by Segrais and Mme de La Fayette: pseudo-historical *milieu*, peopled by "real" persons engaged in actions not recorded by history.

The 1671 edition of the *Journal* contains another passage of introductory material not found in either the 1680 Lyons edition or the various editions of the *Œuvres*. Mlle Desjardins claimed therein to have found a "Ms. de la 1re partie" of the *Journal* which she revised in her own manner, converting "quelques récits en actions, et quelques actions en

---

[5] *Au lecteur* of *Partie I* of the edition of Lyons, 1680, now in the Cornell University Library. The reference to the reigns of Alexander and Augustus is to La Calprenède's *Cassandre* and *Cléopâtre*. Mlle Desjardins refers later in the passage to the *Princesse de Montpensier.*

[6] Ed. of Lyons, 1680, *Partie II*. These introductory remarks were removed from the various editions of the *Œuvres*. Bayle in the *Nouvelles de la république des lettres* praised Mlle Desjardins for warning the reader of the *Journal* that the stories were "de pures fictions" (*Œuvres*, La Haye, 1737, I, 157).

[7] The first *journée* is dated "Mai 1564." Marguerite was then about twelve years old (born 1552).

récits." In an explanation printed with the list of admitted works which appears in the same edition, she confirms this statement, adding: "Je ne prétends point blâmer les livres que je désavoue, mais . . . je déclare n'avoir aucune part à la 3ème et 4ème partie du *Journal amoureux*."[8] Mlle Desjardins' claim then is that she found a manuscript of Part I, revised it, added Part II, allowed some unnamed person to write Parts III and IV, then wrote V and VI. No external evidence exists to disprove her contention, but the work itself argues against it. The finding of a manuscript is, to begin with, one of the oldest literary pretensions. There are no perceptible differences in style or manner between Parts I, II, V, and VI on the one hand, and III and IV on the other. The psychology of the characters, such as it is, is the same. The final words of Part II invite the reader to await Part III; if she intended to write the third part, why should she have permitted someone else to issue it?

There is, however, a reason why Mlle Desjardins should disclaim Parts III and IV, even though she does not wish to "blame" them. Both, as Bayle pointed out in his comment on the above passage, contain "des choses un peu trop libres."[9] Customarily the novelists of the time brushed over or ignored all sexual relations, legitimate or otherwise, between fictional characters; a disembodied passion veiled all evidences of physical desire or satisfaction. Doubtless readers drew their own conclusions, and read between the lines.[10] Mlle Desjardins for the most part endorses this literary prudishness; even when she fails to do so, her characters' questionable actions are so disguised under abstract terms like "bonheur," "douceur," "passion," and the like, that the passage seems mild indeed. For example, in *Partie IV* Tournon describes an amorous assignation with Mme d'Annebault in the following manner:

Je fus chez elle. Je sçavois qu'elle seroit seule, & qu'elle vouloit bien que je la visse: j'entrai dans sa chambre, le soleil n'étoit guères qu'à la moitié du jour, le chaud étoit modéré par un petit vent frais, qui venoit du jardin par une fenêtre, que l'on avoit laissée ouverte à dessein. Mme d'Annebault, n'avoit sur elle qu'un simple déshabillé couleur de rose, garni de rubans verds; son teint étoit vermeil, ses yeux étoient plus animés que de coutume; & le désordre charmant que je remarquois en toute sa personne, me faisoit bien comprendre que la partie étoit toute faite pour

---

[8] Both passages reproduced by Derome, *loc. cit.* The list itself states: "Trois tomes (II, V, VI) du *Journal amoureux*."

[9] Bayle, *Nouvelles lettres sur le calvinisme*, II, 735. He mistakenly asserts that she denies having written one *tome*, instead of two. Cf. Ch. I, above.

[10] Cf. Ch. I, above, and Bayle's remark: "On est persuadé en lisant les Histoires amoureuses, que le Héros va beaucoup plus loin que le Livre ne dit" (*loc. cit.*).

l'amour. Dès qu'elle me vit, sa rougeur augmenta. . . . Que voulez-vous que je vous dise, Monsieur, elle m'aimoit, j'étois amoureux, elle fut persuadée de ma passion; & si elle en avoit douté, j'étois assez ingénieux pour la tirer sur le champ d'une erreur si cruelle: enfin quand vous vous formeriez une idée de plaisir & d'amour la plus tendre & la plus forte qui ait jamais été, vous ne sçauriez encore ni sentir ni exprimer tout ce que notre passion nous fit éprouver de douceurs différentes.[11]

Surely an explicit action could hardly be couched in less specific words. This is the freest portion of the two repudiated books.[12] That such passages were considered licentious by the sophisticated and *galant* public in the age of Louis XIV may seem incredible, but we have Bayle's word for it, and the scrupulous avoidance of bedroom scenes in the fiction of the day is evidence of a tacit ban on anything approaching pornography.[13] It should be remarked that Mlle Desjardins felt no reluctance in admitting the authorship of the Peeping-Tom incident in *Partie IV*, which to modern taste may seem a bit more questionable than the above.[14]

Emphasis on amorous intrigue overshadows everything else throughout the work. Politics and military affairs are referred to in passing, but only as part-time concerns of princes, kings, and high ladies chiefly interested in arousing the interest or jealousy of another member of the court. A certain amount of would-be local color is introduced, much of it false and anachronistic: ballets, comedies, "original" compositions of Ronsard and Marot (who was dead at the time of one of the stories in which he

---

[11] *Le Journal amoureux* (ed. 1741), pp. 281-283.

[12] In *Partie III* Anjou enjoys the favors of Mme d'Urfé in a similar scene: "Monsieur approcha du lit de Mme d'Urfé, qui la trouva dans un état si propre à donner & à recevoir de l'amour, qu'il oublia sa colère & son dépit. L'occasion étoit belle, M. d'Urfé étoit seul, il étoit amoureux, Mme d'Urfé ne se souvint point d'apeller Hermine [her maid], elle n'étoit point insensible, & Monsieur étoit auprès d'elle. Que leur entretien fut touchant, & que . . . .! Mais je ne veux point mettre en vûe le secret de leur conversation" (p. 254).

[13] The taboo is apparent in classical drama as well: cf. Phèdre's lust for Hippolyte, spoken of in the play rather as some rare disease than as plain physical passion. Only the lowest comedy and the vaudeville of such men as Gautier Garguille reflect the libertine side of the classical period, which is nevertheless so apparent in the *lives* of seventeenth-century figures (cf. Tallemant, *op. cit.*).

[14] "Madame se baigna au commencement de cet Été, comme vous pouvez vous en souvenir, & choisit pour le lieu de son bain cette magnifique grotte que le Roi votre pere a fait faire à l'appartement de la Duchesse d' Éstampes. Je sçai le secret de cette fausse niche, d'où par le moyen d'un miroir de réflexion qui est enchassé dans la Roquaille, on peut voir les Dames dans le bain. Le Roi votre pere m'avoit confié cet essai de sa curieuse galanterie. . . . La seule Mlle de Vendôme eut le privilege d'entretenir Madame dans son bain. . . . Elle admiroit la gorge de la Princesse, sa taille, sa jambe . . ." (p. 398).

figures), etc.[15] The festivals "en forme de combat naval" with their lavishness, grottoes, and the like, recall the entertainments of Louis XIV at Versailles rather than those of Charles IX. References to jousts and tourneys sound vaguely authentic, and the historical characters are put through paces which, if scarcely true, at least bear some resemblance to the accounts of the sixteenth century available at the time in the works of Mézeray, Pierre Matthieu, the Père Anselme, de Thou, Jean de Serres, and Davila. Historical "documentation," of the type practised with a great show of erudition by Mlle Desjardins in her next work, the *Annales galantes*, is absent from the *Journal amoureux*.

What little unity of construction the *Journal* might have had was spoiled by the sudden jump in *Partie IV* to the reign of François I, at a period earlier than that of the preceding parts. The plots are monotonous, complicated, and trivial. Although the naïve devices of the heroic novel, present in *Alcidamie*, are here dispensed with, little effort is made to fill the gap with more adult matter. The psychology of the characters seems in many ways more superficial than that of some of the personages of *Alcidamie*. *Histoires intercalées* are shorter and less numerous, but they are still present to interrupt the flow of the narrative. The style is somewhat improved over that of *Alcidamie*; it is straightforward, simple, and clear, with a fair balance between narration, description, and dialogue. Mlle Desjardins found the heroic novel an impossible medium, and recognized its vogue as dying; hence *Alcidamie* was never completed. The historical novel, on the other hand, was scarcely born; its technique was as yet undetermined, free, open to experimentation. Mlle Desjardins' first attempt in the new field showed a certain talent for devising complicated plots, a strong tendency to play up the *galant*, and a complete lack of concern for historical accuracy.

[15] No attempt is made seriously to imitate the style of either poet. Marot is represented as writing a version of the fable of Diana and Actaeon beginning:

> Au tems jadis qu'on vit Dieux & Déesses
> Se profaner aux œuvres des mortels,
> Et maintes-fois partager les foiblesses
> De ceux, qui tous leur dressoient des autels;
> Certain chasseur doué d'une trop bonne vûe,
> Fut d'un beau fols fait animal cornu,
> Pour avoir vû Diane toute nue,
> Puis dévoré par sa meute déçûe. . . .

Ronsard's alleged verses run thus:

> Dieu garde tout cœur innocent,
> De pirate abordant l'Étendart de l'Église,
> Dieu nous sauve de barbe grise
> Cachant désir adolescent. . . .

Les Annales galantes (1670)

La Bruyère, writing facetiously of the loss to polite society caused by the death of Arrias, the *colporteur* of current "échos mondains," the connoisseur of balls and comedies, the perfect *ami des femmes*, asks, "Qui prêtera aux femmes les *Annales galantes* et le *Journal amoureux?*"[16] The question is evidence of the popularity of both works. The *Annales* appeared anonymously in 1670; the work was acknowledged by Mlle Desjardins in her list of 1671, and was reprinted in 1697, 1700, 1702, and in the eighteenth-century editions of the *Œuvres*.[17] The word *galant* appears in many titles prior to 1670, but not, so far as can be traced, the word *annales*.[18]

The *Journal amoureux*, though it contained several separate stories, was cast in the novel form. *Les Annales galantes* is a genuine collection of *contes* or *nouvelles,* each unrelated to the other, and each, unlike the three *nouvelles* which Mlle Desjardins had published separately before 1670 (*Lisandre, Anaxandre,* and *Cléonice*), supposedly a true account of an historical happening. The transition from the frank pseudo-historical inventions of the *Journal amoureux* to the almost scientific pretensions of the *nouvelle historique* is reflected in the *avant-propos* of the *Annales:*

Je déclare . . . que les Annales galantes sont des veritez historiques, dont je marque la source dans la Table que j'ai inserée au commencement de cét Ouvrage. Ce ne sont point des fables revetuës de noms veritables, comme on en a vû un essay depuis quelques mois dans un des plus charmans Ouvrages de nos jours.

Mlle Desjardins mentions specifically the subjects of several stories, affirming their historical authenticity:

Il y a eu autrefois une Comtesse de Castille, et elle suivit en France un Pèlerin. Il y a eu des Fraticelles, et ils ont été condamnez par les Papes Boniface VIII et Clement V pour les crimes que je leur impute. Qu'on ne cherche point un Tableau

---

[16] La Bruyère, *Les Caractères,* ed. Grands Écrivains, I, 289 [written 1688].

[17] The original edition appeared *chez* Barbin, in 3 vols. The others were issued respectively by Hilaire Baritel, Lyons, L. & H. van Dole, La Haye, and Desclassen, Toulouse. The introductory letter was to Mgr de Lionne, Mlle Desjardins' most influential protector, whose death in 1671 was a blow to her fortunes. It states "je ne vous diray point, Mgr, qui est l'auteur de cette Mascarade."

[18] Cf. *Les Diversités galantes* (anon.), 1664; *Les Galanteries diverses* (anon.), 1665; Boulanger's *La Morale galante,* 1669; de Visé's *Nouvelles galantes et comiques,* 1669, etc. Mlle Desjardins' *Recueil de lettres* had borne the description "relations galantes." The word is extremely common in titles after 1671 (cf. Dorothy Dallas, *Le Roman français de 1660 à 1690,* Paris, 1932, pp. 247 ff.). F. Brunot, *Histoire de la langue française,* III, 237 ff., discusses the various meanings of the word *galant* in the seventeenth century.

de l'hypocrisie du siècle dans cette avanture, elle est une relation fidelle d'une hypocrisie ancienne.[19]

Her argument is that many historical events motivated by love and amorous intrigue, which the ordinary historian relates only "en passant," because of "la majesté des matières historiques," may be expanded into stories by the addition of dialogue, encounters, and other "ornemens à la simplicité de l'histoire." In matters of love, according to Mlle Desjardins, man's behavior is more or less stable throughout the ages. Experience and common sense, therefore, allow the historical writer to invent amorous action and dialogue without going too far astray from the historically possible:

> On est homme aujourd'hui comme on l'estoit il y a six cents ans: les loix des Anciens sont les nostres, et on s'aime comme on s'est aimé. . . . Il n'est pas plus extraordinaire de voir un Amant de 1674 faire l'amour comme on le faisoit en 950, que de voir un enfant qui naist cette année estre composée des mesmes parties qui composoient les enfans d'Adam et des Patriarches.[20]

If, in this process, impiety and vice are sometimes apparently pushed "jusqu'à l'effronterie," it is only, according to Mlle Desjardins, "pour donner des couleurs plus fortes à l'impudicité," and thus to inspire horror for evil actions. To interpret her effort in any other way, she states, the readers must "trahir l'intention d'un Auteur qui les aura si bien divertis."

Such then is the conception behind the first genuine collection of *nouvelles historiques* of the seventeenth century. Bayle recognizes her innovations and gives her full credit for her achievement:

> S'étant fait un nouveau goût de Narrations Romanesques, elle . . . y réussit très heureusement. Elle mit à la mode ces petites Historiettes Galantes. . . . Elle fit tomber ces longs et vastes Récits d'Avantures héroïques, guerrières, et amoureuses [comme] Cassandre, Cléopâtre, Cyrus, Clélie, etc. Le nouveau goût qu'elle créa subsiste encore [after 1699]: et . . . on lit encore avec plaisir les premiers Romans qu'elle composa selon sa nouvelle idée: son Journal amoureux, ses Annales galantes, et plusieurs autres.[21]

[19] *Les Annales galantes*, edition of 1700 (all citations are from this edition). The work praised in the first paragraph may be *Zaïde*, which also appeared in 1670. For other historical *nouvelles* of the period immediately following the *Annales*, cf. Dallas, *op. cit.*, pp. 262-266.

[20] P. 4. Mlle Desjardins' paralogism recalls some of the arguments brought out in the quarrel of the ancients and moderns. Editors of the various editions changed the phrase "un Amant de . . ." to suit themselves: the edition of 1702 has "un Amant de 1694," and the edition cited by Dulong (*op. cit.*, p. 79) has "un Amant de 1669," probably the original date, despite the printer's *Avis* of the 1700 edition, which states that "l'Avant-propos fut fait en 1674 lors que cét Ouvrage parut pour la première fois" (a manifest error).

[21] *Dictionnaire*, article "Jardins." Voisenon, *Anecdotes* (*op. cit.*, IV, 94), repeats

Historical fiction had, of course, appeared before Mlle Desjardins, but in sporadic, almost accidental fashion. Aside from the "historical" novels of La Calprenède and the like, and an occasional treatment of a contemporary event like Marguerite de Navarre's use in the *Heptaméron* of the story of Lorenzaccio, or Montchrétien's *L'Écossaise,* historical interest was for the most part confined to works of history proper, or to such compendia of ancient lore and biography as Father Caussin's *Cour Sainte* (1624), which became the source of "historical" plays by La Calprenède, Tristan l'Hermite, and others.[22] Classical tragedy was frequently based on historical events, and its *vraisemblance* resembles closely the air of probability with which Mlle Desjardins sought to surround her *nouvelles,* but the tendency of the seventeenth-century dramatists to depict their own society in the guise of Romans, Greeks, etc., and to abstain completely from the use of local color or historical *milieu* sets the dramatic literature of the period apart, and differentiates it sharply from the new "historical" *genre.* In the latter field, only two instances of something similar to Mlle Desjardins' production may be noted. In 1615, a certain Rosset undertook to write several "histoires autants véritables que tristes," based on recent events, and disguising the names "à fin de n'affliger pas tant les familles de ceux qui en ont donné le sujet."[23] More striking is the Sieur de Grenaille's *Amours historiques des princes* (1642). The *Avertissement* of this work offers the reader "des histoires d'amour, mais qui sont toutes authentiques."[24] Grenaille, a moralist of the Camus school, argued that if a story is to instruct the reader and provide an example for conduct, then a true event may be expected to have a more powerful effect than an imaginary one.[25] Grenaille also listed the historians used as

that it was Mlle Desjardins "qui avec raison a fait perdre le goût des grands Romans." Gallier, *op. cit.,* attributes substantially the same remark to Voltaire. (Cf. Preface, n. 5.)

[22] Cf. Lancaster, *op. cit.,* II (I), 354, and II (II), 799. See also George Hocking's *Father Caussin, his Life, his Cour Sainte, and his Tragoediae Sacrae,* Baltimore, 1934.

[23] Rosset, *Histoires tragiques de ce tems,* 1615, Avant-propos. One of the subjects is Bussy d'Amboise, of whom Mlle Desjardins also wrote (see Ch. VIII, below).

[24] The whole *Avertissement* is reproduced by Magendie, *op. cit.,* pp. 149-150.

[25] "Ce qui a esté peut bien plus toucher que ce qui ne fut et ne sera peutestre jamais" (*ibid.*). Grenaille claimed the authority of no less a writer than Montaigne, who in the essay *De trois bonnes femmes* had written: ". . . et [je] m'estonne que ceux qui s'adonnent à cela [*i.e.,* to the writing of fiction] ne s'avisent de choisir plutost dix mille tres-belles histoires que se rencontrent dans les livres, où ils auroient moins de peine et apporteroient plus de plaisir et de profit" (Montaigne, *Essais,* ed. Villey, II, 561-562).

sources, a procedure followed by Mlle Desjardins in a portion of the *Annales galantes*.[26]

The aristocratic bias of authorship in the seventeenth century, together with the traditional "great man" view of history and other psychological and sociological limitations of the period, helped to prevent the new *genre* from attaining the scope it came to possess in the nineteenth century. But the foundations of the modern historical story and novel were laid by such relatively unknown writers as Grenaille, Mlle Desjardins, Saint-Réal, and Courtilz de Sandras.[27]

Eighteen stories comprise the *Annales galantes*. They are given in order, their periods indicated, and plots sketched:[28]

Partie I, 1. Reign of Ramire XVI of Spain, ca. 950. A French pilgrim on his way to St.-Jacques-de-Compostelle tarries at the château of Dom Fernandez long enough to seduce his wife, the Countess of Castille. She follows the pilgrim back to Paris. Dom Fernandez goes in pursuit of her, and after an interval during which he lives with the pilgrim's sister (who secretly gives the Count's money to her brother), finds the lovers and kills them. He then marries the pilgrim's sister and returns with her to Castille.

Partie I, 2. Reign of Edward I of England. Edward's favorite Ethelvold is sent like Tristan to fetch the King's bride-to-be, Alfrede. Ethelvold, who has fallen in love with the beauty, returns saying she is too ugly to become Queen. Edward asks Ethelvold to marry her, and Ethelvold, asking nothing better, does so, but keeps his bride far from court to conceal his treachery. At last a picture of Alfrede falls into the King's hands, arousing his suspicions. When he beholds Alfrede herself he orders Ethelvold's imprisonment. Ethelvold dies, probably poisoned; Alfrede is made Queen.[29]

[26] Dulong, *op. cit.*, pp. 77-78, and note, recognizes the parallelism between Grenaille and Mlle Desjardins in their treatment of history in fiction, but does not suggest that Mlle Desjardins was familiar with the work of her predecessor. "Le livre de Grenaille," he writes, "paraît avoir eu peu de retentissement et n'avoir pas suscité d'imitateurs." Grenaille's stories dealt with subjects from Portuguese, early French, and Roman history, the preface listing such sources as Vasconcellos, Tacitus, "et tous ceux qui ont parlé de Chilpéric." It is impossible to state whether Mlle Desjardins knew the *Amours historiques*.

[27] Cf. the fortunes of Saint-Réal's *Dom Carlos* and Courtilz's *Mémoires de Monsieur d'Artagnan*, which became sources for romantic novels and plays. It seems strange that the Spanish *drama histórico* had no effect on French fiction in the seventeenth century. Spanish *novelas* were imitated in French, and Spanish *comedias* adapted to the French stage, but the Spanish interest in national history appears to have had no important echo in France. Several of the characters in the *Annales galantes* had appeared in historical plays by Lope or Tirso, but Mlle Desjardins remained unaware of the fact, and esteemed her own innovations, as in fact they were to her public, quite original.

[28] Most of these stories are summarized by Chatenet, *op. cit.*, pp. 112-173. The most famous one, the *Histoire des fraticelles*, is analyzed by the *BUR*, 1776 (II), 193 ff.

[29] An anonymous *Alfrede, Reyne d'Angleterre* appeared in 1678 (cf. R. C. Williams, *Bibliography of the Seventeenth-Century Novel in France*, New York, 1931).

Partie I, 3. Reign of Othon III, ca. 984. Othon falls in love with the Duchesse de Modène; his wife the Empress falls in love with the Duc. The Duc and Duchesse are faithful to each other. The enraged Empress has the Duc killed; the Duchesse then causes the assassination of both the Emperor and the Empress.

Partie II, 1. Reign of Alfonso of Castille, ca. 1083-1127. Three Spanish princesses marry three French lords. Two couples engage in infidelities, and, when the third husband attempts to straighten out their affairs, he returns to find his own wife has deceived him. He kills his wife's lover, and, reflecting that, according to the point of honor, "l'éclat seul fait la honte," retires to the country with her, all three families settling down to a quiet, orderly life.

Partie II, 2. Reign of Frederic Barbarossa, ca. 1154-1159. Frederic and his son are rivals for the favors of Constance, niece of Pope Alexander III. Mlle Desjardins sees in the scorn of Constance for Frederic the beginning of the wars between the Guelfs and the Ghibellines. Frederic's son obtains Constance's hand.

Partie II, 3. Reign of Fernando IX of Castille, ca. 1228. Young Jacques d'Aragon marries Eleanor of Castille, who in order to remain faithful to her lover, convinces Jacques that they should not live together as man and wife. Jacques quietly consoles himself with a lady of the court.

Partie III, 1. Early fourteenth century. During the papacies of Boniface VIII and Clement V, a self-styled religious order, the "Fraticelles," is constituted for the express purpose of seducing the wives of Rome. Like Tartuffe, the "Frérots" attempt to undermine the morals of a matron and enjoy her favors beneath a discreet ecclesiastical mien. Metaphysical and pseudo-religious arguments are used to further the seductions. At last a certain matron, Hortense, using Elvire's device in *Tartuffe,* proves the perfidy of Frère Conrart by inducing him to confess to the seduction of an officer's wife, while the officer lies in hiding.

Partie IV, 1. Reign of Dulcin of Lombardy, ca. 1310. Dulcin and his wife Marguerite la Voluptueuse conduct a court of easy divorce. When Nogaret is offered a divorce from his wife Mariane (who has in disguise been his mistress until his recent discovery of her double rôle), the thought that he can no longer have her reawakens his love, and he refuses to give her up.

Partie IV, 2. Reign of Pedro el Cruel, ca. 1334-1369. Pedro marries a French princess, Blanche, grows weary of her and orders his henchman Nuñez to kill her, so that he may devote his whole attention to Marie de Pudille, his new mistress. Nuñez falls in love with Blanche and plans to save her. Marie learns of this, informs Pedro. Both Nuñez and Blanche are executed, but the King has meanwhile fallen in love with Jeanne de Castro, and Marie loses the advantage which she had hoped would put her on the throne.

Partie V, 1. Jean le Beau, Emperor of Greece, marries a Princess to whom he has made passionate love. When he grows indifferent, the Princess accuses him of no longer loving her. He replies: "Vous parlez comme une héroïne de roman, Madame. . . . Croyez-moi, il faut aimer en gens de bon sens."

Partie V, 2. Period of Amédée VIII, Duke of Savoy. The scene on the shores of Lake Geneva is described in almost romantic style. Amédée's favorite, Savonne, tries to prevent the Duke from taking away his mistress, the wife of the Comte de Moriène. Moriène kills his wife and commits suicide; Savonne is imprisoned and killed.

Partie V, 3. Reign of Pedro el Cruel, ca. 1334-1369. Pedro's son becomes too interested in Agnes de Castro, and the King has him murdered.

Partie V, 4. Reign of Charles VII of France, ca. 1440. The future Louis XI tries to get rid of Agnès Sorel, his father's mistress, by plotting with Chabannes. The latter falls in love with Agnès, and when almost caught in her room is forced to freeze outside a window while inside Charles and Louis discuss Agnès' character. Louis' next agent La Tremouille succeeds in poisoning Agnès.

Partie VI, 1. The scene is laid in Tunisia, at an uncertain period. Féliciane de Ribeiro's family disapproves of her love for Alfonso, but Alfonso, saving her from the evil designs of the Comte d'Atrevalo, wins them over.

Partie VI, 2. Reign of Enrico IV of Castille, ca. 1454-1474. Enrico's supposed daughter Jeanne (really the daughter of the Queen by the Comte de la Cueva) is sent for by Louis XI of France. The Marquis de Villena and a certain count, both victims of Jeanne's infidelity, join forces to expose Jeanne's debauched habits. Jeanne retires to Portugal, where, after further depravities, she enters a convent. There is much complicated cape-and-sword intrigue, with false letters, rendezvous in gardens, etc.

Partie, VII, 1. Reign of Bajazet II, ca. 1500.[30] Two princes are betrothed to girls who are stolen from them by Imirse and Sélim, the sons of Bajazet. In order to win the girls back the princes pose as dervishes, lure Imirse and Sélim into a grotto, and there cut their throats.

Partie VII, 2. Story of the false king, Sebastian of Portugal. He is a soldier who has been saved from death by a Greek princess, Xérine. When Sebastian's impersonation of the dead king proves successful, he grows indifferent to Xérine, who tries to persuade him to abandon his deception and return with her to Africa. He is denounced and imprisoned; she leaves Portugal, and he drinks poison.

Partie VIII, 1. Reign of Mahomet III, early seventeenth century. One of his sons, Jacaya, falls in love with the Italian ambassadress to the Sultan's court. His courtship and his rivalry with the Duc de Mantoue lead him through Transylvania, Italy, and France. Such characters are depicted as the Maréchal de Bassompierre and the Marquis de Strossi. The marriage of Louis XIII to the Spanish Infanta is described.[31]

In her *Avant-propos* to these stories, Mlle Desjardins announces that she intends to indicate her historical sources in a *Table* which, though it may appear to the reader "suspecte de quelque négligence," will never-

---

[30] Segrais' story of Bajazet (*Floridon*) appeared in 1657. Racine's *Bajazet* was first performed two years after the publication of the *Annales galantes*. The plot does not concern the same Bajazet as that of Mlle Desjardins' *nouvelle*. In the preceding story of *Jeanne supposée de Castille* there is an interesting use of the word *scorsonère*, which appears there for the first time in printed French. The problem of the origin of the superstition surrounding the plant and the etymology of the word are discussed in my article "*Scorsonère*, Black Salsify," in *PMLA*, LV (1940), 602-605. Cf. also a reply of Leo Spitzer to the foregoing in *MLN*, LVI (1941), 243-244.

[31] Gallier, *op. cit.*, pp. 55-56, expresses special admiration for the *Histoire de Jacaya*, quoting a passage which appears on p. 522 of the *Annales* to illustrate "la phrase courte, incisive . . . les sentiments mobiles . . . le sarcasme contre les femmes [qui] jaillit avec une verve intarrissable, qui fait penser à certaines boutades de Voltaire."

theless contain "plus de science" than he will have expected of her.
Unfortunately, the sources of only nine of the eighteen stories are given.
The publisher of the 1700 edition laments this fact:

> Quant à ce qui regarde la Table des Matières, il auroit été à souhaiter, que Madame
> de Villedieu nous eut indiqué les sources d'où elle a tiré les Histoires des quatre
> dernières Parties, comme elle a marqué celles des quatres premières.[32]

The *sources* are given by Mlle Desjardins in the following manner:

Table des Matières historiques

Dom Garcia Fernandez Comte de Castille, et la Comtesse sa femme. pag. 1. Hist.
d'Esp. Regne de Ramire XVI Roi d'Oviedo, et IV de Leon, Tom. 1, année 941 jusques
à 956. Ce qu'il y a d'ajoûté à la verité de l'Histoire, est aisé à remarquer pour le
Lecteur.

Alfrede, pag. 19, titre du meme nom. Hist. d'Angl. Regne d'Edgar, ou Édoüard I
liv. VIII fol. 276. Il y a si peu de choses changées en cette Historie, qu'elles ne
meritent pas d'être marquées.

Othon III, petit fils d'Othon le Grand, et Marie sa femme, pag. 49. Frisin, liv. 6.
Sigon. liv. 7 et pour plus grande commodité, abregé de l'Hist. Universelle de Turcelin,
année 984 fol. 323. Il y a plus d'invention dans cette Histoire que dans aucune autre.

[Les Princesses de Castille] Hist. d'Esp. Regne d'Alphonse VI du nom, III roi de
Cast. et XX de Leon; année 1083, jusques en 1127.

[Barbarossa] Sigeb. en sa Chro. Frisin en l'Hist. de Frederic. Sigon. liv. 12.
Abregé de Turcelin année 1154.

[Jacques d'Aragon] Hist. d'Esp. Regne de Ferdinand IX Roi de Castille environ
l'an 1228. Cette histoire est fondée presque mot à mot sur la verité.

[Les Fraticelles] . . . Platus en fait un chapitre entier, Baronius qu'après l'Evangile,
on regarde comme un Historien sacré, rapporte des particuliers de leur débauche.

[Dulcin et Marguerite la Voluptueuse] Annales ecclesiastiques 1310. S. Ant. Arch.
de Flor. liv. 20 et pour la commodité de toute sorte de Lecteurs, Abr. de Turcel.
Regne de Henri VII Emp. d'Occ.

[Pedro el Cruel] Hist. d'Esp. . . . [1334-1369]. . . . Il n'y a que l'amour de Nugnez
supposé.[33]

Abruptly, without apology or explanation, the *Table* ends at this point.
The remaining stories are merely listed with the numbers of the pages
on which they begin.

What are these sources, and to what extent did Mlle Desjardins make
use of them? The first two, the "Hist. d'Esp." and the "Hist. d'Angl.,"
defy any specific identification. General histories of Spain were numerous,
as were works on England. To indicate the "Tom." or "fol." of so vague
a title could have benefited a contemporary reader no more than a modern

---

[32] *Les Annales galantes*, edition of 1700, *Avis*.

[33] *Ibid.*, unpaginated preface. The page numbers refer to the beginnings of the
stories mentioned.

scholar, and betrays a somewhat suspicious capriciousness.[34] The books which she mentions by name are, on the whole, the works of rather recondite and imposing authorities. Most of them are rare today. They may be identified as follows: (1) *Frisin.* Abrahamus Frisius, or Fries, whose *Chronologiae secundum norman Sacrae Scriptae* appeared in 1613. Since I find no trace of a French translation, I suspect Mlle Desjardins found Frisius referred to by another author, and used his name for effect. (2) *Sigon.* Carlo Sigonio, author of *Historiarium de occidentali impero*, 1579: rare, and apparently untranslated. (3) *Turcelin.* Orazio Torsellino, author of many historical works. The *abrégé* referred to is almost certainly Coulon's translation of his *Histoire universelle*, a source which can be unquestionably verified.[35] (4) *Sigeb.* Sigebertus' *Chronicon ab anno 381 ad 1556* was published in 1556. There is no evidence of a French translation. (5) *Platus.* Jerome Piatti, or Hieronymus Platus, a Jesuit, published two works: *De bono status religiosi* (1590) and *De Cardinalis dignitate et officio* (1602), neither of which contains either "un chapitre entier" on the Fraticelli, or indeed any mention of the sect.[36] (6) *Baronius.* Baronius' *Ecclesiastical Annals* originally extended no further than the year 1198, more than a century before the appearance of the sect of the Fraticelli. The work of his continuers (Raynaldus, Bzovius, Spondamus, and others) was, however, generally included under the same title. Mlle Desjardins' source was not Baronius, but Raynaldus.[37] (7)

[34] Dulong, *op. cit.*, pp. 155 ff. mentions in connection with the Dom Carlos legend many source books of Spanish history which had wide circulation in the seventeenth century, such as Turquet de Mayerne's *Histoire générale de l'Espagne*, 1586, 1608, etc., and du Verdier's *Abrégé de l'histoire d'Espagne*, 1659. For works on English history, cf. G. Ascoli, *La Grande-Bretagne devant l'opinion française au XVIIe siècle*, 2 vols., Paris, 1930, especially the bibliography in Vol. II.

[35] Editions of the *Histoire universelle, traduite et continuée par le sieur Coulon* appeared in 1648 and 1654. Mlle Desjardins refers to the story of Othon as on "fol. 323." It begins on p. 324 of the 1654 edition.

[36] There were numerous French translations, *abréges, analyses, extraits*, etc., of *De bono status religiosi* issued during the first part of the seventeenth century. Père Girard's translation of 1644 was reprinted at Avignon in 1848; I have examined three of the four volumes in this edition, as well as a rare copy of the first edition (Rome, Iacobum Tornerium, 1590), but find no reference to the Fraticelli. Mlle Desjardins was apparently making use of the name of Platus to add authority to her statement that her story was based on historical fact. A fully annotated edition of *De Cardinalis dignitate et officio* (Rome, 1836), with an exhaustive index, contains nothing about the Fraticelli. The only other known works of Platus are a letter on St. Louis de Gonzague in the *Acta sanctorum*, IV, 896-911, and a biography of William Elphinston, not published until 1881. The Ms. of a lost work, *De bono status conjugalis*, was destroyed during the life of the author (cf. *Bibliothèque de la Compagnie de Jésus*, Paris, 1895, VI, 691-697).

[37] The 1758 edition of Baronius and his continuers ("Mansi edition") contains

S. Ant. Arch. de Flor. Apparently some "Archives de Florence." The reference has the appearance of having been copied by Mlle Desjardins from the margin of some general historical work, possibly Torsellino's. The excessively fragmentary abbreviations of marginal notes of the sixteenth and seventeenth centuries often make it impossible to identify the references.

Of the numerous "sources" alleged for the first nine stories, only two, the Raynaldus continuation of Baronius, and the *abrégé* of Torsellino, can be clearly traced to French versions readily available to Mlle Desjardins.[38] From these she took the backgrounds for three stories (*Othon, Dulcin,* and *Les Fraticelles*) and the chief characters for one (*Othon*). In the case of *Dulcin,* her "background" was taken from the following passage of Torsellino:

> Dulcin et sa femme Marguerite introduirent dans la Lombardie les embrassemens communs & illicites de toutes sortes d'hommes & de femmes indifferemment sans aucune distinction des personnes à la façon des bestes. Et desia cette sale et honteuse secte, seduite par la douceur de la lubricité se repandoit bien avant par le grand nombre qui suivoit le chef de cette vie licentieuse, lors que le Legat du Pape prit les armes contre eux, dissipa leurs troupes & punit severement les principaux autheurs de ces dissolutions.[39]

To this she added the Italianesque *nouvelle* of Nogaret and his mistress who is really his wife. For *Othon,* Mlle Desjardins also found the elements of her plot in this source, but not content to leave the story in its original simplicity, complicated it by doubling the Empress' passion for the Comte de Modène with that of the Emperor for the Comtesse. Torsellino's account runs thus:

numerous references to the Fraticelli which undoubtedly provided Mlle Desjardins with the background for her story. Cf. Vols. V-VIII of Raynaldus' continuation, *passim.* (Cf. "Fraticellorum haeresis," "cultus sordidus," "simulata virtus in vitia degenerans," "addictos se contemplationi fingunt," "eorum hypocrisis," "a Bonifacio VIII damnata," "a Clemente VI jubentur reprimi," etc.). A French *abrégé* of the *Annales,* possibly the direct source used by Mlle Desjardins, appeared in 1655. For the story of Dulcin and Marguerite, Mlle Desjardins seems to have utilized the *Annales* less than the *abrégé* of Torsellino's *Histoire universelle* (cf. below). Baronius had been used as a source for historical fiction by La Calprenède in the writing of *Faramond* (cf. S. Pitou, *La Calprenède's "Faramond,"* Baltimore, 1938).

[38] Mlle Desjardins claimed that she knew no language other than French: cf. Chapters I and II, above. Platus existed in French, but she made no use of his work.

[39] *Histoire universelle depuis la création du monde jusques à l'an 1598,* par le P. Horace Turcelin de la Cie de Jésus, traduite et continuée par le sieur Coulon, Rouen, 1654 (2 vols.), I, 406. Mlle Desjardins' reference to her own story in the *Avant-propos* of the *Annales* corresponds almost textually to the above passage: "Dulcin et Marguerite avoient introduit l'usage de s'accoupler avec toutes sortes de personnes sans choix, et sans distinction. . . ."

Le commencement du regne d'Othon fut remarquable par un acte de iustice tres-extraordinaire. L'Imperatrice Marie avoit essayé par tous moyens d'attirer à son amour le Comte de Modene, sans le pouvoir iamais gagner. Et comme il advient pour l'ordinaire, l'amour s'estant changé en haine, elle accusa ce Seigneur deuant son mary, & le chargea du crime, dont elle seule estoit coupable. Le Comte ayant plus de passion pour l'honneur que pour sa propre vie, apres avoir communiqué cette affaire avec sa femme, eut la tête trenchée par le commandement de l'Empereur trop credule. Quelque temps après cette execution, la femme du Comte s'alla presenter à l'Empereur . . . & portant un fer ardent dans ses mains sans en estre bruslée, elle donna une preuve indubitable de l'innocence de son mary. . . . L'Empereur . . . condamna l'Imperatrice à estre bruslée toute vive, pour sa calomnie, & pour sa lubricité.[40]

The story of Frère Conrart of the Fraticelli and the disclosure of his lascivious hypocrisy by the matron Hortense has struck both Chatenet and Dulong with its similarity to the plot of Molière's *Tartuffe*.[41] The existence of the sect itself, its corrupt practices, its hypocritical poses, and its ultimate denunciation by the Pope: these details were all found by Mlle Desjardins in Raynaldus.[42] She is careful to assert in her preface that the story concerns "une hypocrisie ancienne," and not one "du siècle." Nevertheless, the discourse of the Frérot Conrart when he attempts to seduce Hortense contains many of the same arguments used by Tartuffe to Elvire in Molière's play. Both hypocrites affirm that love, being a divine manifestation, can only bring one closer to God.[43] Both seek to remind the objects of their desire that priestly discretion makes an excellent cloak for adultery, and both argue that undisclosed sin is harmless, the only offense arising from scandal.[44] The first of the duties of the Fraticelli is, in fact, "sauver les apparences," and a Frérot, if he writes

---

[40] Torsellino, *op. cit.*, I, 324. Mlle Desjardins' Empress, "se voyant méprisée par un homme qu'elle avoit crû combler d'honneur," makes the same Phèdre-like accusation (*Annales galantes*, p. 65).

[41] Chatenet, *op. cit.*, p. 140; Dulong, *op. cit.*, p. 79.

[42] Cf. above, n. 37. Chatenet says nothing of Mlle Desjardins' sources; Dulong mentions her list of them ("mainte authorité imposante") but implies that she was only making a show of erudition (as in some cases she undoubtedly was). Direct proof of Mlle Desjardins' use of historical sources is here presented for the first time.

[43] Cf. "L'Amour est aussi naturelle à l'homme que la vie," etc., in the passage in *Les Annales galantes*, pp. 184 ff., and Tartuffe's "un homme est de chair," and ". . .je n'ai pas pu vous voir, parfaite créature, Sans admirer en vous l'auteur de la nature" (III, 3).

[44] *Les Annales galantes*, p. 186: "Aimez ce que vous trouverez aimable, écrivez des poulets, donnez des rendez-vous, il n'importe, ce ne sont pas ces choses qui soient criminelles, c'est la connoissance que vous en donnez qui fait le crime." *Tartuffe* (IV, 5): "Le scandale du monde est ce qui fait l'offense, Et ce n'est pas pécher que pécher en silence." Cf. also Tartuffe's "Les gens comme nous brûlent d'un feu discret" (III, 3).

a madrigal with one hand, must be able to pen a prayer at the same time with the other (p. 162).

The influence of *Tartuffe*, already clear, becomes unmistakable in the scene of the unmasking of Frère Conrart. Hortense leads the Frérot into an avowal of his true intentions, which is overheard by an officer whose wife Conrart has seduced and who has exhibited the same stubborn reluctance to believe evil of Frère Conrart as had Orgon to accept the perfidy of *le pauvre homme*. It would be illogical, in view of the rather extensive documentation undertaken by Mlle Desjardins for this story in such sources as Raynaldus, to assume that her basic intention was to imitate Molière, as she had done, for example, in the *Récit de la farce des Précieuses*. What probably happened was that, with her locale and period selected, the authoress attributed to the sect she found described as wicked and hypocritical a variant of the outstanding example of religious hypocrisy with which she was familiar, that of *Tartuffe*. Despite its resemblances to Molière's work, the story of the Fraticelli has little literary merit: the atmosphere of *galanterie* and the particularization of the plot prevent it from approaching, at any time, the merits of a social satire or a comedy of manners.

The remaining stories of the *Annales galantes* require little comment. Research may uncover the sources of additional *nouvelles*, but it seems unlikely that in any case the employment of sources and the technique of construction would differ much, if at all, from Mlle Desjardins' procedure in the stories examined above. Such is Mlle Desjardins' first contribution to "les historiettes, les nouvelles et les romans historiques, ornés des agrémens que la verité peut souffrir," for which she was praised by Langlet du Fresnoy.[45] Her mixing of fact and fiction brought a denunciation from Bayle, who thought the new practice corrupted the taste of the young for history "et fait qu'on n'ose croire ce qui est au fond croiable."[46] Her precedent of listing her historical sources was followed by Saint-Réal in *Dom Carlos* and elsewhere, though she herself, in her one later historical novel, *Les Désordres de l'amour*, omits any list of

---

[45] L'abbé Nicholas Langlet du Fresnoy, *De l'usage des romans*, Amsterdam, 1734, I, 201. As early as 1664 Sorel wrote that people were beginning "à connoistre ce que c'estoit des choses Vraysembables, par des petites narrations dont le mode vient, qui s'appeloient des Nouvelles" (*Bibliothèque françoise*, p. 160). He himself had written *nouvelles* in 1623. He declares further that "les Nouvelles qui sont un peu longues et qui rapportent les avantures de plusieurs personnes ensemble, sont prises pour des petits romans" (*ibid.*, p. 168).

[46] *Dictionnaire*, article "Jardins," and *Nouvelles de la république des lettres*, I, 405.

sources. M. Dulong, who refers to the *Annales galantes* in connection with Saint-Réal, sums up its merits in a flattering yet substantially just critical estimate which deserves citation:

Le livre tient assez bien les promesses de la préface. Au sortir des fadeurs et des extravagances du roman héroïque, il apporte à l'esprit un repos plein d'agrément. Mme de Villedieu a peu de style, mais, d'instinct, elle sait conter. Elle badine avec grâce et ne se prend pas au sérieux plus qu'il ne convient. On ne rencontre chez elle ni la préciosité affectée, ni les sentiments guindés.[47] Sa morale est facile et l'amour, dans ses récits, a toujours raison. . . .[48] Amie de Molière, elle partage les indulgences du grand homme pour les expansions de la libre nature et sa haine pour les hypocrites.[49] Tel qu'il est, avec son allure ironique et légère et sa franche inspiration, l'ouvrage de Mme de Villedieu mérite une place honorable dans la littérature romanesque du XVIIe siècle. Il est encore un de ceux dont les changements de la mode ont le moins fané les attraits.[50]

Les Désordres de l'amour (1675)

Some uncertainty exists as to the earliest date of publication of *Les Désordres de l'amour*. Graesse, who is almost certainly mistaken, gives the date of the first edition as 1670.[51] Miss Dallas, whose testimony may be accepted as reliable, mentions handling one volume of a 1675 edition *chez* Barbin which, in the absence of contradictory evidence, must be regarded as the first.[52]

Readers of the work were not offered an explanatory preface or defense such as that which accompanied the *Journal amoureux* and the *Annales galantes*. Those familiar with the "method" of the two preceding works doubtless recognized that it remained substantially the same; others must have drawn their inferences directly from the text. Again the basic plots

[47] This assertion hardly applies to all of Mlle Desjardins' works; cf. the discussion of *Alcidamie*, and elsewhere.

[48] Not, however, in the *Fraticelles*, where bourgeois virtue triumphs.

[49] This is an exaggeration. Mlle Desjardins' relationship with Molière cannot be termed one of friendship, nor was she indignant at the hypocrisies of the *Fraticelles*. Her attitude was one of amusement, and the cult, with its "règles d'amour" and the like, would have welcomed many of Mlle Desjardins' fictional heroes.

[50] Dulong, *op. cit.*, p. 79.

[51] *Loc. cit.* His compendium also assigns *Les Annales galantes de Grèce* to the year 1668 instead of 1687, the date of the *privilège* discovered by Derome.

[52] *Op. cit.*, p. 189, note. The copy is owned by Magne, whose bibliography gives 1676 as the date of the first edition. The Bib. Nat. contains a Toulouse edition of 1702, *chez* Desclassen. An English translation of the last of the three stories of the *Désordres* appeared as early as 1677, entitled *The Disorders of Love, truly expressed in the unfortunate amours of Givry with Mademoiselle de Guise* ("Made English from the French. London. Printed for James Magnes and Richard Bently, 1677"). The work is not mentioned in Mlle Desjardins' list of 1671.

are drawn from history, and filled in with dialogue and incidents in keeping with the characters and with well-known events. Instead of writing many stories placed in various epochs, Mlle Desjardins confines herself here to three *nouvelles*, all based on sixteenth-century French history, and develops each in a fuller and more orderly fashion. There is less of the Italianesque *conte* in the *Désordres*, and more of the psychological novel. Irony and *badinage* are put aside for analysis of character and emotion. The stories of the *Annales* are "realistic" in the grosser sense of the word; those of the *Désordres* reveal a trend toward that realism of the personality which gives significance and value to such a work as the *Princesse de Clèves*, published almost simultaneously.

There are four *Parties* in the *Désordres*, relating three stories (the third story taking up two *Parties*, *III* and *IV*). Each *Partie* runs to about 50 pages.[53]

Partie I. "Que l'Amour est le ressort de toutes les autres passions de l'Ame." Henri III shows an interest in the Protestant Princesse de Condé, alarming Catherine de' Medici, the Queen Mother. Catherine persuades the beautiful Mme de Sauve to flirt with Henri to distract his attention. Two of his former mistresses, Mlle de Chateauneuf and Mlle d'Elbeuf, enraged with jealousy, form a plot with the Duc de Guise and Henri de Navarre: the King of Navarre is to make passionate love to Mme de Sauve, then scorn her. He is to announce his scorn for her after a ballet in which he will play Apollo and she "la méprisée Clitie," telling her that the allegory is only too true. Instead, he falls in love with her. A fourth lover is added when Monsieur, the King's brother, also falls in love with Mme de Sauve. Each reproaches her for infidelity, but she manages to persuade each in turn that he alone is the object of her love. The King's favorite, Dugua, sees Guise leaving Mme de Sauve's apartments at night. This news is communicated to Marguerite de Navarre, who loves Guise and angrily reveals his affair with Mme de Sauve to Monsieur. Mme de Sauve is able to persuade Monsieur that the rumor is false, meanwhile writing letters to Henri de Navarre offering to give up Guise, and to Guise offering to break off relations with Henri de Navarre. This complex amorous situation is interrupted by a rapid account of the war which ended in the peace of 1576, victimizing the Duc de Guise, and thus inclining him to sympathy with the Ligue. Thus, concludes the author, the foundations of the religious and civil wars of a later period were laid down by a "fatale passion," and the war of religion "eut ses sources dans les intrigues d'amour que je viens d'écrire."

Partie II. "Qu'on ne peut donner si peu de puissance à l'Amour qu'il n'en abuse." During the reign of Charles IX the Marquis de Termes marries a young girl from a neighboring estate whom he had not met "lorsqu'il la fiança," but with whom he quickly fell in love. The Marquise becomes pale and ill, and seems about to languish

---

[53] The *Désordres de l'amour* has been used in the 1741 edition of Mlle Desjardins' *Œuvres*, I, 1-214.

away. When the Marquis questions her about her illness, she finally confesses to him that she had been in love with, and indeed still loves, the nephew of the Marquis, young Bellegarde, whom she would have married had her father not insisted through avarice on her match with Termes. She apologizes for the state of her feelings, and insists she has tried to forget Bellegarde and be a good wife, only to find love stronger than her will. Termes generously proposes divorce, but she refuses, urging him to forgive her so that she may try again to become "la femme que je dois être." The Marquis is killed shortly thereafter at the battle of Jarnac. His will names Bellegarde his heir, on condition that he marry the Marquise.

Termes' heirs contest the will. A rumor accuses the Marquise of poisoning her husband. Her father denounces her. Nevertheless, she follows Bellegarde, now banished from Court, to Savoy, "et se trouva la femme du jeune Marquis, sans qu'on ait bien sçu si elle avoit trouvé le secret de la devenir en conscience." After a period of happiness their relations are troubled by boredom and restlessness on the part of Bellegarde and an intense, unjustifiable jealousy on the part of the Marquise. Charles IX dies (1574) and Henri III makes Bellegarde a Maréchal. He becomes involved in a plot against the Queen Mother; his wife intercepts a letter revealing this fact and carries it to Catherine, hoping thus to secure revenge on the lover who has turned against her. The Queen Mother, in Lyons, upbraids Bellegarde for his treachery to her, at the same time giving him proof of his wife's perfidy.[54]

Bussy d'Amboise falls in love with the Marquise. Bellegarde hears of this, and arranges what Bussy supposes to be a rendezvous with her. A servant girl is to meet Bussy, but the Marquise learns of the plot and arrives herself, sending Bussy firmly away as Bellegarde listens from concealment. Failing in his design to prove the marquise unfaithful and thus be rid of her, and having incurred the wrath of Bussy and his powerful friend Monsieur, Bellegarde retires to Savoy and in a sudden coup seizes the marquisate of Saluces. The Marquise is ordered off to a convent by the Queen Mother. Once again, love has been shown as the mainspring of historical action, having in this example placed "un obstacle secret à la Paix générale du Royaume."

Partie III. "Qu'il n'y a point de désespoir où l'Amour ne soit capable de jeter un homme bien amoureux." Givry d'Anglure, former friend of the Guises, now fights against them in the wars of the Ligue. His mistress Mme de Maugiron writes to him constantly and one day he loses her letters, only to have them returned by the opposing side, each bearing a *maxime* written in an unfamiliar hand. The verses trouble him. He learns from Bellegarde (the nephew of the one in Part II) that they were written by Mlle de Guise, and the seeds of his fatal love are sown. In fear that she may be in need of food, Givry permits a shipment of wheat to enter Paris, delaying the capture of the city and provoking the anger of the King, who nevertheless forgives him on hearing his sentimental explanation. During a truce (1589) Bellegarde and Givry visit Mlle de Guise. Later Givry sends her perfume and a message, to have both returned coldly. In despair, and now wounded, he persuades the King to allow the Chevalier d'Oise, a prisoner, to go back and enquire why Mlle de Guise has

---

[54] A different story forms the basis of Chapman's *Bussy d'Ambois*, 1607 (cf. also Dumas' *Dame de Montsoreau*). In Chapman, Bussy is summoned to a rendezvous by a letter which Montsoreau forces his wife to write, and is there killed.

rejected his attentions. She sends word that Givry has written her an offending letter, an accusation which Givry is at a loss to understand.

Partie IV. (No motto.) In an interlude in the fighting, Givry retires to his estate at Brie. The Guises pass through. Givry asks an explanation of Mlle de Guise's disfavor, and she shows him an impertinent love letter which she thinks he has sent her. Givry recognizes Bellegarde's handwriting. Learning this, Mlle de Guise feels an awakening interest, not in Givry, but in Bellegarde. Bellegarde turns aside Givry's accusation of treachery. Mme de Maugiron overhears Mlle de Guise confess her love for Bellegarde to her *suivante*, and urges her former lover to cease sighing after a woman who loves another. She, too, a victim of a "fatale passion," tells Givry: "Vous reviendrez quelque jour à moi." Givry, however, insists he would rather find a third mistress than return to Mme de Maugiron.

When Henri IV enters Paris, Bellegarde and Givry quarrel over who shall defend Mlle de Guise's house from the soldiers and the rabble. Mlle de Guise accuses Givry of misbehavior, and makes her indifference to him plain. In spite of this, Givry later forces his way into her bedroom, falls to his knees, and makes passionate declarations of love. Mlle de Guise, in great anger, orders him to withdraw forever. He does so, and in the next battle [Laon], deliberately seeks his death, leaving a letter for Mlle de Guise, which is, however, never delivered. Mme de Maugiron falls into a languor and dies. The King bitterly accuses Mlle de Guise of killing Givry. Such is the last example of the evil effects of the passion of love.

These are the historical periods in *schéma:*

Partie I. Mme de Sauve, Duc de Guise, Henri III: ca. 1574.
Partie II. Marquise de Termes, Bellegarde: ca. 1570-1580.
Parties III et IV. Givry, Mlle de Guise: ca. 1589.

The single reference made by Mlle Desjardins to any source for the *Désordres* occurs at the end of *Partie I*, where she mentions "les Mémoires sur lesquels je fais ce Commentaire" (I, 60). Mme de Sauve is mentioned by Brantôme, Pierre Matthieu, L'Estoile, Dupleix, de Thou, and in the *Mémoires* of Marguerite de Valois. But the body of Mlle Desjardins' intrigue appears to derive directly from Mézeray's *Histoire de France,* which gives the following account of Mme de Sauve, containing all the elements of Mlle Desjardins' story:

De toutes les beautés qui brilloient alors à la Cour, la Dame de Sauves, la plus éclatante et la plus spirituelle, mais la plus inconstante et la plus vaine, n'employoit pas moins ses attraits pour les intentions de la Reine que pour sa propre satisfaction: se jouant de tous ses mourans avec un empire si absolu, qu'elle ne perdoit pas un, quoi qu'elle acquist toûjours de nouveaux.[55] Le premier de tous estoit le Duc de

[55] Le Laboureur's *Tombeau des personnes illustres*, Paris, 1642, p. 205, contains this note on Charlotte de Beaune, Marquise de Noirmoutier, and Baronne de Sauve: "Fille de Messire Iacques de Beaune Vicomte de Tours, et Baron de Samblançay, et d'une fille de la maison Illustre et ancienne de Sade, autrement appellée de Sado en Provence, de laquelle estoit la belle Laure, tant aymée de Petrarque."

Guise, si galant et si brave. . . . Mais comme la Reine avoit ordonné à cette Dame d'adoucir les ressentiments du Roy de Navarre, elle s'en estoit si bien acquitée, que le Duc en avoit pris une violente jalousie. . . . Après cela, il se lia d'amitié avec son rival: lequel de son costé n'adressant pas ses désirs à un seul objet, se rencontra en concurrence, et en consequent en picque, avec Monsieur, premierement pour une autre Dame; puis encore à deux mois de là pour la mesme de Sauves. . . .[56]

Very little invention sufficed to transform this account into fiction. Mlle Desjardins added a few names found in Brantôme and the like, contrived incidents and dialogue, and cast the whole into the framework of her pseudo-theory that the moving power in history is chiefly love, "ressort de toutes les autres passions de l'Ame," and that love leads to a fatal *désordre* if not to ruin.

Partie I contains little of literary or psychological interest. The level of style and emotion is about that of the *Annales galantes*. There are the usual *maximes*, a few letters, a ballet-festival scene like that in the second part of the *Journal amoureux* ("une Comédie Italienne" is presented), and much conversation in a precious, elegiac manner:

Hé! de grace, Madame, poursuivit le Duc d'un air inquiet, laissez-moi dans l'oubli où il vous a plû me mettre, et ne cherchez point à vous justifier d'une legereté que je ne vous reproche pas (p. 35).

There is a reference to certain verses by Marot "sur le mepris que le Duc témoignoit d'abord pour les retours de Mme de Sauve" (p. 47), but Mlle Desjardins does not on this occasion transcribe for the reader her gratuitous contribution to the poet's works.[57]

The second *Partie* of the *Désordres*, with its obvious resemblance to *La Princesse de Clèves*, has aroused much critical comment. The controversy dates from the very appearance of the latter work, and hinges upon whether Mlle Desjardins' story may be either the source or the principal inspiration of Mme de La Fayette's more famous novel. The points of similarity are many: both the Marquise de Termes and the Princesse de Clèves are married to worthy men who love them, but whom they cannot love, because their affections are attracted elsewhere by fatal *amour d'inclination* for younger men. Both women grow listless and unhappy; both, when questioned by their husbands about their sadness and unsociability, *confess* their illicit but repressed love for another. In each case the husband, a generous, contemplative type, offers

[56] Mézeray, *Histoire de France*, Paris, 1643-1651, III, 361-362.

[57] Cf. Ch. II, above. A Mme de Sauve is indeed mentioned by Marot, but she is of a preceding generation. Marot died in 1544, about thirty years before the action of *Partie I*.

to withdraw from the situation; in each the wife refuses this proposal and promises to be as good a wife as possible under the circumstances. At this point the similarity ceases. Though both husbands die, Termes in a battle and Clèves from heartbreak, the women behave quite differently thereafter. The Marquise de Termes joins her lover, and lives to regret this second stage of her life. The Princesse de Clèves decides not to marry Nemours, and one of the reasons she herself gives to him for her decision is her fear of precisely the sort of outcome of their relationship as that which occurred in the case of the Marquise and Bellegarde. It is almost as if, having the situation to relive, the heroine had profited from experience and now knew which course to choose.

Mlle Desjardins, who has been criticized for not having had the "artistic insight" of Mme de La Fayette, and of carrying the narrative beyond the most effective stopping place (*i. e.*, the point at which *La Princesse de Clèves* ends), was in so doing not constructing a story but following history. Whereas Mme de La Fayette took from historical sources only the background, "atmosphere," and certain intercalated anecdotes of *La Princesse de Clèves,* creating (or borrowing?) the main plot,[58] Mlle Desjardins was retracing the account of Bellegarde and the Marquise de Termes as given by Brantôme and by Mézeray, at least in the latter part of the story. Brantôme devotes a chapter to Bellegarde's disgrace, his retirement to Savoy, his negotiations with Catherine de' Medici, and his seizure of the marquisate of Saluces. He mentions that Bellegarde married the widow of his grand-uncle, the Marquise de Termes, and that he treated her ill. Mézeray also writes:

[Bellegarde] . . . estoit revenu en Savoye, auprès de la veuve de Termes son oncle, l'une des plus belles femmes du monde, qu'il avoit enlevée de Languedoc en ce païs-là. . . . Il l'épousa . . . mais aussitôt après il la traita si mal qu'il laissa toûjours à douter s'il la tenoit pour légitime.[59]

Mlle Desjardins' principal inventions occur in the first part of the story: the "amitié tendre hors le mariage," the wife's coolness, her confession, her husband's generous attitude—in fact, all the psychological apparatus which resembles so closely the work of Mme de La Fayette—

---

[58] Cf. H. Chamard and G. Rudler, "La documentation sur le XVIe siècle chez un romancier du XVIIe, les sources historiques de *La Princesse de Clèves,*" *Revue du seizième siècle*, 1914, pp. 92 ff. and 289 ff., and 1917-1918, pp. 1 ff. and 231 ff.

[59] *Op. cit.,* III, 353. Brantôme's account is in his *Histoire des hommes illustres et grands capitaines.* None of the critics who have dealt with the problem of similarities between the *Désordres* and the *Princesse de Clèves* has noted the existence of historical sources for the outcome of Mlle Desjardins' story.

the famous *aveu* and its implications. It is idle to conjecture where Mlle Desjardins might have ended her story had she not been attempting to follow history, but one may suppose she would have carried it on to something like its present conclusion, since one of her favorite themes, found in as early a work as *Alcidamie,* is the degeneration of a great passion as a lover's ardour cools and his mistress struggles desperately to hold him.

Was the *Désordres de l'amour* the source of the situation of the *aveu* in the *Princesse de Clèves?* The first point in the problem is the date of the two works. We are forced to reject Graesse's date of 1670 for the *Désordres* in favor of the certain date of 1675.[60] There is no question but that the publication date of the *Princesse de Clèves* was March 8, 1678,[61] whatever may have been its date of composition. Mme de La

[60] Cf. above. A. Praviel, in an article on "Mme de Villedieu et la *Princesse de Clèves,*" *Revue littéraire,* 1898 (cited by H. Ashton, *Mme de La Fayette,* Cambridge, 1922, p. 164), assigns to the *Désordres* the impossible date of 1664.

[61] Jules le Petit's *Bibliographie des principales éditions originales d'écrivains français,* Paris, 1927, and A. Tchmerzine's *Bibliographie d'éditions originales et rares d'auteurs français,* Paris, 1932, both reproduce the title page of the *Princesse de Clèves* in facsimile, giving the *privilège* ("16 janvier 1678) and *achevé* ("8 mars 1678"). The preface of the printer (Barbin) implies that the work had circulated to some extent in Ms., but the novel is almost certainly not as old as would be implied by Mme de Sévigné's letter of Mar. 16, 1672, with its curious statement "je ne fais pas des *Princesses de Clèves* et *de Montpensier.*" The *Princesse de Montpensier* appeared in 1672, and was accordingly quite in place in Mme de Sévigné's letter of 1672, but how could she have known of the *Princesse de Clèves* at that date, if it was not published until 1678? Notwithstanding the *privilège* uncovered by Magne (*Le Cœur et l'esprit de Mme de La Fayette,* Paris, 1927, p. 195, n. 2) given in 1672 for a *Prince de Clèves,* which Magne takes to be evidence that Segrais was then already working on what was to become the *Princesse de Clèves,* it seems probable that the original text of the letter in question was "je ne fais pas des *Zaïde* et des *Princesse de Montpensier,*" the text having been altered by the eighteenth-century editor of Mme de Sévigné's letters, Perrin, whose copy is alone extant. Supporting this view is the correspondence between Mme de Sévigné and Bussy-Rabutin of a later date. In a letter dated Mar. 18, 1678, Mme de Sévigné refers to the *Princesse de Clèves* as "un petit livre que Barbin nous a donné depuis deux jours." Bussy's reply and the letters between the two during the weeks following are full of comments on the book which was to both obviously a novelty: Bussy finds the *aveu* "extravagant," etc. Cf. *Œuvres de Mme de Sévigné,* Gds. Éc. ed., II, 533, V, 424, 462, and *passim.* The earliest true evidence of the existence of the *Princesse de Clèves* in Ms. form is a letter of Mme de Scudéry, who, on Dec. 8, 1677, announced that "M. de La Rochefoucauld et Mme de La Fayette" had just completed "un roman des galanteries de la cour de Henri second" (see Lalanne's edition of Bussy's *Correspondance,* III, 451). To Ashton (cf. *op. cit.,* p. 166) this letter is the strongest proof that Mme de La Fayette is indeed the chief author of the *Princesse de Clèves.* We are not here concerned with the thorny problem of the single, multiple, or dubious authorship of the work, as discussed by such critics as Perrero, Hémon, and Ashton, but will refer to it simply as the work of Mme de La Fayette. (See, in this connection, Marcel Langlois, "Quel est l'auteur de la *Princesse de Clèves?,*" *Mercure de France,* CCXC (1939), 58-82, recapitulating the arguments and proposing Fontenelle

Fayette's work was printed, then, some three years after that of Mlle Desjardins, and it is in the realm of possibility that Mme de La Fayette may have read the *Désordres de l'amour*, deriving from it the situation of the *aveu*. Could the influence have been exerted in the opposite direction, Mlle Desjardins having had access, before 1675, to a manuscript of the *Princesse de Clèves?* It seems improbable in the extreme that a work, unknown to the intimate circle of Mme de La Fayette herself until the end of 1677, and familiar to such a personage as Mme de Sévigné only after its publication in 1678, could have fallen at the early date of 1675 into the hands of Mlle Desjardins.[62] Moreover, no real evidence exists to prove that the *Princesse de Clèves* had been either begun or finished as early as 1675.[63]

as the author, and my reply, "Marcel Langlois' Untenable Attribution of *La Princesse de Clèves* to Fontenelle," *MLN*, LXI (1946), 267-270.

[62] Ashton, *op. cit.*, pp. 163 ff., does, however, suggest this unlikely hypothesis, alleging that "Mme de Villedieu, qui travaillait vite," may have profited from "une indiscrétion due au fait que Mme de La Fayette communiquait facilement son manuscrit." Though Ashton assumes the prior publication of the *Désordres*, he assigns to it no certain date, and seems unfamiliar with its text, except for the actual scene of the *aveu*, which he reproduces in an appendix "tel que M. Praviel l'a donné dans son article." He devotes much space to proving that the *aveu* is an integral part of the *Princesse de Clèves*, and could not have been added "après coup." But an examination of the *Désordres* would have shown that Mlle Desjardins could scarcely have added it to *her* novel in short order, if there had indeed been any way in which she might have known of the other work. Besides, the three years' interval between the *Désordres* and the *Princesse de Clèves* could certainly not be termed "après coup." The bias of critics like Ashton and Raynal in favor of Mme de La Fayette leads them to deny the very real possibility that she may have borrowed a device of plot from a minor contemporary writer.

[63] Cf. n. 61, above. This problem of sources is not a modern one. Shortly after the publication of the *Princesse de Clèves*, Jean-Baptiste de Valincourt brought out an extensive criticism of the novel entitled *Lettres à la Marquise de * * * au sujet de la Princesse de Clèves*, Paris, 1678. In it he alleged that the *Désordres* was the source of the *aveu* of Mme de La Fayette's work, and drew a parallel between the two situations. Soon the abbé de Charnes issued his *Conversations sur la critique de la Princesse de Clèves*, Paris, 1679, and, to defend Mme de La Fayette from Valincourt's charge of borrowing, advanced the same unsubstantiated argument used by Ashton, suggesting that the indebtedness, if any, was the reverse. De Charnes writes: "Ce qu'il y a de seur à l'égard de l'Auteur de la *Princesse de Clèves* & que je sçay de bonne part, c'est qu'il avoit fait son Histoire longtems avant l'impression du livre des *Désordres de l'amour*." But we have only his word for it. Émile Faguet in 1909 tried to investigate Valincourt's assertion, but was unable to locate a copy of the *Désordres;* cf. his article "Un Critique homme du monde au XVIIe siècle (Valincourt)," *Revue des Deux Mondes*, May 15, 1909, pp. 372 ff. André Beaunier (*L'Amie de La Rochefoucauld*, Paris, 1927, p. 197) makes the strange claim that "l'aveu de Mme de Termes n'a presque nulle analogie avec celui de Mme de Clèves," although in the same breath he cites the *Désordres* as proof that the idea of such a confession was current ("Il semble que cette idée-là fût, comme on dit, dans l'air"). Miss Dallas expresses the same opinion: "Il n'y a pas d'analogie" (*op. cit.*, p. 191). Marie-Aline Raynal (*Le Talent de Mme de La Fayette*, Paris, 1926) refuses to admit the *Désordres* as a source, seeing only "un rapport assez lointain" (p. 235).

The problem is further complicated by the fact that in Donneau de Visé's *Mercure galant* of January, 1678, there was published a twenty-one-page item with the appearance of a *fait divers* but called in the table of contents *La Vertu malheureuse, histoire*. It purports to be a true account of the remarkable actions of a noblewoman who had withdrawn to a convent shortly before ("il y a quelques jours"). The story is practically a *schéma* of the plot of the *Princesse de Clèves*, except that the scene is contemporary. Most critics are of the opinion that *La Vertu malheureuse* is a deliberate conversion by a journalist (probably de Visé himself) of the plot of the *Princesse de Clèves* (read in manuscript by virtue of some "leakage" from Mme de La Fayette's circle in late 1677) into a false news account. What has not been pointed out, and what renders the solution of the problem of the *Désordres* and the *Princesse de Clèves* even more difficult, is the fact that *La Vertu malheureuse* forms a kind of bridge between the works of Mlle Desjardins and Mme de La Fayette. It contains a number of plot elements from *both novels*, combined in such a fashion as to suggest that the author was basing his composition on an account which was closer to the *Désordres de l'amour* than the plot of the *Princesse de Clèves* is in its present version.[64]

[64] *La Vertu malheureuse* was first discussed in relationship to the *Princesse de Clèves* by Fernand Baldensperger, "À propos de l'*aveu* de la *Princesse de Clèves*," *Revue de philologie française et de littérature*, XV (1901), 26-31. He makes no mention of the *Désordres de l'amour*. Rejecting the idea that the account in the *Mercure galant* could have been Mme de La Fayette's direct source (because of insufficient time), Baldensperger conjectures that the real story behind it might have struck the author of the *Princesse de Clèves* as of unusual psychological interest, and worthy of inclusion in a novel, constituting thus a source from real life. The critic then goes on to propose a counter theory, namely, that de Visé, or whoever wrote *La Vertu malheureuse*, invented the story from pre-publication knowledge of the *Princesse de Clèves*, either through hearsay or from some "fuite" or leakage of a Ms. copy from Mme de La Fayette's circle. Beaunier (*op. cit.*, p. 201) affirms that the "nouvelle . . . est d'un plagiare," an opinion in which he is followed by Dallas (*op. cit.*, p. 203). Ashton (*op. cit.*, p. 164) goes so far as to suggest that some "indiscrétion de Mme de La Fayette" may have given the idea to both de Visé and Mlle Desjardins, ignoring the chronological improbability of such a conjecture. A careful comparison of *La Vertu malheureuse* with the *Désordres* and with the *Princesse de Clèves* discloses that up to and including the scene of the *aveu*, the anonymous story is closer to the *Désordres*, and that thereafter, in its conclusion, it more closely resembles the *Princesse de Clèves*. One might almost conclude that *Vertu* represents a stage in the transformation of the plot of the *Désordres* into that of the *Princesse de Clèves*. How it got into print, disguised as a *fait divers*, remains a mystery. Another point which has puzzled critics is why, when the idea of a wife's confession to her husband had already been publicized in the *Mercure galant* (and, it may be added, in the *Désordres* three years before), the *aveu* of the *Princesse de Clèves* provoked the "espèce de stupeur . . . chez les lecteurs" which Baldensperger describes. Ashton tries to dismiss the matter as more the reaction of one reader, Bussy-Rabutin, than of the general public, but his view is controverted by much additional testimony,

From the standpoints of chronology and of internal and external evidence the *Désordres de l'amour* may have suggested the *aveu* in the *Princesse de Clèves*. Is there another possible source, antedating both works? Critics have mentioned the well-known (but not strikingly similar) confession of a wife to a husband in Corneille's *Polyeucte* (1642).[65] Mme de La Fayette herself, in her *Princesse de Montpensier* (1662), has her heroine confess to a friend, the Duc de Chabannes, her love for a man other than her husband.[66] Both the *Désordres* and the *Princesse de Clèves* contain evidence that the author felt the heroine's *aveu* to be something unique and noteworthy: Mlle Desjardins writes, "Des aveux si rares et si ingénus pénétrèrent le Marquis d'une douleur inexprimable . . ," and Mme de Clèves says to her husband, "Je vais vous faire un aveu que l'on n'a jamais fait à un mari."[67] Wherever the conception of such a confession (now a commonplace of the novel) may have originated, the first specific example of it in a published work of prose fiction is incontestably that contained in Mlle Desjardins' *Désordres de l'amour*.

Too much importance must not be attached to the *aveu*, nor must it be elevated to the status of a criterion. The device or innovation does not in itself suffice to make of the *Désordres de l'amour* a masterpiece. What raises the *Princesse de Clèves* above it in merit is a whole complex atmosphere of tone, style, organization, and psychology which outstrips

especially the numerous "réponses à l'*aveu*" sent in by readers of the *Mercure galant* for its extraordinary issue of July, 1678 (cf. Langlois, *loc. cit.*, and especially Beaunier, *op. cit.*, pp. 202 ff. for discussion and analyses of these letters). The *Mercure*, during the early months of 1678, displayed a singular interest in the *Princesse de Clèves*, yet never chose to point out that as early as January of that year it had run what amounted to a synopsis of the novel, nor did it explain the mystery of where it obtained that synopsis, or how it happened to be disguised as a true account.

[65] Suggested first by the abbé de Charnes, *op. cit.*, Pauline (*Polyeucte*, II, 4) tells her husband that her former suitor, Sévère, falsely reported dead and now returned, "a toujours le droit de nous charmer." This *aveu*, despite Voltaire's indignant commentary, seems hardly comparable to that of either Mme de Termes or of Mme de Clèves. Nor is the innocent revelation of love made by Agnès to her guardian in *L'École des femmes* a likely source. Beaunier (*op. cit.*, p. 198) follows de Charnes: "Je veux qu'elle [Mme de Clèves] ait une dette, qui ne la ruine pas, envers la Pauline de Corneille; mais elle ne doit rien à Mme de Termes."

[66] By a curious circumstance, the first line of the *Princesse de Montpensier* contains both of the important words of the title of Mlle Desjardins' novel: "Pendant que la guerre civile déchiroit la France sous le règne de Charles IX, *l'amour* ne laissoit pas de trouver sa place parmi tant de *désordres*. . . ." (Italics mine.) Mme de La Fayette's further preoccupation with the theme of confession is shown in her posthumous *Comtesse de Tende* (1741), which Ashton, Raynal, and Beaunier believe to have been written in order to justify the *aveu* of the *Princesse de Clèves*. The Comtesse, however, waits until she is with child by her lover before confessing!

[67] Mlle Desjardins, *Œuvres*, I, 70; *Romans et nouvelles de Mme de La Fayette*, ed. L.-S. Auger, Paris, n.d., p. 354.

anything in the lesser novel. The *Princesse* is not without its faults, chief among which is the inclusion of historical anecdotes which have little bearing on the main story, but its superior elegance and charm are instantly apparent. The significance of a work like the *Désordres* in the literary history of the French novel lies less in its intrinsic value as an artistic achievement than in the light it throws on the tentative efforts and approximations which frequently precede works of art. Literary manuals have not hesitated to describe the *Princesse de Clèves* in terms which suggest that it was a highly unique production, the "first psychological novel," and one which deviated abruptly, thanks to the genius of Mme de La Fayette, from the preciosity and bombast of the heroic novel which preceded it. The sole explanation for such a sudden literary attainment would presumably lie in the genius of its author. Such a view does not fit the facts of literary history. Behind the perfection of a novel like the *Princesse de Clèves* lies a long period of preparation for such a "psychological" and sentimental masterpiece, extending as far back as Hélisenne de Crenne's *Angoysses douloureuses* (1538) and that mammoth source of so many fictional trends in the seventeenth century, *L'Astrée*.[68] The heroic novel itself is not without its "psychological" aspects, and the rapidly developing *genre* of the historical novel and *nouvelle,* as we have seen, strove for realism of characterization (always, of course, within the framework of seventeenth-century psychological conceptions). Classical tragedy likewise directed attention to the personality of the individual, exalting its importance, subtilizing its mental processes, integrating its driving forces and controls until it ran like a jeweled watch movement. Within his closed system, Racine is a more sensitive psychologist than any novelist of the period.[69] Outside of the drama,

[68] Cf. Reynier, *op. cit.*, and Magendie, *op. cit.*, *passim.*

[69] That two distinct "psychologies" may be found in seventeenth-century literature, one in the rationalistic classical tragedy, and the other in the *roman historique,* the realistic novel, etc., becomes apparent on close examination. Classical Racinian tragedy permits only the "well-made" character, in whom every desire, fear, and potentiality is neatly in its place, readily available when the moment arrives which will call it forth. There are no "irrational" personages; even a Hamlet would be unthinkable. In certain works of prose fiction, on the other hand, characters pursue courses of action less clearly motivated, and their *état d'âme* lends itself less easily to logical analysis. Chamard and Rudler in their above-mentioned article point out that Valincourt's criticism of the *Princesse de Clèves* attacked it precisely because it did not show the same "*vraisemblance*" with regard to history and the motivation of action as did the classical tragedy, which had "rendu les esprits terriblement difficiles à cet égard" ("L'Histoire et la fiction dans la *Princesse de Clèves*," *Revue du seizième siècle,* 1917, p. 242). The abyss between the psychology of a Racine and that of a Proust demonstrates clearly that, of the two opposing systems, it is the

in novels and short stories, new problems and new personality types came into vogue. Extra-marital relationships and other domestic difficulties were treated in fiction on a plane more accessible to the average reader than that of the classical stage. Types like the understanding husband (less noble, more sentimentally appealing than a Polyeucte, and without his religio-mystic tendencies) became more common. The devastating *désordres* produced by love differed materially in fiction from those of a play like *Phèdre*, for example. The dramatic climax gave way to a series of more "realistic" events like those of Mlle Desjardins' novel. Historical fiction, with its scene laid in France itself (not in Greece or Rome), and in the not-too-distant past, turned out to be the entering wedge with which something approaching realism was introduced into literature. The *Princesse de Clèves*, far from being a unique and startling product, was in reality the culmination of many tendencies already present in fiction. Although other similar examples could be cited, Mlle Desjardins' *Désordres de l'amour* is the work to which it bears the closest resemblance, and to which it may owe a sizable literary debt.[70]

The story of Mlle de Guise and Givry (Parts III-IV) was a part of the fictional and word-of-mouth tradition of the seventeenth century. Although historians and writers of memoirs refer at some length to Givry, extolling his courage, his knowledge of languages and mathematics, and deploring his unfortunate death, they do not mention his unrequited love for Mlle de Guise.[71] Curiously enough, the first reference to such a love occurs in a novel attributed to Mlle de Guise herself, *Les Amours du grand Alcandre*, a *roman à clef* which appeared in 1629 and was later reissued as *Les Amours de Henri IV*, with the characters unmasked and given their real names.[72] At the beginning of Mlle de Guise's work a number of incidents

growing art of prose fiction which has taken precedence, especially since the advent of romanticism and modern psychological and psychoanalytic research. The heroes of French classical tragedy, so rationally constructed and motivated with such meticulous care, are now like museum pieces, beautiful but outmoded.

[70] For the development of the conception of the *honnête homme* type of understanding husband, and the prevalence of marital problems as subjects for novels and *nouvelles*, cf. Dallas, *op. cit.*, and, to a lesser extent, Magendie, *op. cit.*

[71] Cf. Mézeray, *op. cit.*, III, 1117, Cheverny's *Mémoires* (Michaud collection), X, 538, etc. He is in Le Laboureur's *Tombeau* (cf. above). On his death Passerat wrote a *Consolation à Mme de Givry*, Masson a *Givrii . . . elogium*, and Dinet an *Oraison funèbre*. Durand, Passerat, du Peyrat, and Richelet published in 1594 a *Tombeau de feu Monsieur de Givry*. Davila's *Guerres civiles de France*, translated into French in 1647, also mentions Givry.

[72] I have seen only the second version. Since Magendie, *op. cit.*, p. 123, states that

found in the *Désordres* story occur, including Givry's admission of food into Paris, the interference of Bellegarde in the affair, and Mlle de Guise's subsequent favoring of Bellegarde. The character of Mlle de Guise is depicted much as it is in Mlle Desjardins' novel, but Givry is dealt with harshly.[73] Mlle Desjardins rearranges the order of events, and inserts the devices of lost verses, love evoked by mere descriptions, counterfeit letters, etc. But the passionate inevitability of Mlle de Guise's love for Bellegarde is in both works the source of Givry's tragic despair.[74]

That Mlle Desjardins may have taken the *données* of the story of Givry from oral tradition as well as from such a printed source as *Les Amours de Henri IV* is proved by the laconic account of the episode in Tallemant's *Historiettes*, to the manuscript of which Mlle Desjardins could not have had access:

Mlle de Guise, depuis princesse de Conty, fut cajollée de plusieurs personnes, et entre autres du brave Givry. . . . Elle le méprisa, et Bellegarde acheva l'avanture. . . . Enfin, Givry, voyant qu'elle le quittoit, luy escrivoit un billet que je mettray ici, parce que c'est un des plus beaux billets qu'on puisse trouver:
Vous verrez en apprenant la fin de ma vie, etc.
En effet, il s'engagea si fort parmy les ennemis au siège de Laon, qu'il y fut tué.[75]

More astonishing than the mere similarity of Tallemant's version to that of the *Désordres* is the fact that the letter referred to above appears word for word the same in Mlle Desjardins' novel (p. 211). I have searched in vain for some common source from which both Tallemant and Mlle Desjardins might have copied verbatim a letter attributed to Givry; it

Alcandre was also called *Les Avantures de la cour de Perse*, it may be assumed that the original *décor* was oriental. Hauser lists the work as a literary source book for the period of Henri IV.

[73] "Ayant favorisé autant qu'il avoit peü tout ce qu'il pensoit estre agréable à mademoiselle de Guise, jusques à faire passer des vivres dans Paris qui en estoit souvent en nécessité [Givry], receut d'elle un si mauvais visage et un si apparent mépris que cela rabatit beaucoup de la vanité dont il faisoit profession." *Les Amours de Henri IV*, in Lafaist and Danjon's *Archives curieuses de l'histoire de France depuis Louis IX à Louis XVIII*, Paris, 1837, XIV, 318. Cf. Mlle Desjardins, *Œuvres*, I, 145 ff.

[74] In *Les Amours de Henri IV* the first meeting of Bellegarde and Mlle de Guise is described in this romantic fashion: "Bellegarde s'y trouva aussi. . . . Mlle de Guise, qui faisoit profession de mépriser tout le monde, sentit . . . à la veue de ce chevalier qu'elle pouvoit aymer autre chose qu'un Roy, et dès cette heure-là ils eurent tous les deux de l'amour l'un pour l'autre; estrange effet des passions ausquelles on ne résiste point!" As the novel progresses Givry disappears from the scene, and a situation entirely dissimilar to any in the *Désordres* arises. Bellegarde is accused of collusion in the death of Mlle de Guise's father, and the two lovers are faced with a problem like that of Rodrigue and Chimène in the *Cid*, first performed in 1636, some years after the appearance of *Les Amours de Henri IV*.

[75] *Op. cit.*, I, 81 ff.

may some day turn up. There is little likelihood that the letter is a genuine historical document. It may have circulated, however, among the friends of Mme de Rambouillet, coming to be accepted as genuine and eventually falling into the hands of both Tallemant and Mlle Desjardins.[76]

More interesting to the historian of fiction than either the unloved Givry or the disdainful Mlle de Guise is the character of Givry's ex-mistress, Mme de Maugiron. She appears to be without literary precedent, invented by Mlle Desjardins out of whole cloth. She is the *honnête femme* counterpart of the generous husband type represented by the Marquis de Termes and later by Clèves. When Givry plans to abandon her, she asks him for a rendezvous. Expecting reproaches, he comes prepared to avoid them, but the interview has another outcome:

> Elle n'avoit jamais été si belle . . . que ce soir-là. Givry s'étonna dans son âme, qu'avec tant de charmes, et beaucoup d'amour, elle n'eût pû le retenir; et croyant qu'elle venoit lui en faire des reproches. . . . Épargnez-vous la peine . . . lui dit-il . . . et sans porter vos bontés jusques à venir me reprocher mon inconstance, abandonnez-moi à mes dissipations et à mes tiedeurs. Je pourrois vous y abandonner en effet, repartit Madame de Maugiron, si elles étoient mes uniques rivales. Je ne sçai même si les soumissions de mon cœur n'iroient pas jusques à me consoler de mes malheurs, par votre félicité, et si je ne vous pardonnerois point votre amour pour Mademoiselle de Guise, si elle daignoit y répondre. Mais je ne puis vous abandonner à ses mépris, et aux trahisons de votre ami Bellegarde. . . .[77]

When Givry tries to protest,

> Non, non, interrompit Madame de Maugiron, ce n'est plus avec moi qu'il faut affecter ces déguisements.

Givry is at last forced to be brutal with her, and when she declares, "Vous reviendrez quelque jour à moi," he replies,

> S'il faut vous avouer toutes mes indifferences, je pense que j'aimerois plutôt une troisième personne, que je ne retournerois à vous.

This cruel rebuff provokes Mme de Maugiron to a remarkable confession of her "fatale passion," the avowal of an Isolde to a Tristan grown faithless and indifferent:

---

[76] Monmerqué fails to assign any date to the composition by Tallemant of his article on Givry. It seems extremely unlikely that Tallemant would have copied the letter from the *Désordres*, a book known to the public, and have sought to pass it off as genuine. On the other hand, it is curious that Mlle Desjardins made no special point of the authenticity of the document, if she copied it from a reputedly genuine Ms.

[77] There is a faint echo here of the interview between Pyrrhus and Hermione in *Andromaque*, IV, 4.

Pousse tes duretées plus loin, reprit Madame de Maugiron, en versant quelques larmes, et ajoute que tu me hais plus que tu ne m'as aimée. . . . Je ne t'en aimerai pas moins pour cela; ma fatale passion n'a aucun espoir pour subsister, et il y a longtems que sans lui elle semble reprendre de nouvelles forces. Tu ne m'en dois aucune reconnoissance, ce n'est pas un amour volontaire. . . .[78]

Decidedly, this woman has a place among the unusual heroines of the seventeenth-century novel. Rarely outside of the *Princesse de Clèves* is such sincerity of emotion, at once romantic and self-analytical, to be found. Madame de Maugiron embodies, if imperfectly, the passion of a woman out of Racine, transposed into a contemporary, "realistic" situation. Hers is indeed an *âme sensible*. Her counterpart will not appear again until the creation of such romantic figures as the heroine of *Adolphe*, well over a century later.

Some six additional historical novels of the period have been attributed to Mlle Desjardins:

Le Prince de Condé
Mlle d'Alençon (sometimes called *Le Comte de Dunois*)
Mlle de Tournon
Dom Carlos
Astérie, ou Tamerlan
Le Journal amoureux d'Espagne.[79]

It is possible, however, to state with considerable certainty that *Le Prince de Condé* is by Boursault, *Mlle d'Alençon* and *Mlle de Tournon* by Vaumorière, *Dom Carlos* by Saint-Réal, and *Astérie* by Mlle de la Roche. *Le Journal amoureux d'Espagne*, with its title obviously patterned after Mlle Desjardins' *Journal amoureux*, is by an unknown author, though it is often attributed to Mlle de la Roche.[80]

Les Désordres de l'amour, which the *BUR* mistakenly calls her first novel, was probably, in reality, her last.[81] No more novels were published until after her death (1683), and these may have been written earlier than 1675. They are in her earlier style. In the *Désordres*, Mlle

---

[78] *Œuvres*, I, 185-187.

[79] Cf. *Œuvres*, XI and XII, wherein most of these novels appear. The only historical novel mistakenly assigned to Mlle Desjardins in Magne's bibliography is *Le Comte de Dunois*. The *BUR* has several false attributions.

[80] Cf. *Le Journal des sçavans*, Dec. 17, 1703, where an unsigned article on the authorship of the above works appears (an article reproduced by Derome, *loc. cit.*, and attributed to the publisher of Mlle Desjardins' works, Barbin). Further evidence is afforded by the appearance of these works in the *Œuvres* of the authors to whom they are here assigned. Cf. also Magne's bibliography in his *Mme de Villedieu*, p. 418. For *Dom Carlos*, see Dulong, *op. cit.*

[81] *BUR*, 1776, II (2), 169 ff.

Desjardins reached the pinnacle, modest as it was, of her art. Style, psychology, characterization, incident—all are developed to the farthest point of which she was capable. That she was moving in a direction which might have led to real artistic achievement is shown by the success of Mme de La Fayette's *Princesse de Clèves*, a work similar in many ways, and the conception of which, with its mixture of historical "research" and invented plot, is illuminated significantly by the lesser work. The plain fact is that the talent of Mlle Desjardins was not of the quality necessary to produce a masterpiece.[82]

[82] Two minor historical *nouvelles* (*Bussy d'Amboise* and *L'Amirale de Brion et d'Andelot*) by Mlle Desjardins appeared in *Les Amours des grands hommes* (1671) and are discussed in Ch. VIII, below. Relevant to the fortune of *Les Désordres* are the following details: An anonymous imitation of the work appeared at Liége, 1686, under the title *Les Nouveaux Désordres de l'amour*. Bayle reviewed it in September, 1686, and pointed out the borrowing in the title (*Œuvres*, I, 650). The abbé de la Porte, *Histoire littéraire des dames françoises*, II, 24, states in an article on Mlle Desjardins dealing with the *Désordres*, "Je crois . . . que les *Désordres de l'amour* ont fourni l'intrigue d'une pièce intitulée *Le Caprice*, mise au théâtre il y a quelques années." The reference is to *Le Caprice ou l'Épreuve dangereuse, comédie en 3 actes, par M. [J. J. C.] Renout, representée sur le Théâtre français le 28 juin 1762*, Paris, 1762, a Marivaux-like play concerning the efforts of the Baronne de Folmont to keep her lover from falling in love with another woman by arousing his jealousy. The plot bears a superficial resemblance to *Partie I* of the *Désordres*. The rather extensive article on Mlle Desjardins in the abbé de la Porte's work also points out the similarity of a passage in the *Exilez* to Voltaire's *Le Mondain* (cf. Ch. VIII, below), traces a dubious parallel between another scene in that novel and an episode in Dancourt's *Galant jardinier*, and seeks to find in Molière's *École des maris* the plot of the story of Hortensius and Martia in *Les Amours des grands hommes* (cf. Ch. VIII, below). Mme de Tencin later employed the title *Les Malheurs de l'amour*, and Campion wrote a comedy *Les Désordres de l'amour, ou les heureux imprudents*, Charleville, 1774. Neither work has any connection with Mlle Desjardins' novel.

CHAPTER VI

NOUVELLES: GALANTERIE AND RÉALISME MONDAIN

Lisandre (1663?)

The first edition of *Lisandre, nouvelle* is not extant, and it is impossible to fix exactly its date of composition. It is dedicated, like *Manlius* (1662), to the Duchesse de Montpensier, and was doubtless written during Mademoiselle's "exile" at Saint-Fargeau in 1662.[1] *Lisandre* must have been published before 1671, for it is on Mlle Desjardins' list of that date. It is placed, moreover, fourth in a series of thirteen items arranged roughly in chronological order.[2] It seems reasonable to suppose that it appeared between 1662 and 1669, and since Marie-Catherine in 1662 was obviously courting the favors of Mademoiselle, it is not unlikely that it followed soon upon *Manlius*, perhaps as early as 1663. Miss Dallas, indeed, lists an edition of 1663.[3]

Several indications of the favor in which Mlle Desjardins was held by the Duchesse de Montpensier are found in the poems added to the first *Recueil de poésies* in the edition of 1664.[4] One poem is headed by the comment, "Je me suis engagée à plus que je ne pensois, quand j'ai promis à V.A.R. de lui mander quelques nouvelles du Parnasse."[5] A letter of mixed prose and verse to Mme de Montglas contains a description of Mme de la Mothe's estate of Beaumont, with the comment:

Et pour vous montrer, Madame, que c'est sans fiction poetique que je vous fais cette description, vous sçaurez, s'il vous plaît, que j'ai été rendre mes respects à MADEMOISELLE, qui a passé à Beaumont chez Madame la Maréchale de la Motte, et que pendant trois jours sa Cour a été composé de Madame de Montmorency, de

---

[1] Cf. *Mémoires* of Mme de Montpensier, year 1662.

[2] Cf. Derome, *loc. cit.* See Ch. I, above. Magne, *op. cit.*, p. 223, n. 4, assigns to *Lisandre* the date "de 1670 à 1676." It could not have appeared after 1671. On Mlle Desjardins' list, only *Anaxandre* is demonstrably not in chronological order; it appeared in 1667, and is listed after *Cléonice*, which appeared in 1669. *Lisandre* is the first piece of fiction mentioned on the list after *Alcidamie.*

[3] *Op. cit.*, p. 258: "*Lisandre, Nouvelle*, Paris, Claude Barbin, 1663, in-12." She does not state where this edition is to be found, and writes elsewhere (*op. cit.*, p. 114) that *Lisandre* is "une petite nouvelle dont nous ne connaissons pas la première édition." Williams, *op. cit.*, gives 1663, without substantiation.

[4] Called "pièces nouvelles" and published with the first *Recueil* in her *Œuvres*, II, 241 ff. See Magne, *op. cit.*, p. 223, n. 2.

[5] *Œuvres*, II, 246.

Monsieur et de Madame de Sevigny, de Mademoiselle de la Trousse, et de vingt autres personnes. . . .[6]

The dedications of *Manlius* and *Lisandre* were therefore natural steps in Mlle Desjardins' efforts to obtain recognition and royal favor.

The dedicatory letter of *Lisandre* states that Mlle Desjardins feels a duty and a desire to entertain the Duchesse, and implies that beneath the names in her little story lie contemporary actions and personages:

Comme votre ALTESSE ROYALE doit mieux sçavoir les nouvelles de la Cour que moi, et que les nouvelles de la Ville sont indignes de votre curiosité . . . je croi que V. A. R. se divertira mieux, à la lecture d'une petite Histoire qui m'a été écrite depuis quelques jours par une de mes amies, je ne sçai point les veritables noms des personnes qui la composent. On s'est si bien persuadé que toute ma discrétion ne seroit pas à l'épreuve du moindre de vos ordres, qu'on n'a point voulu confier ce secret, et ce que je sçai seulement, c'est que l'homme dont j'ai à vous parler s'appelle Lisandre; à juger de lui par sa maniere de faire l'amour, c'est un homme de la Cour, qui est beaucoup plus spirituel que sincere, et plus galand qu'amoureux. . . . Je ne sçai mesme dans quel lieu les avantures de Lisandre lui sont arrivées; on me mande que c'est dans un agréable endroit du monde, où la liberté de dire qu'on aime est si bien établie, que le mot d'amour n'offense la pudeur d'aucune des Dames; mais comme cette maxime commence à devenir de tous pays: elle ne me fait point deviner celui de Lisandre. . . .[7]

It is apparent that Mlle Desjardins has not as yet formulated the theories of the historical novel which occupy her in the years following this period. We are given a *nouvelle* very much like the minor stories of *Alcidamie,* involving in an anonymous place a group of characters reduced from heroic to contemporary size, the whole suggesting an adaptation of a Spanish *novela.* We are in much the same world as that, for example, of the story *La Belle Invisible* in Scarron's *Roman comique:*

Lisandre, traveling for pleasure and to satisfy his curiosity about the world, stops in an unnamed city and joins the ranks of suitors around the beautiful Lisidore. Piqued at her continued indifference to him, he makes a speech to her in praise of his own virtues, announces his readiness to serve her should she call on him, and with a great show of nonchalance goes off to a solitary place near the city. There, brooding in a garden, he sees Artenire and is immediately drawn to her languorous beauty. He picks up her handkerchief, begins a conversation with her, and discovers she is from his own city, to which she is shortly to return. He abandons Lisidore and devotes himself to his new mistress, who seeks to discourage him by protesting her "paresse" and her languidness, which make her even more charming to Lisandre. Lisandre weeps before her to no avail. Finally she leaves for home and shortly

---

[6] *Ibid.,* p. 248.
[7] *Ibid.,* V, 449-450.

afterwards sends for Lisandre to join her. He goes to the given address and finds, instead of Artenire, two beautiful girls, Dorise and Cloriane. No one has ever heard of Artenire, nor can Lisandre find any trace of her elsewhere. His grief is soothed instantly by the loveliness of Dorise and Cloriane, and after a short soul-struggle he abandons his search for Artenire and begins to visit the two girls.

Many suitors surround both: "La Cour de Cloriane étoit donc la plus grosse, mais celle de Dorise étoit la plus illustre." After hesitating a while, Lisandre decides to woo Cloriane. He sends her a *billet* in verse, but the messenger gives it of course to Dorise and the two sisters dispute amicably over his affections. When both women appear before him and demand that he commit himself, he cannot bring himself to say which he prefers, and ambiguously allows each to think she is his desire. When he is alone with Dorise he feels he prefers her; when he sees both together, Cloriane is his choice. He pays suit to both.

At last the sisters go to a remote spot in a garden and compare the attentions and favors Lisandre has shown each of them. They perceive a lady walking alone and ask her to judge which of them Lisandre loves. To their astonishment the unknown lady already knows their story and even quotes the verses Lisandre has sent to them. At this point Lisandre appears and is astonished to recognize Artenire, for whom he had indeed originally written the verses. The two sisters scold him soundly, and in great embarrassment Lisandre flees.

Hoping to win Artenire, Lisandre returns to the garden, but talking with her he learns "des choses qui lui ôterent pour jamais l'espérance qu'il avoit conçue." The implication is that Artenire is of too high rank to marry Lisandre.

The story ends with the quotation of an elegy ascribed to Artenire, lamenting the social bonds which keep her from returning Lisandre's love.

"Voilà, Mademoiselle," adds Mlle Desjardins, "tout ce que je sçai des avantures de Lisandre. . . . Je vous supplie . . . de regarder tout cela comme un pur effet de mon imagination. . . ."[8]

That Mlle Desjardins should call Lisandre "un homme de la Cour, qui est beaucoup plus spirituel que sincere, et plus galand qu'amoureux," is evidence of the Hylas-like character of the courtiers of the day. Lisandre is a development of the Lisicrate of *Alcidamie*, grown a little more susceptible, and, it must be feared, a little less witty; and both derive from Hylas. In one story the hero courts no less than four women. In no case is he able to make up his mind; he vacillates between Dorise and Cloriane like a needle between two magnets. Lisandre is really a romantic, a Fantasio, a Pierrot sick for lack of love. Mlle Desjardins sees his secret and describes it admirably:

[Lisandre] passa une partie de la nuit à rêver à son avanture, sans pouvoir y rien comprendre. Il avoit été touché véritablement du merite d'Artenire, et s'il est vrai qu'il y en ait une au monde et qu'elle lise ceci, elle sçaura qu'elle est coupable

8 *Ibid.*, p. 488.

de toutes les inconstances de Lisandre; puisqu'assurément, il étoit en son pouvoir de l'arrêter pour jamais. Il étoit même si disposé, qu'il consulta plus de quinze jours, s'il devoit oublier cette trompeuse, ou s'il devoit aimer toute sa vie la belle idée qui lui en étoit restée. Mais *il n'avoit pas un cœur qui pût demeurer vuide;* et puis il rendit deux ou trois visites à ces deux nouvelles connoissances, dans lesquelles il leur trouva tant de charmes, qu'il se résolut à s'abandonner à sa destinée. . . .[9]

His overweening vanity is also amusing, and the author has depicted it with gentle irony. When Lisidore shows no interest in him, this is his protest:

Je suis, comme vous voyez, un Amant assez commode, et l'on m'a souvent dit que ma façon de faire l'amour n'est pas la moins agréable de toutes; mais puisqu'elle ne vous a pas semblé telle, je me résigne aux ordres du destin, adieu, Madame; si par hazard vous ne vous trouvez pas bien de votre Amant, vous n'aurez qu'à m'en avertir. . . .[10]

In this one little speech we hear the voices of the insulted *Inconstant,* the pretended *Parfait Amant,* and the embryonic *Ami des femmes.*

The heroines of *Lisandre,* with the exception of Artenire, are not new or remarkable. Lisidore is the usual impassive, dignified, almost haughty *Dame* who listens equitably to all her suitors and commits herself to none. Her main trait is preoccupation, which she carries so far as to talk with people "avec autant de tranquillité, que si elle eût été dans le fond d'un désert," and to leave a suitor kneeling before her for half an hour before remembering to ask him to rise (pp. 454-455).

Artenire is mysterious, unpredictable, and as languid as the Lady of the Camellias. We would call her neurasthenic; in the terminology of her period she is a "Maîtresse paresseuse." Her secret is that she loves beneath her rank, but since we do not learn this until the end of the story, the effect of her disappearances and evasions is merely that of caprice. This is Mlle Desjardins' description of her:

Lisandre . . . rêvoit encore à Lisidore . . . lorsqu'il vit une Dame seule traverser l'allée où il étoit; quelque profonde que fût sa rêverie, la vue d'une Dame l'en tira fort aisément, et il connut même d'abord que celle qui venoit de passer, étoit de la plus belle taille qu'on puisse avoir; et qu'elle marchoit avec un certain air languissant et négligé qui lui plaisoit infiniment . . . .

[He picks up her handkerchief and speaks to her.]

À ce discours cette inconnue tourne sur lui de grands yeux bleus, les mieux

[9] *Ibid.,* pp. 467-468 (italics mine).

[10] *Ibid.,* p. 458. Through an error in the pagination of Vol. V of the 1741 edition the page is numbered 468.

fendus et les plus languissans qu'il eût vû de sa vie. . . . Car il y avoit longtems qu'il s'étoit fait un portrait d'une Maîtresse paresseuse qui lui faisoit souhaiter avec passion d'en trouver une de cette espece. . . .[11]

It is difficult to distinguish between Dorise and Cloriane; both have that colorless perfection of Mlle Desjardins' early heroines, and one sympathizes with Lisandre's inability to choose between them. Neither is really interested in Lisandre, but they quarrel over his affections as a test of their attractiveness. Lisandre, who had previously spaced his infidelities over a period of time, is faithful and unfaithful to both simultaneously. The essential triviality and shallowness of the whole school of amorous fiction of the day is here manifest: an *Inconstant* vainly trying to choose between two almost identical flirts—variations in a superficial game of "love." It is the *esprit badin et galant* in all its emptiness.

The style of *Lisandre* is flat and mediocre, lacking in wit and tasteless in phrase. Character analysis is almost absent, except for the rare passages like those quoted earlier in the sketches of Lisandre and Artenire. The plot, doubtless an invention of Mlle Desjardins herself, is loosely constructed and has little inherent interest. The incidental verses are below the author's usual level.[12] Here is a sample from the "Élégie" written by Artenire lamenting the loss of Lisandre:

> Noble orgueil d'un haut rang, importune chimere,
> Qui bornez à vos lieux tout ce qui peut nous plaire,
> Obstacles immortels pour nos plus doux plaisirs,
> Cruel, qui captivez jusques à nos désirs,
> Impérieux devoir . . . etc.[13]

Lisandre, although one of the earliest seventeenth-century *nouvelles* to be issued separately, does not represent an important step in the development of fiction towards a shorter form. It is hardly more, as suggested earlier, than an *histoire intercalée* removed from its *cadre* and standing alone. None of the realism, psychological analysis, or historical feeling which characterize the first successful short novels of Mlle Desjardins is yet apparent.

---

[11] *Ibid.,* pp. 460-461. Artenire is not, however, a pale lily; she even speaks of her own "embonpoint," attributing it to her "paresse."

[12] The restet "Je vous dirai, Madame, pour nouvelle," p. 471, was reproduced in the *Recueil Barbin,* 1692, IV, 246; and the "Madrigal" ("Vous offrir quelques fleurs") on p. 479 appeared in the same collection on p. 215. (See Lachèvre's *Bibliographie des recueils . . .* and Magne, *op. cit.,* p. 223, n. 4.)

[13] *Œuvres,* V, 486-487. Cf. the *stances* of the Infanta in the *Cid,* V, 2.

Anaxandre (1667)

Anaxandre was first published in 1667.[14] Langlet du Fresnoy in his *De l'usage des romans* lists an edition of Brussels in 1667.[15] The dedicatory letter leads one to suppose a Belgian edition was published; it is to those "Dames de la Cour de Bruxelles" of whom she speaks so unflatteringly in the *Recueil de lettres*.[16] The *nouvelle* seems to have had no further editions, and it does not appear in the collected works. Robinet's *Gazette* announced the publication of the work, but the index to Baron Rothschild's *Continuateurs de Loret* listed it as a play, thus leading Magne to identify it with the lost tragedy *Agis* mentioned in the *Lettres* at this time as a work in progress.[17] It is included in Mlle Desjardins' list of 1671. There are 83 numbered pages of large print, and several pages of an unpaginated dedicatory letter.

We have mentioned the unfavorable reception accorded to Mlle Desjardins by the ladies of the Pays-Bas, the rumors which were circulated about her, and the suspicions aroused by her literary activities.[18] *Anaxandre* was presented as a kind of homage designed to reassure the doubting Belgian public.[19] Several details in the introductory letter to *Anaxandre* are worth brief attention. First, the author is obviously conscious now of having her own literary style and technique; she speaks frankly of "une Histoire de ma façon." The reader is told, furthermore, that "ce n'est pas . . . la suite des Avantures d'Alcidamie que je vous présente," a statement which may mean that Mlle Desjardins still contemplated at this date (1667) completing her earlier work. Her description of the adventures of Anaxandre as "plus galantes qu'Héroïques" shows plainly that she recognized the new *genre* of the "galant" as contrasted with the "Héroïque," which she dismisses rather summarily

[14] *Anaxandre, nouvelle.* Par Mademoiselle Des-Iardins, Paris, Iean Ribov. The *achevé* is dated June 20, 1667. A copy of this rare work is in the Library of Congress. This is the edition used here.

[15] Cf. Dallas, *op. cit.*, p. 258.

[16] *Lettre I, XII*, etc. See Ch. II, above. Mlle Desjardins was in Brussels during April, 1667.

[17] Robinet, *Lettre du 26 juin 1667.* He refers to the Ribou edition. Cf. also Magne, *op. cit.*, p. 337 and note; Mlle Desjardins' *Recueil de lettres*, p. 121. *Agis* is mentioned in a letter dated June 12; *Anaxandre* was probably already in the press. Cf. also the index to Baron Rothschild's *Continuateurs de Loret*, where it is described as a "pièce."

[18] Cf. the citations from the dedication of *Anaxandre* in Ch. II, above.

[19] *Anaxandre*, unpag. ded. letter. The name Anaxandre had been used by Boisrobert in 1629 (*Histoire indienne d'Anaxandre et d'Orazie*).

as little else than "l'Art Militaire." We saw earlier (Chapter V) how the term *galant* appeared in titles and increased in popularity from 1664 on. Anaxandre is one of the earliest and most typical of the "héros galants." He speaks in the first person, and for fifteen pages addresses complimentary remarks to the ladies of Brussels, quotes a few verses, and offers, because "i'ay fait l'amour en tant de manières, et sous tant de climats diferens," to tell them whatever sort of story they would like.[20] When he finishes quoting an "Élégie" which begins,

> Estes-vous donc absent, cher objet de ma flame?[21]

—they express curiosity about the hero and heroine. Anaxandre begins their story:

Iris and Clidamis are Daphnis-and-Chloe-like lovers, who, after a happy youth together, discover the true extent of their love when, at a masked ball, sheer attraction leads them to each other. Clidamis is sent away to a garrison. Anaxandre arrives in the city and seeks to meet Iris after he reads some of her poems. The perfect *galant* is aided by an old device from the heroic novel: he saves Iris from a runaway sled during a "Course de traîneaux." He falls in love with her, and, to rid her mind of thoughts of Clidamis, tells her the latter is unfaithful to her. When Anaxandre feels he is gradually supplanting Clidamis in Iris' affections, he discovers a long letter in verse and prose written by Iris to Clidamis which shows plainly that she still loves her first lover. Anaxandre removes the letter and leaves in its place a passionate declaration of his love for Iris. Iris fails to read this and thinking it the one she had written to Clidamis, mails it to him. Clidamis returns and confronts Iris with the letter; his innocence is proved and the lovers are reunited. Anaxandre abandons "cette Ville fatale" forever.

A short afternote thanks "Monsieur le Comte de M. . . ." [Marcin] and "le Comte de G. . . ." [Gourville] for their kindness to the authoress.[22]

Anaxandre, though hardly a story of psychological analysis, nevertheless approaches more closely than *Lisandre* the method and outlook of Mlle Desjardins' best work, the *Désordres de l'amour.* There is less of the *badinage* and triviality of *Lisandre;* though the main character, Anaxandre, is a superficial trifler, the minor characters are moved by real passion. The story is not unlike the last one of the *Désordres,* with Anaxandre as a Bellegarde who does not win the lady, but loses her to a luckier Givry, or Clidamis. The pessimism of some of Mlle Desjardins'

---

[20] *Anaxandre,* pp. 1 ff.

[21] *Ibid.,* p. 11, "Élégie en forme de songe." The first *Recueil,* 1662, contained several elegies, very similar in tone, with the same hero, Clidamis.

[22] For Mlle Desjardins' relations with the Marcins and Gourville, cf. Ch. I, above, and the *Recueil de lettres, passim.*

later stories has not yet shown itself, but her acceptance of Anaxandre's brazen account of his perfidious actions indicates that she expects little from men, at least from the worldly, cynical variety she calls "des hommes de la Cour."

Anaxandre contains a number of verses, most of which appeared again in the *Recueil* of 1669. They are among the author's best, coming as they do in the middle of her most fertile period of poetry writing (1660-1670). Most are of the amorous-didactic type so popular at the time:

> Soyez tous avertis que l'Amour vous ordonne . . . (p. 10).
> La tendresse peut seule aspirer à l'honneur . . . (p. 10).
> Ne murmurez iamais de vous trouver soumis . . . (p. 30).

Some are laments, like the "Estes-vous donc absent" quoted earlier; several are quite pastoral in tone, an unusual effect in Mlle Desjardins' verse:

> Du pied d'un Oranger, au bord d'une Fontaine . . . (p. 39).
> Dans un charmant Climat qu'un eternel Printemps . . . (p. 39).[23]

Anaxandre marks an advance in the technique of Mlle Desjardins, and foreshadows her best work. Though it shows that the authoress was conscious of a personal manner, it cannot be regarded as an exact indication of the direction in which she was moving, for before we reach the historical and psychological novels we find such throwbacks as *Cléonice*, a sort of heroic *nouvelle*, and the long, graeco-roman novel, *Carmante*. Mlle Desjardins never, in fact, completely outgrew the heroic novel, but rather developed along with it a psychological-historical competitor.

Cléonice (1669)

Cléonice ou le roman galant, nouvelle appeared in 1669, dedicated to the Duchesse de Nemours.[24] It is a rather curious work; in it Mlle Desjardins attempts to retain most of the outward forms of the heroic novel, and yet to describe only what is reasonable and *vraisemblable*. As a would-be attack on the *roman héroïque* it is somewhat spoiled by dealing too much with heroic material and in the heroic *milieu*. The author describes her aims in the quite informal beginning of the *nouvelle*:

---

[23] This is the longest of the pastoral poems (20 stanzas, 10 pages). See Ch. II, above.

[24] Copy in the Bib. Nat. Published by Barbin. Cf. Magne, *op. cit.*, p. 414. For use of the word *galant* in titles at the time, cf. Ch. V, above, and Dallas, *op. cit.*, pp. 247 ff.

Déjà le Soleil commençoit à dorer de ses Rayons, les côteaux délicieux de la Fameuse . . . etc.

Mais pardon, ma grande Princesse, je le prens sur le ton d'un Roman dans les formes, et c'est une nouvelle Galante que j'ai résolu d'ecrire. . . .

Vous ne verrez point de Trones renversez, ni de Nations détruites: vous verrez seulement des résolutions surmontées, et des mérites triomphans; et bien que je considere la bravoure, comme une qualité nécessaire à un honneste homme: je vous déclare, que si mon Héros est attaqué par vingt Cavaliers, et qu'il ne soit défendu que par trois ou quatre, il sera contraint de leur ceder, comme s'il n'étoit point le Héros de ma Nouvelle. Accomodez, s'il vous plait, vos idées au vraisemblable, puisque c'est un ouvrage de ma main qui doit les remplir, et souffrez que je m'éloigne de la Fable et du Prodige, puisque c'est une avanture de nos derniers siecles dont j'ai à vous faire le récit. Je nommerai mon Héroïne Cléonice, ou de quel autre nom de Roman il vous plaira. . . . Vous sçavez que les Noms Allégoriques, ont un son plus agréable pour l'oreille que les noms connus; il faut exciter la curiosité du Lecteur, pour divertir son imagination. Et le mystere est si fort de l'essence d'une avanture amoureuse, qu'on ne diroit pas je vous aime, sur le bon ton, si le Tircis, ou la Climene, n'assaisonnoient une conversation d'amour. C'est donc sous le nom de Cléonice que [notre héroïne] va se présenter à votre Altesse. Je me passerois bien de faire son portrait, si cette nouvelle n'étoit vûe que de vous; mais comme l'impression est un destin inévitable pour tout ce qui part de ma plume, je crois qu'il est bon d'apprendre à tout Lecteur mal informé, que Cléonice étoit d'une taille. . . .[25]

Mlle Desjardins' beginning recalls the first sentence of Scarron's *Roman comique*, which also ridicules the pretentious device of starting a novel with a rhetorical description of the sunset:

Le soleil avait achevé plus de la moitié de sa course, et son char, ayant attrapé le penchant du monde . . . etc. Pour parler plus humainement et plus intelligiblement, il était entre cinq et six. . . .

She continues in a fashion similar to that of the preface of *Anaxandre*, warning the reader that he is not to expect an ordinary heroic novel, and promising realism, psychological analysis, and a certain optimistic rewarding of virtue. She lives up to these promises only to a limited extent, for on the whole her theories are more ambitious than her practice, and the story falls into the pitfalls it condemns.

The author's defense of "les Noms Allégoriques" is a flat contradiction of her opinions as expressed in another work of the same year, the *Journal amoureux*. In the latter novel she makes a pretense of using real names for the same reasons advanced above in favor of fictitious ones:

[25] *Œuvres*, I, 461-463.

L'on n'a inséré des noms connus, que pour flatter plus agreablement vostre imagination . . . et l'Auteur n'ayant que vostre divertissement pour objet, etc.[26]

In *Cléonice* Mlle Desjardins pretends to hide a real story beneath fictitious names to give it more "mystere" and to provoke the reader's curiosity; in the *Journal amoureux* she clothes an invented story in real names to obtain the reader's sympathy and interest. Which technique did she really favor? The answer is given by her procedure during the next few years, when she turns to real events, narrated without changing the characters' names.

A few remarks at the end of the story anticipate the theories expressed in the *Désordres de l'amour* concerning the importance of love intrigues in the political affairs of nations:

> Si jamais la verité de cette nouvelle est developée, et que quelque sçavant dans l'Histoire de nos derniers siecles s'avise de reconnoître un Général fameux, sous le nom de Célidor, il trouvera que cette avanture a été le nœud d'une alliance éternelle, entre les deux couronnes qui étoient en guerre, et que du commun consentement des deux Rois, le pays de Cléonice a été érigé en Souveraineté neutre, qui sert encore de monument à l'hospitalite de cette belle Fille, et à la gloire des deux Étrangers.[27]

This is the same kind of argument as that used by Mlle Desjardins some five years later to prove that the Religious Wars had their origin in the affairs of Mme de Sauve, etc.[28]

Mlle Desjardins promises to take up the further adventures of two minor characters, Arianire and Florise, in another story:

> Je me reserve à m'informer de ce que sont devenues ces belles Parentes de Cléonice, pour la premiere nouvelle que je prendrai la liberté de vous presenter.[29]

This promise was not fulfilled, nor were there, indeed, any further dedications to the Duchesse de Nemours.[30]

Here is a summary of *Cléonice:*

> Cléonice is the reigning princess of a land constantly attacked by an opposing monarch, Sicamber. Her father and brothers have already been killed by Sicamber.

---

[26] *Journal amoureux*, Au Lecteur. See Ch. V, above.

[27] *Œuvres*, I, 548-549. Mlle Desjardins may be referring to the settlement made following the War of Devolution (1667-1668).

[28] See Ch. V, above.

[29] *Œuvres*, I, 550.

[30] Mlle Desjardins had dedicated *Carmante* to her in 1668. Magne, *op. cit.*, p. 370, note, uses the dedication of the *Comte de Dunois* (1671) to Mme de Nemours as an argument for Mlle Desjardins' authorship of the work, but we have contemporary evidence that it is by Vaumorière (in the *Journal des sçavans*, Dec. 17, 1703).

Her main support is General Artambare, who loves her and considers her his fiancée. Cléonice is saved from the enemy by a mysterious stranger, who turns out to be Célidor, son of Sicamber, later captured by Artambare and held as a hostage. Cléonice resists the strong attractions she feels toward Célidor until he rescues her from a burning palace.[31] She finds a box belonging to Célidor containing letters and a portrait of herself, disclosing his love for her. She learns also that Célidor gave himself up to Artambare so that Sicamber would not dare make too violent an attack on Cléonice's forces, fearing a reprisal on his son. When each knows of the other's love, they contrive to meet regularly in a garden. Artambare learns of this and comes secretly to overhear them. Enraged, he imprisons Célidor and threatens to put him to death unless Cléonice marries him, Artambare. Sicamber marches secretly to Cléonice's palace, captures her, and starts negotiations with Artambare for the release of his son. The two parties argue across a small stream. Artambare's own forces prevent him when he attempts to kill Célidor, and in a rage the general kills himself. Cléonice and Célidor are married and the two opposing countries reconciled, Cléonice's country being converted into a neutral land.

The heroic outlines of this plot are evident; it reads like an episode out of *Faramond* or *Cléopâtre*. Yet Mlle Desjardins succeeds in injecting into it a certain amount of her specialty, the *galant*. Most of the conversation and many of the minor incidents are in this "new style." Here are a few examples—first, Cléonice's first sight of Célidor and its effect on her:

> Elle ouvroit déjà la bouche, pour ordonner qu'on perçât Célidor de mille coups en sa présence, lorsque les graces de sa Personne l'ayant forcée malgré elle d'arrester les yeux sur son visage plus long-tems qu'elle ne l'avoit résolu; elle pâlit, elle rougit, la voix lui mourut dans la bouche; et chancelant sur la selle comme si elle eût été surprise d'une maladie inopinée, elle n'eut pas la force de prononcer une seule parole.[32]

After Célidor has saved her life, the heroine debates with herself thus:

> Que ferai-je pour accorder deux choses si opposées? Comment la reconnoissance et la haine peuvent-elles habiter ensemble dans un même cœur, pour la même personne?[33]

The broad outlines of the plot seem hardly to concern Mlle Desjardins; her whole attention is centered on the progress of the main love affair, and on the little *galant* episodes—conversations, riddles, games, etc.— which make Cléonice's court resemble that of *Alcidamie*. Célidor spends his time while a captive of Artambare, not in prison, but walking about

---

[31] There is a similar incident in the *Mémoires de Henriette-Sylvie de Molière* (see Ch. VII, below). Rescues were a much overworked device.

[32] *Œuvres*, I, 471-472.

[33] *Ibid.*, p. 476.

the garden composing love verses, writing *billets,* and solving riddles. The incident of the *Rebus* is typical; it shows the preoccupation with games, the sort of philosophic-moral discussions over them, and the general pattern of behavior of the characters in *Cléonice* during the lulls between heroic savings of lives, battles, etc. Célidor, concealed on the terrace, overhears this conversation between Cléonice and her friend Eurillas:

> Non, je ne me picque point de pénétration, j'ai peut-être assez de bon sens, pour décider judicieusement des choses apparentes, mais je n'ai point assez de subtilité pour dévelloper les obscures, et quelque cours que la mode ait donné au *Rebus,* je vous répete encore qu'il n'est ni de mon goût, ni de mon génie. Mais, Madame, interrompit Eurillas, le *Rebus* ne peut être mis au nombre de ces obscuritez, que vous vous deffendez de pénétrer, j'avoue qu'il renferme un sens caché qui tient de l'énigme, et de l'allégorie; mais comme il a une apparence réelle, il ne doit pas être confondu avec ces énigmes ordinaires, qui ne consistent que dans le sens et dans les paroles. Je tombe d'accord de ce que vous dites, reprit Cléonice; mais bien qu'il soit vrai que le *Rebus* a une obscurité moins embarassante, que celle de l'énigme ou du mot retourné, je suis si ennemie de la dissimulation en général que je l'évite dans chaque chose en particulier. . . .

We are at last presented with the *Rebus* in question:

> Par example, poursuivit-il, en tirant des tablettes de sa poche, et en les présantant à Cléonice; Voilà un Cœur, un Œil, et le mot de Pas écrit entre les deux.

Cléonice admits she cannot solve it, and continues her arguments against all such obscurities. She asks:

> À quoi sert-il de se rendre obscur, pour les gens dont on veut bien être entendu? Sommes-nous parmi les premiers Egyptiens, pour parler des Hieroglifes?

While they talk thus, Célidor has solved the riddle and makes a song about it:

> Pendant que ces discours se tenoient sur la terrasse, leur Auditeur secret ne s'endormit pas sous son portique. Il avoit entendu le sens du *Rebus,* sitôt qu'il l'avoit ouï proposer. . . . Il fit des vers impromptu . . . et s'approchant d'un écho qui étoit au coin de cette terrasse . . . il chanta les paroles qui suivent.

CHANSON

Si comme nous, vous pouviez voir, Mesdames,
Vos yeux d'où naissent tant de Flâmes,
Ce *Rebus* si caché ne le paroîtroit pas.
Hélas! il grave dans nos âmes,
Que quand on a vû vos appas,
De l'Œil, au Cœur, l'amour ne fait qu'un pas.[34]

[34] *Ibid.,* pp. 481-485. None of the characters seems to experience a feeling of anticlimax at the precious solution.

Cléonice of course recognizes Célidor's voice, and the *inclination* which she feels towards him is strengthened. Later the inevitable "Boëte" is found, containing a portrait of Cléonice and the other evidence of Célidor's love for her. The heroine is herself a poet, and while like Chimène she struggles against the tenderness she feels for her sworn enemy, she composes a passionate "Élégie." It is interesting because of its would-be strong emotional content. Mlle Desjardins could turn ordinary *vers*, especially of the didactic, maxim-like variety; but real expression of intense feeling was beyond her:

ÉLÉGIE

Lâche et foible courroux, infidelle vengeance,
Sur qui mon cœur trahi, prenoit tant d'assurance,
Vous, à qui je commis ma gloire et mon repos,
Hélas! qu'avez-vous fait, de ces sacrés dépôts?
Où sont ces mouvements, d'un orgueil invincible . . . etc.

Mais, ô cruel Amour? Quels sont tes privileges,
N'est-il rien de sacré pour les feux sacrileges:
La haine, la raison, le sexe, et le devoir,
Ne peuvent-ils sauver un cœur de ton pouvoir . . . etc.

O Dieu! comment sortir d'une captivité,
Dont ma propre raison fait la félicité?
Qui me délivrera de ce péril extrême,
Si tout ce que je suis combat contre moi-même?
Cédons, fierté, cédons à ce puissant effort,
La tendresse a son heure, aussi bien que la mort.[35]

Worthy of comment is the manner in which Mlle Desjardins turns the spotlight of interest from one of her principal characters to the other. After subjecting the reader to a rather lengthy examination of Cléonice's feelings, the author turns to Célidor and gives us what is almost a *monologue intérieur:*

Pendant que la belle Cléonice abandonnoit son âme à des mouvemens si passionez, l'amoureux Célidor étoit dans une inquiétude, qui ne devoit rien à la sienne. . . .

Il apprit bientôt et que sa boëte étoit trouvée, et qu'elle étoit entre les main de Cléonice. Tout ce que la crainte et l'esperance peuvent faire naître de plus violent dans un cœur passionné, Célidor le sentit à cette nouvelle. Il ne pouvoit douter que cette Peinture n'apprit le secret de son âme. . . . Nous portons rarement le Portrait d'une personne qui nous est indifférente. De sorte que l'amour ayant cela de propre, qu'il aime à se découvrir, il y avoit des moments où il ne pouvoit s'empêcher de sentir quelque plaisir de cette avanture. Mais quand il se représentoit la haine que

[35] *Ibid.,* pp. 502-506. The lines echo feebly the Cornelian and Racinian drama.

Cléonice avoit toujours fait éclater contre lui . . . il lui sembloit bien qu'on ne le traitoit pas trop sévérement pour un homme dont on connoissoit l'amour. . . . Est-ce mépris, disoit-il en lui-même? est-ce complaisance pour ton amour? La tranquillité apparente de Cléonice, lui faisoit croire le premier; et certaines rougeurs imprévûes . . . lui faisoit espérer l'autre . . . etc.[36]

Such passages as this show us the technique of the novel as we know it today growing beneath our eyes: these minute contributions, insignificant in themselves, each improving ever so slightly on previous techniques and devices, are assimilated into the fictional frame of mind of any period, and form a part of the tradition on which later and greater artists unconsciously build. The apparently simple procedure of transferring the reader's attention from one character's mind to another was arrived at only through a slow evolutionary process; the thoughts of characters other than the principal one were, at this period, usually presented only through conversations or *récits*. Even to go inside the mind of the hero or heroine alone was a novelty; to examine the thought processes of both in a single story was technically a very bold stroke.

Here and there in the story are further points of interest. Célidor's love affects not only his temper, but his cleanliness and appearance:

L'inquiétude qui naît des commencemens de l'amour . . . inspire le désir de plaire; elle donne du génie pour des divertissements, elle augmente la propreté. . . . On ne peut rien imaginer de plus magnifique et de mieux entendu que l'étoit sa parure. Un soir qu'il avoit un habit d'une nouvelle mode, qui l'avoit exposé tout le jour aux louanges de la compagnie. . . .[37]

Célidor provokes in Cléonice, however, only an unpleasant reaction; she becomes "aigre et contredisante" and begins to denounce finery and pretentious dress until she sounds like a female Misanthrope railing at the insincerities of the world:

Hé! grand Dieu, n'y a-t-il pas assez de sujets de louanges dans les qualitez de l'âme des gens qu'on veut louer, sans qu'il soit besoin d'en chercher dans les choses qui leur sont étrangeres? C'est la manie du siecle, Madame, interrompit Eurillas, nous ne devons plus rien à votre sexe là-dessus, et cette maxime est devenue si à la mode, qu'on croiroit faire injure à une personne, si on lui voyoit une parure nouvelle, sans en faire le panégirique. En rendant ce défaut général, poursuivit Cléonice, vous ne nous ôtez rien de son extravagance. Car il est certain que si vous avez quelque part à cette foiblesse, vous la tenez de passer la moitié de sa vie à louer des choses qui doivent être regardées comme indifférentes. . . .

---

[36] *Ibid.*, pp. 506 ff.
[37] *Ibid.*, p. 509.

Célidor defends fine dress in women, but places it beneath other consider-
ations in his evaluation of men:

> L'ajustement est si fort du partage d'une Dame, que c'est la louer, par une
> qualité essentielle, que de la louer de s'habiller galament. Mais pour nous autres,
> il nous faut tant de qualitez éminentes pour plaire, que celle de la propreté ne devroit
> y entrer que par un effet du tempérament. Il est plus beau d'être né propre, que
> d'être né sale, et mal-séant. Mais il est à mon gré bien indigne d'un honnête homme,
> de faire son capital de sa Garniture et de ses Canons, et d'employer plus de tems à
> assortir ses rubans, qu'à polir son language, ou à s'efforcer de régler ses mœurs.[38]

The discussion continues—another of those little courtly essays, disguised
as conversations, which Mlle Desjardins found so necessary to her *galant*
style.

Some of the sessions of Cléonice's court are held in semi-pastoral surroundings. She sits beneath a "Dome" and her followers gather about her.
There are more games; one of these is the guessing of various "Emblêmes"
which resemble our modern jig-saw puzzles more than anything else.
Quite a baroque metaphor is invented from one of these:

> Célidor lui apportoit tout le tems des Emblêmes, à deviner. . . . Le dernier qui
> avoit été imaginé, étoit un de ces Tableaux qui représentoient des parties informes
> et séparées; lesquelles étant rassemblées par le verre optique, forment un tout
> accompli de plusieurs parties imparfaites. Le sens général de cet Emblême, étoit
> qu'il n'y a rien de si imperceptible à nos sens, que la science, ou l'art, ne puisse
> rendre sensible. Mais le sens mystique de notre Amant, étoit que les soins, les
> regards, et les discours, qui sont considérés par les gens indifférens, comme les
> parties inutiles de l'amour et sans liaison, tracent le Portrait d'un feu très-ardent,
> quand ils sont regardés par les yeux d'une Maîtresse. . . .[39]

Mlle Desjardins has lost none of her flair, so noticeable in *Alcidamie*,
for describing feminine attire. Perhaps no single trait in *Cléonice* is
more amusingly typical of the *galant* style than the sartorial portrait
painted of the heroine just after her capture by Sicamber. What does the
author tell us of the anguish, the sense of danger, the hope that her
capture will free Célidor? Hardly a word. Instead, we read:

> Notre nouvelle captive avoit ce jour-là un manteau d'étoffe blanche, plicé sur les

---

[38] *Ibid.*, pp. 509-511. Magne writes, commenting on Mlle Desjardins' remark that
the elder Zuylichem was "extrêmement propre, et chez luy, et sur sa personne," that
"Cette expression ne doit pas étonner. La propreté existe à l'état rudimentaire au
XVIIe siècle. C'est pourquoi maints auteurs, et Tallemant en particulier, enregistrent
presque toujours dans un portrait cette particularité de l'individu" (*op. cit.*, p. 317,
n. 3).

[39] *Œuvres*, I, 520. "Lesquelles étant rassemblées par le verre optique" probably
means that a magnifying glass was used to aid in putting together the pieces, "par"
having the force of "à l'aide de."

épaules, et doublé d'un crespon gris-de-lin. . . . Un tissu mêlé d'argent et de gris-de-lin
la ceignoit au-dessus les hanches, et marquoit la forme admirable de sa taille . . .
etc.[40]

Cléonice marks a step forward in Mlle Desjardins' efforts to introduce
into the heroic tale that increasingly popular concept in fiction, the
vraisemblable. Much had already been said of the *vraisemblable*, particularly in dramatic criticism (cf. d'Aubignac, etc.) ; and much ground
remained to be covered. Mlle Desjardins was to traverse a good part of
it herself. The progress made in *Cléonice* and the other *nouvelles* was
small, but the direction taken establishes Mlle Desjardins definitely in
the *avant-garde* of fictional writing in her time.

Le Portefeuille (1675?)

Chatenet mentions *Le Portefeuille* in his list of Mlle Desjardins' works,
but does not discuss it at all.[41] Magne accords to it three sentences, all
inaccurate and misleading; he assigns to it the approximate date of 1668,
implies that it is "un recueil de correspondance" like that of the *Lettres*
(1668), and says further: "Il fourmille de préceptes tendres. Il est d'un
bout à l'autre un guide des 'honnestes amants.' "[42]

Le Portefeuille is in reality a *nouvelle* told through a series of letters,
all supposedly written by the Marquis de Naumanoir to his friend, a
provincial count (cf. the pretext of Pascal's *Lettres provinciales*). It is
not a lovers' guide, nor is it an anthology of "préceptes tendres." It is
a realistic story of amorous intrigues among some six or seven characters
drawn from contemporary Parisian society. The date of the first edition
is not known, but a reference to the death of Chapelain fixes the earliest
possible date as March, 1674.[43] A phrase referring to the restaurateur
Frédoc, "qui revient à la mode depuis que l'Opéra se joue au Palais
Royal,"[44] suggests that some time had elapsed between the first presentation of opera at this theatre and the time of the writing of the story,
enough time for the restaurant to become popular. Though the Palais-
Royal was given to Lully in the spring of 1673, the first opera presented

[40] *Ibid.*, pp. 535-536.
[41] *Op. cit.*, p. 100.
[42] *Op. cit.*, p. 351.
[43] On p. 63 of *Le Portefeuille* (*Œuvres*, II) we read: "Je vous mande toutes les
nouvelles. . . . Mlle Marin épousa hier votre aimable parent Monsieur d'Aupede . . .
le pauvre Chapelain est mort, et * * * n'a pas voulu le laisser partir sans compagnie."
[44] *Ibid.*, p. 51.

was *Alceste* in January, 1674.[45] This fact, together with the reference to the death of Chapelain (February 22, 1674), would put the date of composition of *Le Portefeuille* late in 1674, if not in 1675. The story occupies the first 82 pages of the second volume of the edition of the *Œuvres* of 1741.

The short introductory letter resembles that of *Lisandre*, reading in part:

À MADAME *****

J'étois il y a quelques jours au Jardin des Simples, où j'admirois avec une de mes Amies, l'indulgence que l'Hyver a pour nous cette année. . . . Nous entrâmes dans le petit bois, où il y a des sieges, pour nous reposer; et j'y choisissois ma place de l'œil, lorsque j'apperçûs un Portefeuille de velours noir. . . . Je l'ouvris, et j'y trouvois des Lettres si agréables, que je croirois manquer à ce que je vous dois, si je manquois à vous en faire part. . . . Je suis persuadée que les noms en sont supposez, j'ai fait ce qu'il m'a été possible pour deviner les véritables. Mais je n'ai rien imaginé qui m'ait semblé juste. Ce qu'il y a de vrai, c'est que la maniere dont cela est écrit est fort à la mode, et que le caractere des gens qui font les avantures, est celui des gens du grand monde. . . . Votre très-humble et très-obéissante servante,

DESJARDINS DE VILLE-DIEU[46]

We recognize the familiar insistence that the story is a true one, despite the names (as in *Lisandre*), the emphasis on the contemporaneousness of the manner in which the story is written (cf. *Anaxandre*), and on the present-day character of the personages. A similar insistence on contemporary subject matter is found in a number of compositions written in this decade.[47] Although Mlle Desjardins wrote only one complete novel using the contemporary scene (the *Mémoires*, 1672), three of her four *nouvelles* employ it. Of these, *Le Portefeuille* is the most contemporary and "realistic."

There had been at least two compositions in the form of letters published in the years preceding *Le Portefeuille*, the abbé d'Aubignac's *Roman des lettres* (1667),[48] and the *Lettres d'une religieuse portugaise* (1669), one of the first psychological novels.[49] Mlle Desjardins had written and published many *Lettres* herself. They were a commonplace

---

[45] Cf. Étienne Gros, *Quinault*, Paris, 1926, pp. 107-108.

[46] *Œuvres*, II, 1-2.

[47] Cf. the titles *Lupanie, hist. amoureuse de ce temps; La Mère rivale, hist. du temps; Le double cocu, hist. du temps;* etc. (1668-1678).

[48] "Par M.L.D.S.A.D.M." Paris, Loyson, 1667.

[49] Paris, Barbin, *achevé*, Jan. 4, 1669. Matisse is reported at present (1946) working on illustrations for a new edition.

in fiction since the *Astrée*. The idea of a *nouvelle* told by a series of letters was therefore hardly an originality, though it was still something of a novelty.

The story of *Le Portefeuille* is typically *mondain* and *galant*:

Lettre I. The Marquis de Naumanoir relates in his first letter to his "cher Comte" that he has just discovered at the home of his friend Mme de Versomont a letter from his mistress Mme de Montferrier hinting that she has begun or is about to begin a liaison with one of his friends, the Chevalier de Virlay. He charges Virlay with this and the Chevalier admits it, asking Naumanoir why he expects Mme de Montferrier to remain faithful to him forever. Naumanoir reflects on the perfidy of his mistress, decides to give her up, and sends her a farewell sonnet.

Lettre II. Naumanoir begins to console himself for his mistress' loss with Mme de Vareville, Virlay's former mistress. Mme de Montferrier, through coquetry and rage at losing a lover, seeks to get Naumanoir back. Naumanoir spurns her advances, and leaves her abruptly.

Lettre III. Mme de Vareville, hearing of Mme de Montferrier's attempt to regain the affections of Naumanoir, begins to encourage him. Naumanoir tells Virlay of his interview with Mme de Montferrier; Virlay complains to her; she tells him she has merely been making sport of Naumanoir. Naumanoir sends a letter meant for Mme de Montferrier to Mme de Vareville and vice versa. Mme de Vareville is furious with him, and Mme de Montferrier boasts of her reconquest of him.

Lettre IV. Naumanoir in order to clear things up is forced to have it out with Virlay. Much tension is created between Mme de Montferrier and Virlay, but Naumanoir is reconciled with Mme de Vareville.

Lettre V. Virlay finds a party being given by Naumanoir for Mme de Vareville and insists on joining it. He pays more attention than necessary to his former mistress, Mme de Vareville. When Naumanoir scolds him, he protests it was only through politeness.

Lettre VI. Naumanoir learns that Mme de Vareville, behind his back, has herself sought a reconciliation with Virlay. They have been meeting secretly for some time, as Naumanoir discovers when he finds them together.

Lettre VII. Naumanoir accuses Mme de Vareville of the basest perfidy; she has always set herself up as above the tricks and deceptions of coquettes like Mme de Montferrier; she pleads guilty and tells Naumanoir that she has always loved Virlay, and has encouraged him, Naumanoir, only to make Virlay jealous and if possible to win him back.

Lettre VIII. Naumanoir, like "Joconde dans Bocace"[50] returns to his old mistress, Mme de Montferrier, who claims always to have loved him. He discovers that during

---

[50] Mlle Desjardins doubtless refers to the story of Giocondo in Ariosto's *Orlando furioso*, Canto XXVIII. La Fontaine's adaptation of "Joconde ou l'infidélité des femmes" appeared in his *Nouvelles en vers tirées de Boccace et de l'Arioste*, Paris, Barbin, 1665, the title of which was probably responsible for Mlle Desjardins' error. More about the fortune of the story in France is found in the Gds. Éc. edition of La Fontaine, IV, 17 ff. "Joconde" has been used to mean "galant séducteur" (*Grand Larousse*).

their reconciliation both Virlay and Mme de Vareville have shamefully deceived him, using him without his knowledge as go-between, letter carrier, etc.

Lettre IX. Naumanoir has a further complaint against Virlay. Growing dissatisfied with Mme de Montferrier's false ways, Naumanoir has found a little Breton girl who suits his taste. To his astonishment he discovers that she, too, has been having an affair with Virlay. The latter has neglected her and the girl offers to aid Naumanoir in a league against him. She tells him of four or five other affairs Virlay is conducting at the same time and they plan to enlist all the outraged women whom he has abandoned or neglected in their league against him. But Virlay returns to the Bretonne and she renounces the league and Naumanoir.

Lettre X. Naumanoir has retired to the provinces, giving up mistresses, rivals, and love. He encloses a little *Historiette* about gallantry in the provinces, the theme of which is *sauver les apparences:*

La Galanterie sans éclat. A certain Mme d'Albimont has such a great reputation for modesty and circumspection, first as wife, then as widow, that the Marquis d'Altevois resolves to investigate whether she does not conceal some love affair or other beneath her fine appearances. By distributing letters supposed to have been written to her by an unknown admirer, Altevois finally learns from one of his closest friends that he, his friend Coursivaux, has for many years been Mme d'Albimont's lover. Their estates join and they used to meet at night. Altevois verifies the rumor by listening to a conversation between them from a hiding place on a terrace. Coursivaux is questioning her about the letters and she is denying knowledge of them. When Altevois goes to tell his discovery to his mistress, Mlle de Saint-Ormin, he finds that she too has been conducting researches into the life of Mme d'Albimont, and has uncovered a second *affaire*, "qui n'étoit pas moins effective que celle de Coursivaux."

A short *Apostille* added by Naumanoir praises the cleverness of Mme d'Albimont, expresses a wish for a mistress like her, and bids farewell to his friend.

The realism of *Le Portefeuille* is one of *mœurs* and psychology rather than of description or literary technique. The Parisian *décor* is taken for granted; the name of the Palais-Royal or of the Jardin des Simples is deemed sufficient to evoke a familiar picture. The characters dine "chez Deschams" at Saint-Cloud, or "chez Frédoc," both well-known establishments of the day. Even the customary descriptions of the characters' appearance and the heroine's dress are omitted. Motives and actions are the focus of interest. What Mlle Desjardins writes is the story of a typical sequence of love intrigues among the "gens du grand monde." We see them in their shallowness, double-dealings, unsubstantial affections, and little agonies. It is much the same world as that we find in the memoirs of Tallemant des Réaux, or in the letters of Bussy-Rabutin. The only difference, aside from the lack of picturesque detail—Tallemant's specialty—is that Mlle Desjardins' realism respects the literary tradition of the day enough to gloss lightly over the sexual *mœurs* of her characters. On the surface of it, Naumanoir and Virlay spend their secret rendezvous with their mistresses in witty conversations or in exchanging tender looks. Probably no reader was deceived by this pretense; but the literary morality of the day demanded a rather *invraisemblable* absence of sexuality. In the eighteenth century, after the Régence and such writers as Crébillon the younger, polite literature claimed its long unpaid due of pornography, and a love affair became what everyone knew a love affair was. For all Mlle Desjardins' ready reference to Boccaccio, she was probably shocked at his frankness, and would certainly never have dared to imitate it.[51]

That an air of monotony should hang over the characters of *Le Portefeuille* is not surprising. They are all of the same type, and if one seems better than another, it is only a temporary illusion to be shattered by the discovery that he or she has only been covering up some all-too-familiar deception. They are all prepared to give such rational explanations of their conduct, their motives are so plain—and so repetitious—that the reader soon wearies of their mechanical regularity. The plot resembles the game of musical chairs, with everyone trying to change places at once. Here are a few stages of the procedure. When Naumanoir first talks to Mme de Vareville about the perfidy of his mistress Mme de Montferrier, he writes:

Je lui disois fort tendrement ce que j'en pensois, et la priois de souffrir que j'aidasse à sa vengeance et à la mienne. Elle a de l'esprit, et elle entendoit fort bien ce que je voulois dire. Il faut sçavoir, Monsieur le Comte, comme elle reçut cela; elle ne prit point un de ces airs de fausse pruderie, si suspect aux gens de bon sens; elle prit encore moins celui d'une Coquette qui cherche à remplir une place vacante: elle me dit fort obligeamment que si j'avois trouvé son cœur en état de donner à quelqu'un, elle m'auroit préféré à tout le reste du monde . . . et qu'elle me prioit de tourner sur une tendre et solide amitié tout ce que je sentirois pour elle. . . .[52]

The accidental meeting of Mme de Vareville and her ex-lover Virlay, which marks the beginning of their reconciliation, has a certain air of naturalness and pleasing freshness:

Ah! ah, Madame, lui dit-il, je vous y prends donc en régal à S. Cloud avec notre ami Naumanoir. . . . Comment vous portez-vous? . . . que faites-vous? que ne faites-vous pas? en quel état sont vos affaires et vos plaisirs? Tout cela répond-t-il à

[51] Even in her medieval stories (cf. *Les Annales galantes*) she preserves a rather high standard of surface morality, and women accord their lovers only those favors which the reader may care to imagine. See Ch. V, above.

[52] *Œuvres*, II, 12-13.

l'embonpoint et à la fraîcheur de votre visage? Tout répond au moins à la tranquilité de mon âme, poursuivit Madame de Vareville, je désire si peu de chose, que sans en posséder beaucoup, on peut dire que je suis toujours contente. Mais vous, Monsieur le Chevalier. . . .[53]

To complete the episode, I quote Naumanoir's speech to Mme de Vareville when her secret return to Virlay becomes known to him. The woman, once so "douce et modérée," is now worse than a coquette, for she is guilty of hypocrisy and deception:

Quoi? Madame, lui disois-je, vous êtes dissimulée et trompeuse, comme toutes les autres femmes? cette franchise qui semble peinte sur votre visage, et dont j'ai été si douloureusement séduit, n'est qu'un appas pour mieux surprendre les gens que vous trahissez; Madame de Montferrier m'a trahi je l'avoue, mais du moins, elle fait profession ouverte de coquetterie . . . etc.[54]

All the other scenes in the story are variations on the theme: false assurances of friendship, false protestations of love and jealousy and the like. What saves the characters from being completely uninteresting in their superficiality is the undeniable fact that they have, in their way, a sort of style. If anything redeems their immorality—which in a sense is profound—it is that they are capable of friendship and forgiveness. Though Naumanoir would willingly ruin Virlay with one or all of his mistresses, given the chance, he is still his friend, and takes a sort of vicarious pride in Virlay's attractiveness and his amorous prowess. In his words, "Ce chien de garçon a je croi quelque Talisman pour se faire aimer de toutes les femmes." Also, they take their disappointments and deceptions in their stride, and never whine. They are puppets playing a brisk and lively comedy, with no time for tears and heavy responsibilities. It is on the stuff of such characters that the brilliant comedy of the English Restoration is built. What Mlle Desjardins' characters lack is wit and detachment from self, and a little more of the restrained sentimentality we glimpse occasionally in such lines as:

Mais mon pauvre Chevalier, l'amour en avoit autrement ordonné, et je sens bien que le Marquis de Naumonoir, est et sera toujours le foible de mon âme. . . .[55]

Paradoxically, we may say that Naumanoir, Virlay, Mme de Vareville, and Mme de Montferrier are too greatly individualized to appear signifi-

---

[53] *Ibid.*, pp. 40-41. The line "En quel état sont vos affaires et vos plaisirs?" is no doubt the amorous equivalent of the "Comment vont les rentes?" with which the characters greet each other in Dumas' *Question d'argent.*

[54] *Ibid.*, p. 56.

[55] *Ibid.*, p. 35.

cant to the general reader and too much generalized, too typical, to have real individuality. If Mlle Desjardins had made them more conscious of their humanity (in their analyses of each other and of themselves), or had made the reader more conscious of their particularity (through differentiations in their psychologies and personalities), her work might have been saved from obscurity. But her personages are neither one thing nor the other; wherever struck, they ring false or sound hollow. Once again, Mlle Desjardins is seen in the rôle of precursor, this time of the *galant* novel of the eighteenth century. Her theory was sound: to present in unadorned terms a picture of upper-class society as reflected in its love intrigues. But her achievement is slight. We miss even her customary penetration into the processes of the mind. *Mœurs* we find more faithfully depicted elsewhere. *Le Portefeuille* is vitiated by the triviality of a superficial age.

Such are Mlle Desjardins' four *nouvelles*. They are experiments rather than finished products. *Lisandre* and *Anaxandre* marked her return to fiction after *Alcidamie* in 1661 and her three plays (1662-1665). They show plainly what changes were taking place in her literary technique and outlook. She had abandoned the neo-heroic formulae of *Alcidamie*, and had turned her attention to love as the prime mover for her fiction. The *galant*—a sort of gay pseudo-realism—becomes her *manière*, her style. *Cléonice* is a pseudo-historic *nouvelle* with a neo-heroic plot, done in the new manner, an offshoot of the period in which Mlle Desjardins was achieving more substantial effects in the real historic stories of the *Annales galantes*. *Le Portefeuille* brings the *galant* technique to bear on the contemporary scene, and presents the *mœurs* of the day without the nominal disguises of *Lisandre* and *Anaxandre*. Although a failure as a work of art, it is nevertheless of interest as a piece of realistic description of the "gens du grand monde." Had Mlle Desjardins combined the psychological insight of the *Désordres de l'amour* with the subject matter of *Le Portefeuille*, perhaps we should have had the first genuine novel based on characters and events of its own day.

CHAPTER VII

LES MÉMOIRES DE LA VIE DE HENRIETTE-SYLVIE DE MOLIÈRE
(1672) : THE PSEUDO-AUTOBIOGRAPHICAL NOVEL

The list of Mlle Desjardins' acknowledged works, "fidèle jusqu'à la fin d'avril de l'année 1671," does not contain the *Mémoires,* although the *privilège* of the work was granted "le 29 avril 1671." The work itself appeared anonymously on the 16th of May, 1672, in six parts bound together.[1] Other editions followed, in Amsterdam (1672-1674, 1709, 1733), Paris (1674, 1680, 1696), Lyons (1693), and The Hague (1725). The *Mémoires* are in the collected works of 1721 and 1741.[2] They were immediately translated into English.[3] The *Mémoires* have been attributed to Subligny, Baron, and d'Alègre.[4] They are not mentioned

[1] Derome, *op. cit.,* pp. 229-230, cites the *privilège* and *achevé.* Magne, *op. cit.,* p. 416, lists the edition of 1672 ("*Ex meis*") as "6 part. en 1 vol.," but Derome says "les tomes I à IV parurent le 16 mai 1672."

[2] I am unable to determine whether they are in the other collected editions, *rarissimes* at present, of 1702 (Barbin, Paris), 1703 (Toulouse), 1696-1713 (Lyons), etc.

[3] *The memoirs of the life, and rare adventures of Henrietta Sylvia Molière.* As they have been very lately published in French. London, printed for William Crooke, 1672-77. Vol. II has the title: *The memoirs . . . of Henrietta Sylvia Molière.* Written in French by herself. Being the II, III, IV, V, VI and last parts. London, Printed by J. C. for W. Crooke, 1677. (In Yale University Library.)

[4] Magne, *op. cit.,* p. 68, note; Paul Lacroix' notice at the beginning of his edition of the *Récit de la farce des Précieuses;* Antoine Barbier, *Dictionnaire des ouvrages anonymes;* the prefaces to the different *Recueils de la Suze;* Vertron, *op. cit.,* art. "Châte." During the period of intense research into problems concerning Molière which occurred during the publication of the *Moliériste,* Mlle Desjardins' work, apparently because of its title, was credited at least once with being a disguised account of the life of Molière and his wife Armande Béjart. Charles Livet, in an article in *Moliériste,* I (1880), 305 ff., discusses a *nouvelle* entitled *Araspe et Simandre,* published anonymously in 1672, in which frequent allusions to Molière and his troupe occur. The author of the story mentions the *Mémoires de Henriette-Sylvie,* but since he (or she) says nothing about Molière, Livet rightly concluded that Mlle Desjardins' novel had nothing to do with the playwright. A passage in Vol. II of *Araspe* attributed the *Mémoires* to "une femme de qualité et d'un esprit que peu d'autres dans le royaume peuvent égaler." Livet construes the "femme de qualité" as an argument against Mlle Desjardins' authorship of the *Mémoires.* Lacroix in an article "Sur les ouvrages attribués à Subligny," in *Moliériste,* III (1881), 273 ff., attributes them to Subligny, basing his attribution on that of Maupoint in his *Bibliothèque des théâtres,* Paris, 1773. The Chevalier de Mouhy, an eighteenth-century "méprisé" (Mornet, *RHLF,* 1910, p. 475), attributes the work to the comedian-playwright Baron. The abbé d'Allainval in his *Lettres sur Baron et Mlle Lecouvreur* attributes them to d'Alègre (Hauréau, *op. cit.,* p. 33). Hauréau writes: "L'abbé se trompe. Si ce roman n'avait pas été de Catherine, Barbin ne lui aurait pas donné place dans le recueil des Œuvres." Le Pays' letter settles the dispute.

in the list in the *Journal des sçavans* (December 17, 1703), but they continued to appear in the collected editions of Mlle Desjardins' works, and the general impression throughout the eighteenth century was that the work was hers.[5]

There exists, moreover, a letter written to Mlle Desjardins by René Le Pays on June 28, 1665, referring to a work which he calls *"Sylvie"* and which without doubt was the beginning of the *Mémoires*. Internal evidence in the letter shows that the manuscript existed as early as the winter of 1664, when Marie-Catherine was at Lyons:

> 28 juin 1665.—Vous avez esté six mois sans m'écrire, parce que durant six mois vous m'avez creu mort. . . . Depuis que je vous laissay en Provence je n'ay reçu que deux de vos lettres et vous avez deu en recevoir quatre des miennes. Je suis doublement obligé à M. de la Tournelle puisqu'il m'a ressuscité chez vous et qu'il a leu chez moy cette agréable *Sylvie* dont vous luy donnâtes une copie à Lyon; je n'ay rien veu de ma vie de pensé ny d'exprimé plus délicatement.[6]

Magne's conclusion, that "en 1664 le manuscrit était déjà terminé" and that in 1672 she merely added a few details such as the death of Lionne (1671), is not upheld by a reading of the work. According to the dates given by the *Mémoires* themselves, only the first two of six parts could have been written by 1664, as will become apparent in the analysis. Likewise Magne's conclusion that "ces *Mémoires* sont une autobiographie volontairement embrouillée," which he will cite "comme une reference indiscutable," seems an unfortunate inaccuracy in his usually trustworthy biography.[7] Chatenet follows in his footsteps and states that "les *Mémoires* retracent avec exactitude la vie de Mme de Villedieu."[8]

The following summary will show that the composition of the novel, though begun before 1665, continued well into (or was resumed in) the

---

[5] Cf. *BUR*, 1776, II (2), 129 ff. This article also attributes *Astérie* to Mlle de la Roche, *Dom Carlos* to Saint-Réal, and calls Mlle Desjardins' alleged authorship of the *Prince de Condé*, *Mlle d'Alençon*, and *Mlle de Tournon*, "fort douteux." This agrees with the conclusions of the present author. The article does, however, imply that Mlle Desjardins wrote Préchac's *Illustre Parisienne*.

[6] In Le Pays' *Nouvelles œuvres*, II, 42 ff. Cf. Magne, *op. cit.*, p. 68, note, p. 268, note, and p. 372. Le Pays' letter contains interesting references to Mlle Desjardins' animated fashion of writing letters: "Moy qui vous ay veue au milieu d'une foule, sur la table d'une cuisine, faire dix despesches de suite sans vous asseoir et sans cesser de nous entretenir, mais des despesches qui n'eussent pas cédé aux lettres de nos maistresses les Sarrazins, les Marignys et les Voitures." The playing of *Le Favory* is also mentioned: "Puisque l'on a joué vostre *Favory* à Versailles, obligez-moy de me mander quel en a esté le succes." Cf. Ch. II, above.

[7] *Op. cit.*, p. 68, note. Cf. also Ch. I, above.

[8] *Op. cit.*, p. 247.

year 1671, without sudden jumps or additions, and that most of the action fills the years between these two dates. It will also show that, though faint suggestions of Mlle Desjardins' own life may be discerned in the novel, it cannot be regarded as intentionally autobiographical: neither the characters, their motives, nor their actions have any counterpart in the real life of its author. Writing a kind of realistic, picaresque *roman d'aventures*, using the contemporary scene, and narrating it in the first person singular, Mlle Desjardins quite understandably refers to persons and places she has known and visited; but we search in vain to find any confessions of the secrets of her life. One has only to compare the account of her life given in Chapter I with the *Mémoires de la vie de Henriette-Sylvie de Molière* to reject the idea that the *Mémoires* are pure autobiography.

Though the *Mémoires* are addressed throughout to "Votre Altesse, Madame," the introductory letter is concluded "Adieu, Monsieur." It contains several remarks of interest:

> . . . à Paris où j'ai eu la folie de consentir qu'on me fît imprimer. . . . De quoi veut-il [l'imprimeur] que je lui compose une Préface, je n'ai plus rien à dire aux Lecteurs. . . . Si je n'ai pü me dispenser d'y parler de quelques personnes vivantes, je crois qu'il n'y en a pas une, qui en un besoin, ne me pardonnât volontiers la liberté que j'ai prise, et à tout événement, je serai le garant de l'ouvrage de ce côté-là. . . . Je finis, car on m'attend pour achever de déjeuner: Adieu, Monsieur, vous êtes le plus obligeant du monde.[9]

The first paragraphs refer to the "médisances qui déchirent ma réputation par tout," and state that the writer intends to answer this slander and vindicate herself despite "le siecle." "Je ne cacherai rien," she writes, "non pas même des plus folles avantures où j'aurai eu quelque part." She hints that Madame was moved "à m'honorer de ses lettres . . . dans l'espérance d'une réponse de ce caractere." Then follows an *incipit* worthy of Jean-Jacques Rousseau:

> Pour commencer, je n'ai jamais bien sçu qui j'étois; je sçai seulement que je ne suis pas une personne qui ait de communes destinées; que ma naissance, mon éducation et mes mariages ont été l'effet d'autant d'avantures extraordinaires.

This clear note of *préromantisme*, struck firmly, begins the work.

---

[9] *Œuvres*, VII, 1. The two people who most probably would have been addressed as Votre Altesse, Madame, were Henriette de France and Henriette d'Angleterre (with whom Mlle Desjardins had certain relations; see Ch. I, above), but both died before 1671, and the narrative continues to be addressed to "Madame" after that date is passed. The picture given above of the author writing a note to be used as a preface, while waiting for lunch, is similar to that sketched by Le Pays in the letter quoted above.

Partie I. Named Henriette for a reason known only to her mother, and Sylvie because she was born "à l'entrée d'un bois appellé le bois de Sylves," Henriette-Sylvie acquires the surname Molière from "ceux qui se donnerent le soin de m'élever, et qui le portoient eux-même." She traces of herself an attractive portrait: black eyes, laughing mouth, unpainted cheeks, "quasi une beauté achevée."[10] Strange circumstances surrounded her birth; in July, 1647, four men and two women took her mother to a peasant's hut near Montpellier. During the night Sylvie was born; the next day the party left, abandoning the baby to the peasant wife and giving her a small sum of money. When Sylvie reaches the age of five [1652], the Duc de Candale, while hunting, sees her, fancies her, and manages shortly thereafter to have her substituted for the dying daughter of a financier, Molière. Molière in later years discovers his wife to be the mistress of the Marquis de Birague, tells Sylvie that she is a foundling, and tries to seduce her. She shoots him twice, flees on horseback, is protected by Birague. Unwilling to remain at his château, she enters a convent; Birague becomes increasingly attentive to her. Molière dies of his wounds and Sylvie hopes to inherit part of the estate, but Mme de Molière discovers Birague's treachery and announces publicly that Sylvie is not her daughter. Sylvie finds refuge in the château of Mme d'Englesac, widowed sister of the abbess of her convent.

Here she meets Mme d'Englesac's son. They fall in love; Birague warns Mme d'Englesac, who asks Sylvie to discourage her son's advances. When Sylvie resists him, Englesac sets fire to the château, so that in saving Sylvie he may have an opportunity to speak with her alone and declare his love. Sylvie resists no longer, and secretly the two lovers enjoy their first happiness. Birague duels with Englesac; a new edict has been issued against duels and Englesac is banished to Piedmont. The Comtesse, his mother, discovers her son's relations with Sylvie and the latter flees to a convent. Birague continues his attentions. We are in Avignon, through which the Court passes en route to the Île de la Conférence in Languedoc, where the Spanish Infanta was to meet the King. Fouquet loves another nun in the same convent and together with Birague effects the escape of both women. Disguised as merchants' wives, they follow the Court as far as Toulouse. At this point Sylvie remarks that her reputation is beginning to suffer.

A lady from Brussels, the ex-mistress of the same Candale who had found Sylvie and befriended her in 1652, reads of Sylvie in the "Gazettes d'Histoire" following the outcries of the Molière family against her, and comes to Languedoc to search her out. They meet finally in Bordeaux and become intimate friends. Sylvie and her friend Mme de Seville go to Paris by carriage to witness the "entrée de leurs Majestés" into Paris [1660]. Some time later they leave for Brussels, Mme de Seville planning to adopt Sylvie.

Partie II. Among Sylvie's visitors at Brussels are the Prince d'Aremberg, the Duc d'Arschot, the Duc de Croüy, Dom Antoine de Cordoue, and "le Gouverneur lui-même."[11] A rich Spanish widower, Dom Fernando Gonzales de Menèze, pays ardent

[10] *Œuvres*, VII, 7. The similarity between this portrait and the self-portrait of Mlle Desjardins printed in 1659 (quoted in Ch. I, above) is a further proof of her authorship of the *Mémoires*.

[11] Mlle Desjardins mentions in her *Recueil de lettres* meeting the first two, Aremberg and Arschot, in 1667; see Ch. I, above.

court to Sylvie and she marries him within ten days of their meeting. Meanwhile Englesac has gone through Savoy and Switzerland to the Imperial Court of Germany. He learns of Sylvie's marriage, attempts to kill himself, is prevented, comes to Brussels and in disguise secures employment in the service of Menèze. When they come face to face and Sylvie tells him he must leave Brussels, Englesac faints and remains in this state near Sylvie's bed for over an hour. As he revives, Mme de Seville comes to see Sylvie; Englesac hides in a closet and later escapes. Later at a dinner "le sieur de ——— qui s'étoit retiré à Bruxelles depuis la disgrace de Monsieur Fouquet"[12] recognizes Englesac, who is acting as maître d'hôtel, and greets him aloud. Menèze accuses Sylvie of infidelity and forces Englesac to leave Brussels. Sylvie's reputation suffers a further blow and Menèze begins to mistreat her. "Enfin mon nom est devenu l'exécration des honnêtes gens et la fable de toutes les Cours de l'Europe, jusqu'à le mettre sous la Presse, et à faire des Romans de ma vie" (p. 78).

In January, 1664, Sylvie discovers that Menèze plans to imprison her in a country house. With her *suivante* Merinville she flees through Luxembourg to Nancy, both disguised as men. They take with them 100,000 écus worth of jewels. An alarm is raised; Sylvie impersonates the German prince, de Salmes, and the two proceed toward Paris through Champagne. En route they encounter the mistress of M. de Vilacerf, also disguised as a man. She mistakes Sylvie for her rival and attacks her; hence "une nouvelle qui courut à la Cour en ce tems-là, que deux Dames déguisées s'étoient battues en duel pour un Amant."

The two women enter a pension outside of Paris, retaining their disguises. The Abbess of Sylvie's first convent appears, and not recognizing Sylvie in male attire, makes advances to her. Finally "il fallut . . . que je lui fisse connoître que je n'étois qu'une femme" (p. 90).

Sylvie, still disguised as the Prince de Salmes, rents a house in Paris, joins the Court, and goes to Versailles for the *Plaisirs de l'Ile Enchantée* [May 7, 1664] and the *Princesse d'Élide*. A lady makes advances toward Sylvie and she is at a loss to know how to handle the situation when Englesac arrives in Paris and saves the day by impersonating Sylvie at a nocturnal rendezvous with the amorous lady. "Il m'informoit a son retour de ce qui s'étoit passé entre eux. (Que je suis imprudente, de rapporter tout cela à Votre Altesse!)" But the lady's husband learns of her actions and surprises her while she is talking privately with Sylvie. The lady flees; the husband orders Sylvie stripped ("pour me faire souffrir une mort plus longue et plus cruelle"). When he perceives she is a woman he orders his men to withdraw, begs her pardon, and even makes advances. His wife, informed of the event, thinks her husband is telling a cowardly lie, until the servants affirm his account, when she is amazed. News of the event causes Sylvie to abandon her disguise and take up that of the Marquise de Castelanne. She takes refuge with the Duc de Guise. Menèze persuades the Queen Mother to have her sent back to Flanders, but Englesac spirits her away en route. Then the Marquise de Seville finds them and tells them the news of Menèze's death. She offers Sylvie a dowry so that she may marry Englesac.

---

[12] For further references to Fouquet, cf. the discussion of *Le Favory* in Ch. IV, above.

Partie III. Englesac goes to Languedoc to appease his mother, Sylvie to Brussels to arrange her inheritance and to dispel the evil rumors concerning her behavior. Her example becomes popular and women begin fleeing their husbands disguised as men, among them the Comtesse de Cardonnoy. Menèze's nephew contests her inheritance. Meanwhile Birague has persuaded Englesac's mother that the boy should marry a cousin of his. Englesac to gain time courts the cousin; Birague sees that news of this reaches Sylvie, who, piqued, stops writing. Birague has Englesac's letters intercepted and a great misunderstanding results, separating the lovers. Sylvie goes to Montpellier to see Englesac, but finds he has left for Brussels to see her. Sylvie enters her old convent, and on hearing of the illness of her rival for Englesac's affections goes to her, only to find Englesac himself kneeling at the bed protesting his love. The sick girl urges Englesac to marry Sylvie, then dies. Englesac tells Sylvie he had come to Montpellier to marry Birague's cousin because in Paris the real Prince de Salmes had told him he had been Sylvie's lover. The lovers go to Paris planning to be married secretly. Mme d'Englesac hurries after them, distributes copies of the "Romans" on Sylvie's life, gives out a long list of well-known men as Sylvie's ex-lovers. The Queen Mother, incensed, has Englesac arrested, but spares Sylvie after the latter has made a long and eloquent plea. Several men attempt to seduce Sylvie, and the news, with its significance turned, gets back to Englesac. Sylvie becomes involved in a seance of Black Magic.[13] Englesac, listening to his mother, believes the scandal about Sylvie, and, released, goes to join the Dutch army against England [1666]. Mme de Seville falls in love with an eighteen-year-old boy and Sylvie's attempts to dissuade her from marrying him alienate her friend. News comes that Englesac has been washed overboard in a naval battle occurring in June, 1666. But "nous le ressusciterons, s'il vous plaît, quand il sera tems" (p. 162).

Sylvie has still to cope with her *importuns* and lovers, chief among them Birague and Signac, a *rapporteur*. Birague, learning that Signac and Sylvie are to go "chez une femme Devineresse ou Astrologue, comme on voudra la nommer, femme sçavante, à ce qu'on disoit, qu'on appelloit la Dame Voisin" (p. 167), goes ahead of them, tells la Voisin Sylvie's past and pays her to astonish Sylvie, then urge her to get rid of Signac and heed the pleas of a widower of her acquaintance, who will shortly save her from robbers. This la Voisin does in her "Cabinet des Oracles." Birague then stages a mock battle with paid men across the street from Sylvie's house and prepares to reap his reward.[14] But Sylvie, still in love with Englesac, sends him away. Meanwhile Signac having found Englesac, arranges a rendezvous with Sylvie for himself and sends Englesac to fill it. The lovers, overjoyed, decide they must marry without delay, and without telling the Comtesse d'Englesac.

Partie IV. They are married "sans aucune cérémonie," but Englesac finds he is impotent—"c'est-à-dire, Madame, qu'il se trouva marié inutilement, et qu'un cruel

---

[13] See below, and cf. the reference to la Voisin, Ch. I, above.

[14] Mlle Desjardins states that a similar device is found in the *Astrée*. It is in the "Histoire de la tromperie de Climante."

charme avoit été jeté sur nous par quelqu'un de nos ennemis."[15] Pressure is brought to bear by the Comtesse, Birague, and others to persuade Sylvie to break the marriage; even Englesac urges it. The lovers quarrel. While Englesac is away Signac calls on Sylvie; Englesac returns to hear Signac declare his love for her, rushes to them both and begs Sylvie to leave him and marry Signac, then leaves abruptly to join the army anew. Signac wishes Sylvie to have a child by him, since "une habile femme ne meurt jamais sans héritier." The Comtesse urges the Marquis de Villars to woo Sylvie and then abandon her, but he gains such respect for her that he confesses the ruse. Sylvie is in constant fear of being kidnapped by the Comtesse d'Englesac's agents. She and Merinville leave their Hôtel de Hollande at Paris and go in search of Englesac. Their equipage breaks down in the forest and a man calling himself the Prince of Portugal comes up, telling Sylvie that la Voisin had predicted he would fall in love with a person shown him in a glass, who resembles her. Mme de Seville's young lover, Sainte-Fère, passes by, then Mme de Seville herself, pursuing him. All leave for Avesnes, where the Queen is. Sainte-Fère dies at the siege of Douay. Englesac returns with the charm "rompu par un Juif." Signac in despair goes to the siege of Lille, where he dies. After the defeat of General Marcin, Englesac, Sylvie, and Mme de Seville go to Paris, Sylvie *enceinte*.

Sylvie then begins to taste the fate of Cinthie, Almanzaïde, the Marquise de Termes and other heroines of Mlle Desjardins: her husband-lover tires of her. The Comtesse, Englesac's mother, spreads scandalous rumors which Birague vainly tries to stifle. "Je ne sçai si ces faux bruits refroidirent le Comte d'Englesac, ou si le mariage fit seul ce changement, mais il se dégoûta, comme c'est la coutume: et dès que je lui plus moins, plusieurs autres femmes vinrent à lui plaire beaucoup" (p. 195). Sylvie on one occasion substitutes for one of her husband's mistresses, and receives an expensive diamond *poinçon* for her favors. On another, preceding Englesac to a rendezvous, she discovers such a beautiful woman waiting for him that she begins conversation with her and the two become fast friends. Walking disguised under the *Portiques* of the Place Royale at night Sylvie encounters the Prince de Salmes, and to her astonishment hears from him a long account of an affair he pretends to have had with her. When the Prince comes to dinner Sylvie twits him, and he becomes thereafter one of her suitors. The Marquis de Castelau is another, and he publicly attributes to her a scarf given him by the Comtesse de Seville. Salmes is duped by an *entrepreneuse* who contracts to gain Sylvie's favors for him, and Sylvie writes, "je ne sçai comment, je fus livrée . . . [Je ne sçai] si l'obscurité seule y contribua, ou si on se servit de magie" (p. 205). When Salmes later makes advances to her, Sylvie rebukes him, and he spreads the story of what he believes to have been his rendezvous with her. The Comtesse d'Englesac begins a new suit to break her son's marriage because of his age. Other lovers cause ambiguous situations to arise, one by sending Sylvie a purse of gold and not admitting her return of it. Sylvie's child is born, but soon dies, and rumors spread that it was not by Englesac. The suit waged by the Comtesse is moved to Grenoble, and with Englesac grown cold and indifferent, Sylvie sets out to defend it there. An en-

---

[15] She adds a touching comment: "Que les hommes sont fous, de se croire méprisables là-dessus, parce qu'ils se méprisent. J'eus beau jurer au Comte d'Englesac que ce malheur ne me touchoit point, comme il étoit vrai."

counter with a Swedish *Walmestre*, whose abandoned mistress is following him disguised as a page, is reported to the scandalmongers and embellished to Sylvie's
discredit. Englesac comes to Grenoble and the two discuss their plans to live apart
and take lovers and mistresses. Sylvie feigns a loss of interest in her husband, and
takes heart when he chides her for levity when various men begin paying her
attention. The Comtesse d'Englesac arrives: Englesac leaves Grenoble and writes
Sylvie an amorous letter, telling her he has written his mother begging her to desist
in her suits. Sylvie goes to see the Comtesse, makes a long plea capped by a declaration that the Comtesse would never be able to do her as much harm as she had
good in giving birth to Englesac. The Comtesse is touched and makes friends with
Sylvie. Englesac is sent for, but he has already left for Candia with the army. The
Comtesse and Birague unite to re-establish Sylvie's reputation, and the girl goes with
her mother-in-law to Languedoc. But the Comtesse dies.

The Comtesse d'Englesac's heirs cry out that she had gone insane before her
death, and that Sylvie should be excluded from any inheritance. Sylvie goes to
Marseilles to live with an aunt of Englesac, but this woman becomes so difficult that
Sylvie returns to Grenoble. There she attempts to win for a former lover the
affections of an eighteen-year-old girl who is in love with a Marquis she cannot
hope to marry. The girl agrees to give up her Marquis and gives Sylvie what she
pretends is a letter bidding him farewell. It turns out, however, to be only a new
declaration of love, and the girl maliciously spreads the rumor that Sylvie has tried
to take the Marquis away from her. Englesac hears this through his aunt and sends
back from Candia a procuration to break his marriage. Sylvie wishes to go to Candia
to find her husband and explain, but she learns that, after committing many new
infidelities, he is dead.

Partie V. Scandals spring up on every side; each new suitor for Sylvie's hand
puts another rumor into circulation. She goes to Lyons and seeks solitude with
a nun; the two have long talks about love, fidelity, etc. A pretended woman-
hater, the Comte de Tavanes, joins their company, and to substantiate his anti-
feminine convictions, relates the story of his deception by his best friend. He is
not long, however, in confessing that it is all merely a ruse to enlist Sylvie's interest
and sympathy, and that he is in love with her. The Chevalier de la Mothe becomes
a suitor, and seeing letters from Sylvie drop from Tavanes' pocket, quarrels with
him.

Sylvie, with her *suivante* Merinville, leaves for Paris by the *Coche d'eau*. She meets
the "fameux Desbarreaux,"[16] who tells her Tavanes has been boasting of an affair
with her and displaying letters written by her to Englesac, which Tavanes secured
by bribing a page. Des Barreaux discourses hotly on the perfidy of women and other
topics. The people on the boat divert themselves by persuading a simple "mary de
Montpellier" that his wife is unfaithful to him, relieving him at last by telling him
the truth. At Paris Sylvie is met by an *écuyer* bearing a present of jewels from
Mme de Seville. Soon afterwards Mme de Seville dies of a poisoned love potion.
Sylvie meets Mgr de Lionne in 1670, and "ce généreux Ministre trouva quelque
chose dans ma physionomie qui lui plut." He aids her in her *procès*. More *importuns*

---

[16] See Ch. I, above.

and lovers make their appearance; typical is the Chevalier du Buisson: "Il affectoit les grimaces des Amans heureux; il faisoit le mistérieux et le faux discret; il s'ôtoit d'auprès de moi quand il s'appercevoit qu'on avoit remarqué qu'il y fût; on le surprenoit toujours lisant quelque lettre, qu'il cachoit aussitôt qu'on l'avoit regardé" (p. 277).

This suitor even forges letters to win a wager that he can seduce Sylvie, and is rebuked by her publicly to his shame. A *fausse Prude*, a former mistress of du Buisson, circulates scandal about Sylvie. Lionne dies,[17] and all Sylvie's advantages gained through him—an income, a share in the inheritance, etc.,—are revoked by the heirs of the Comtesse.

Sylvie decides to go to Brussels and sue for the estate of Mme de Seville. She learns that the Comtesse's heirs have had a warrant for her arrest issued there, and seeks refuge in Liége, "Païs neutre," until her friends can have the warrant revoked. She goes *incognita* to Spa, and there associates with the Comte de Marcin and the Princesse de Nassau. Conjectures arise as to her identity; a "Milord Anglois" pretends to be related to her and offers her "une retraite en Angleterre" (p. 295). This man's pretentious affectations give rise to the scorn of a *bourgeois* of Liége, who discourses on the advantages of being middle class. Mme de Seville's chief heiress marries a powerful noble and Sylvie, discouraged, despairs of her suit. She decides to enter a convent in Cologne, and, with her friend the Abbess and Merinville, sets out for that city.

Partie VI. They are stopped at Mauberge by news that the Prince de Liége and the King of France are besieging Cologne because of the city's refusal to allow its elector to enter. Sylvie meets the Chanoinesses of the Collège de Flandre, who take no vows against marriage or lovers. One of them relates how a friend of her lover tried to save her for the latter by pretending love himself when in the absence of his friend she showed signs of faltering interest, and how each man lost interest in her and tried to give her to the other. The Abbess tells her story, too, one of an unhappy marriage forced by a mother desirous of marrying the man who was really in love with her daughter, and of a tender, platonic friendship between the Abbess and the lover she could not have. Sylvie meets a man who tells her many adventures supposed to have happened to her: "il me fit voyager habillée en homme, dans je ne sçai combien de Villes d'Italie," etc. (p. 331). Sylvie's *incognita* is broken and she takes refuge with a certain Dom Pedre, who falls in love with her and keeps her prisoner in his château near Liége. She finally escapes disguised as the young brother of Dom Pedre, and finds refuge, still disguised, at the château of the Baron de Raste. There an heir of Mme de Seville who has fallen in love with her discovers her plight and enables her to escape to a convent in Cologne. He offers to provide her with whatever she wishes. Sylvie then concludes: "Mais, Madame, si je continue dans l'humeur où je suis, je ne . . . prendrai jamais d'autre [condition] que celle où je suis. Je la trouve douce, le Couvent ne me paroît plus ce qu'il m'avoit paru dans une vûe éloignée, et je pourrois dire qu'il ne manqueroit rien au repos de mon esprit, si je pouvois vous dire de près, comme je vous l'écris, que personne du monde n'est dévouée à Votre Altesse avec tant de zele et

---

[17] In 1671. The event could hardly have been added *après coup*.

tant de soumission, que sa très-humble et très-obéissante servante, Henriette-Sylvie de Moliere" (pp. 375-376).

What part of the foregoing narrative may be deemed autobiographical? A comparison of it with the facts of Mlle Desjardins' life forces one to answer: little, if any. The legend that the *Mémoires* are a disguised account of Mlle Desjardins' own life begins with Magne, who, as we have seen, makes several wholly unwarranted statements about the work. It seems obvious that Sylvie's peregrinations in Languedoc have nothing whatever to do with Molière's *Illustre Théâtre*. It seems equally obvious that the manuscript was not "déjà terminé" (Magne) in 1664 and touched up again for publication in 1672, for, according to its own chronology, the body of the work (from the middle of *Partie II* to the end of *Partie VI*) lies between those dates. René Le Pays, in 1664, must have read only the beginning. Chatenet accepts Magne's categorical statement that the *Mémoires* are an autobiography, adding however that "l'imagination . . . se laisse aller ici à sa complète fantaisie," and that "derrière la fiction, on sent une histoire 'vécue.' "[18] These remarks are true, but they hardly support the argument; they merely affirm the realistic temper of the novel.

The most important events in Mlle Desjardins' life have no counterpart in the *Mémoires*. Her arrival in Paris, literary beginnings, meeting and affair with Villedieu: surely these do not resemble the first part of the novel. Englesac is no Villedieu; the latter was a sophisticated soldier (whose musical family lived on the bohemian fringe of the day), already married, realistic, cynical; Englesac was a spoiled booby, dominated by his aristocratic family and full of absurd idealism and impulsiveness. The circumstances of their relationships with their mistresses, in life and in the novel, are wholly different. There is no hint in *Sylvie* of a literary career.

In the *Mémoires*, Sylvie makes two trips to the Low Countries, one in 1662 or thereabouts, staying until 1664, and the other in 1671, just before the end of the novel. Neither resembles very closely the actual trip made by Mlle Desjardins in 1667. A certain amount of "atmosphere" derives naturally from her first-hand knowledge of Holland and Belgium, and the *Mémoires* contain references to persons whom she met or knew in real life: the Prince d'Aremberg, the Duc d'Arschot, the Comte de Marcin, and others. The grateful eulogies of Lionne are likewise a frank

[18] *Op. cit.*, pp. 225, 246.

reference to her own life, but Mlle Desjardins does not construct her novel around such infrequent mentions. Sylvie does not meet Lionne until 1670, about a year before his death (September 1, 1671). Marie-Catherine had known Lionne since 1663 or 1664, and *Le Favory*, played in April, 1665, was dedicated to him.

Stretching the point to call the novel "une autobiographie volontaire-ment embrouillée" (Magne) seems, then, unwarranted. The elements are not the same. Mlle Desjardins' life contained no Englesac, Birague, Molière (the financier), Menèze, Mme de Seville, etc., and certainly none of the adventures, imprisonments, escapes, disguises (though there is a legend that she once pursued Villedieu in men's clothes), and false deaths which form the fabric of the *Mémoires*. On the other hand, it contained its own startling events, of which no trace is to be found in *Sylvie*. The conclusion must be that Mlle Desjardins, instead of writing an auto-biography, wrote a picaresque novel using a contemporary heroine not unlike herself, giving the account realistic color by making liberal use of places, persons, and perhaps in a few ambiguous passages, events, known to her in real life. The device of the first person, the title *Mémoires*, the air of an "histoire vécue" which surrounds the novel: all these are part of the technique of composition of the pseudo-autobio-graphical novel. What could be more natural, since she herself had been to Brussels and Spa, than to work into her novel of contemporary scene a description of these gay and interesting cities?

But not all the background of the *Mémoires* was necessarily lifted from the author's own experience. A point in proof is her long account of the *fêtes* at Versailles in the spring of 1664, at the occasion of the presenta-tion of the *Plaisirs de l'Île Enchantée*, including *La Princesse d'Élide*. Reading the novel, one assumes Mlle Desjardins must have been present, so exact is the description. Yet all her information came from a con-temporary account of the festival, Marigny's *Relation*, published June 17, 1664. A side-by-side comparison will make this clear:

SYLVIE	MARIGNY
On avoit orné de quatre grands porti-ques de verdures . . . un rond, auquel quatre allées spacieuses aboutissoient en-tre de hautes palissades. . . .	L'on avoit élevé dans les quatres ave-nues du rond de grandes portiques. . . .

[Entrance of King and suite, King as Ariosto's *Roger*.]

Apre celà paroissoit un Apollon dans un char . . . et ayant les quatre âges à ses pieds: le Temps, comme on le dépeint, en étoit le Conducteur. . . . Un long accompagnement le suivoit; puis venoient les Pages des Chevaliers avec les lances et les devises; puis une troupe de Bergers chargés des diverses pieces de la Barriere, qu'on dressa pour la Course; on courut jusqu'au soir.

La nuit venue, et un nombre prodigieux de flambeaux de cire blanche avec plus de quatre mille bougies ayant éclairé le lieu, on ouït un agréable concert. . . . Toute la suite du Soleil dansa dans le rond une belle entrée de Ballet. Puis le Printemps vint, et c'étoit la pauvre du Parc qui le representoit; elle montoit . . . un superbe cheval d'Espagne; l'Esté sur un éléphant; l'Automne sur un chameau, et l'Hyver sur on Ours, venoient après, avec une suite, composée d'une infinité de personnes, qui portoient sur leurs têtes de grands bassins pour la collation. Les premiers couverts de fleurs et faits en corbeilles, étoient portés par les Jardiniers, les autres par des Moissoneurs, ceux de l'Automne par des Vendangeurs. . . . Les Controlleurs généraux, sous les noms de l'Abondance, de la Joie, de la Propreté, et de la Bonne-chere, firent aussi-tôt couvrir une table d'inventions nouvelles de toutes ces choses, le tout par les mains des Plaisirs, des Jeux, des ris, et des Délices. . . .

Comme le second jour on représentoit le Comédie de la Princesse d'Élide, je me trouvai placée entre deux belles femmes. . . .

Après les paladins, l'on vit entrer Apollon sur un char. . . . Apollon avoit à ses pieds les quatre Siècles. . . . Milet, le premier Conducteur . . . étoit vêtu comme l'on peint le Temps. . . . Le char étoit . . . suivi des Pages des Chevaliers portants leurs lances et les écus de leurs devises, et de vingt pasteurs chargés des pièces de la barrière. . . . Lorsque les paladins voulurent courre la bague. . . .

La nuit étant survenue, le camp fut éclairé d'un nombre infini de lumières . . . et l'on vit entrer . . . Lully, à la tête d'une grande troupe de concertants. . . . Et en même temps l'on vit arriver . . . les quatre Saisons: le Printemps sur un grand cheval d'Espagne, l'Été sur un éléphant, l'Automne sur un chameau, et l'Hiver sur un ours; les Saisons étoient accompagnées de douze jardiniers, douze moissoneurs, douze vendangeurs et douze vieillards; ils marquoient la différence de leurs saisons par des fleurs, des épis, des fruits et des glaces, et portoient sur leurs têtes les bassins de la collation. . . . Les controlleurs de la maison du Roi, qui représentoient l'Abondance, la Joie, la Propreté et la Bonne Chère, firent apporter vis-à-vis du haut dais, de l'autre côté du rond, une grande table . . . ornée de festons, et enrichie d'un nombre infini de fleurs; et sitôt qu'elle fut couverte par les Jeux, les Ris et les Délices, l'on ouvrit le milieu de la barrière. . . .

Le jour suivant on eut le divertissement de la comédie. . . .[19]

The close similarity between these two passages, in the phraseology, descriptive adjectives, and even verbs, proves that one was taken quite consciously from the other; no series of coincidences could have resulted in two passages which are so nearly alike. Those facts not mentioned in

[19] Mlle Desjardins, *Œuvres*, VII, 93 ff. Marigny, *Relation des Plaisirs de l'Ile Enchantée*, in the Despois edition of Molière, IV, 251 ff.

Marigny were obtainable in the printed version of the *Plaisirs*, or in other *relations*.[20] If Mlle Desjardins was indeed present at Versailles in 1664, she must have used Marigny's account to refresh her memory, for her *"relation"* owes its whole structure and texture to his.

Sylvie is, then, assuredly not an autobiography, but rather a realistic novel, strongly picaresque in manner, stemming from the current of the "realistic" comic novel of Scarron and Sorel. Sylvie herself is a female Lazarillo de Tormes, moving in a higher social circle, and with a far more limited view of the world. She is never actually hungry or in need of money (the two besetting characteristics of the average *pícaro*), but she must fight for survival among jealous husbands, unfaithful lovers, suing mothers-in-law, and a host of *importuns*. Although her money comes from jewel caskets and sundry gifts, the supply is always threatened, and the heroine, though not reduced to want, must scheme and cajole to keep her source of income from being shut off entirely. Her weapons are not cunning and deception so much as beauty, coquetry, and charm. She loses not her employ, but rather her husband or lover. She is not chased by an angry household, but by malicious gossip and rumors. She is a Lazarillo once removed, a *pícara* of the luxury sphere.

That Dallas should place the picaresque *Sylvie* among the "Romans badins et galants" of the period serves to show the extent to which interest in amorous and "social" intrigue had supplanted the earlier, more vigorous and realistic motivations of *Francion*, *Guzmán*, the *Roman comique*, or the *Roman bourgeois*. The characters of *Sylvie*, while speaking a rather natural dialogue and going through a series of sometimes quite plausible events, never impress us as essentially real, because the intrigues in which they take part had value and significance only for the average readers of the day when they were conceived. There is no appeal to "constant" values; there is, indeed, far less psychological analysis, far fewer keen observations of character, than in Mlle Desjardins' other novels of the period: the *Journal amoureux*, the *Annales galantes*, and the *Désordres de l'amour*. Critics have frequently mentioned the fervent emotionalism of the *Mémoires*. Chatenet writes:

[20] See the edition of Molière mentioned above, IV, 109 ff. Saint-Aignan is mentioned as the director of the *fête*, a fact found in the *Mémoires*, and la du Parc is stated to have been Le Printemps. The fact that Mlle Desjardins refers to her as "la pauvre du Parc" dates the composition of the passage after the actress' death in 1668. Other *relations* were the *Livret de la Fête*, 1664 (cf. Molière, *Œuvres*, IV, 234), and the account in the *Gazette de Loret*, May 21, 1664.

Ce qu'il y eut de désordonné ou de passionné dans cette existence un peu exception-
nelle, même au dix-septième siècle, on le retrouve dans les *Mémoires d'Henriette-*
Sylvie de Molière. . . .[21]

And Miss Dallas:

. . . son ouvrage [*Sylvie*] . . . est remarquable . . . surtout par des accents de passion
sincère. Elle a ressenti des émotions vraies et décrit souvent ses situations du roman
de sa propre vie. . . .[22]

I find few traces of such sincerity and passion in the work, almost none
in comparison with the *Désordres*, for example. Sylvie is a calculating
minx, and her unshakable "love" for Englesac never rings true, either
in her expressed attitude or her actions. The secondary stories are mostly
a sort of modernized *fabliaux*, and contain little emotion. Why the critics
have united to discover in the *Mémoires* a set of heart-rending personal
confessions remains a mystery; on cold analysis, nothing in the work
supports such a misleading view.

A few remnants of the heroic novel are found in *Sylvie*, chiefly in the
use of *histoires intercalées*. The author is quite conscious of this indebtedness. When Sylvie is about to tell her story to Mme de Seville, she says:

J'avois tout sujet de craindre l'indiscrétion ordinaire à ces esprits héroïques, ayant
remarqué dans les livres qu'ils contoient toujours leurs histoires aux premiers inconnus
sans aucune précaution.[23]

Elsewhere she mentions the "traverses," of which she has enough to
"fournir un gros Roman."[24]

Few of the events of the *Mémoires* possess any interest for the modern
reader, even from an historical viewpoint. The *relation* of the *fête* at
Versailles, as we have seen, is secondhand. The rare descriptions of
mœurs in the sections concerning the Pays-Bas are surpassed many times
by Mlle Desjardins' own *Lettres*. Though much of the action of the novel
takes place in the provinces, there is little background material or local
color. Nothing in the psychology of the characters is particularly new
or significant; their "realism" is left unheightened by either shrewd gen-
eralization or careful observation. About the only original feature is
Sylvie herself. She indeed seems to be a new type. She was popular,
and her career was imitated at least once.[25]

---

[21] *Op. cit.*, p. 247.
[22] *Op. cit.*, p. 119.
[23] *Œuvres*, VII, *Partie II.*
[24] *Ibid.*
[25] By Préchac, in *L'Héroïne mousquetaire, histoire véritable de Mlle Christine,*

Sylvie contains two references to la Voisin, "Divineresse ou Astrologue," which suggest that Mlle Desjardins herself may have known her (see Chapter I, above). Not much is said about her, but a divining ceremony ("de la Magie noire") witnessed by Sylvie hints that Marie-Catherine had at least seen something of the magical practises of her day. Wishing to foretell the outcome of an amorous intrigue, Sylvie, the Baronne de Saint-de-Fer, and Mme Feronne secure a mare in foal, carry it to a stable near the Pont-Marie, and there wait for it to foal its colt, in order to inspect the "je ne sçai quoy qu'on . . . avoit fait accroire que le Poulain apporteroit au front en naissant." The account continues:

Nous y avions déjà passé la nuit à faire des sentinelles ridicules autour de la Jument: ce qui m'effrayoit et me faisoit soupçonner que mes amies fussent folles. Nous devions continuer cette extravagante cérémonie, jusq'au terme de la naissance du précieux animal.[26]

There are few such passages, however, to relieve the monotony of the book. The encounter with Des Barreaux, a few *traits de mœurs* observed in Holland, an occasional amusing adventure—these are the spare attractions of the *Mémoires*. The heroine, although an original type, is not a wholly successful creation, perhaps because her actions, extravagant as they are, hide a soul commonplace in its outlook and fundamentally bourgeois in the midst of its bohemianism. A rapid style, superficial characters, picaresque adventures, surface realism: such is the stuff of the *Mémoires de Henriette-Sylvie de Molière*. Somewhere among intersecting tendencies, abortive attempts, unrealized forms—between *Lazarillo*, *Francion*, and the *Roman bourgeois* on the one side, and *Gil Blas*, *Manon Lescaut*, and the modern picaresque novel on the other—may be placed this work of Mlle Desjardins, a memorial to a luckless talent.

---

comtesse de Meyrac, 1677. Dulong writes, "Il y raconte, non sans verve, la biographie d'une dame béarnaise qui court le monde, habillée en homme, et que la fortune sépare obstinement d'un gentilhomme espagnol, son amant" (*op. cit.*, p. 353).

[26] *Œuvres*, VII, 153 ff. The effect on Sylvie's reputation is bad: "On ne laissa point de me charger libéralement de tout, et d'ajouter à mes autres fameuses qualitez celle d'une honnête Sorciere: pardonnez-moi de ce gros et déplaisant mot, dont je n'ai pu ici me passer." Littré's dictionary gives examples of "sorcière" from Corneille, La Fontaine, Malebranche, etc., with no indication that it was ever regarded as a "gros et déplaisant mot."

CHAPTER VIII

ROMANS: GRAECO-ROMAN AND EXOTIC NOVELS AND NOUVELLES; POSTHUMOUS WORKS

Carmante (1668)

Carmante, histoire grecque par Mlle des Jardins, dédiée à S. A. S. Mme la Duchesse de Nemours appeared in two volumes published by Barbin in 1668.[1] The authoress acknowledged it as her own work in her list of 1671, where it appears after *Anaxandre* (1667) and before the *Recueil de lettres* (1668).[2] It was not published again until the editions of the collected works of Mlle Desjardins began to appear in 1702. In the opinion of Hauréau, *Carmante* "ne paraît pas avoir obtenu toute l'estime qu'il méritoit."[3] Kretschmar, on the other hand, considers its lack of success deserved, and blames Mlle Desjardins for her failure to keep abreast of the times; to him the work is too Arcadian and too reminiscent of the *Astrée* to find approval with a public becoming accustomed to a different psychological tone in its fiction.[4] This criticism is valid; *Carmante*, Mlle Desjardins' first novel after *Alcidamie*, suffers from an excess, not only of Arcadianism, but also of outmoded technique derived from the heroic novel of Scudéry and La Calprenède.[5] An enthusiastic nineteenth-century critic has called *Carmante* and *Alcidamie*, recognizing their similarity in *genre*, "des adorables idylles qu'on croirait tombées du pinceau d'Ovide."[6] The *BUR*, which analyzed it as a "Roman d'amour," calls it "un petit roman" not unworthy of attention.[7] It is

[1] Copy in the Bib. de Versailles. For Mlle Desjardins' relations with the Duchesse de Nemours, cf. Ch. I, above.

[2] See Ch. I, above.

[3] *Op. cit.*, IV, 34.

[4] *Op. cit.*, p. 40. Kretschmar speaks erroneously of the appearance of the *Princesse de Clèves* "zwei Jahre vor dem Erscheinen der *Carmante*." Mme de La Fayette's work appeared in 1678.

[5] It must be recalled however that the decade 1660-1670 saw the appearance of both *Faramond* and *Almahide*. It is from 1670 on that the public taste of Paris swings almost completely away from the heroic, toward the historical-psychological, novel.

[6] É. Neveu, "Mlle Desjardins," in Baratte's *Poètes normands*, Paris, 1846.

[7] *BUR*, March, 1776, p. 133, and May, 1776, pp. 147 ff. (analysis). The introductory remarks criticize the construction of Mlle Desjardins' novels and the writer complains that "il semble qu'elle ne travailloit pas sur un plan arrêté."

not, however, a short novel, but one of her longest.[8] The following account is greatly condensed:

At Légée, a village in Arcadia, a feast for Pan and Syrinx, at which Queen Carmante is expected, is being prepared. A young shepherd, Cléophile, who is really Prince Evandre, tells his story to Simas. As children, he and Carmante, daughter of the King of Arcadia, had fallen in love; Argos the King had so favored Evandre as a son-in-law that he had offered him his daughter's hand and, to the neglect of his own son Tessandre, the throne. Argos dies and Tessandre seizes the throne, banishing Evandre, whose own throne has been usurped by his step-brother Palans. Evandre goes to Latium and becomes commander of the troops. He hears that Tessandre is about to marry Carmante to Palans, tries to prevent it, but fails when an illness renders him unconscious at the time of the wedding. In his sorrow he lets the rumor spread that he has died of his sickness, and leaves for foreign lands. Now after two years he has come to Arcadia disguised as a shepherd. He has met Theocritus, the poet-philosopher, who has withdrawn to Légée because of unrequited love for Ardelie, a slave of his father. There they spend their time composing verses, talking, and telling their stories, in a world peopled by "attardés et égarés" of the *Astrée:* Licoris, Cyparisse, Timente, Iphise, etc. At last Theocritus points out to Carmante Cléophile's resemblance to the "dead" Evandre; the two meet at night in the grove of Diana and Carmante recognizes her former lover, confessing that she still loves him. King Palans is found dead in the same grove, and Evandre is accused of his murder; Tessandre has recognized him and becomes his principal accuser. Theocritus and Simas win over a majority of the populace to Evandre's side, and force Nicostrate, betrothed to Arcaste, Palans' sister, and next in line for the throne, to flee the land. Evandre finds an ally in the Roman Albius Turnus, who arrives in Arcadia and tells his story. The King of Carthage had entrusted to him his daughter Perselide, but she has been captured by pirates. The Oracle of Delphi has told Albius that he will receive Perselide from the hands of a certain Ardelie when Evandre's misfortunes are ended. Thus he has a motive for coming to Evandre's assistance. Carmante wishes to marry Evandre at once, but is dissuaded by Prince Timoleon, who is also disappointed in love for Ardelie through his rival Hermocrate. Theocritus and Albius go to seek troops. Theocritus by accident finds Ardelie on an island, and learns from a slave that she is really Perselide, daughter of Pygmalion, King of Carthage. He takes her back to Arcadia and to Albius, fulfilling the provisions of the Oracle for Evandre's success.[9] Albius in turn gives her to her lover Timoleon.

Carmante wishes to convince the populace of Evandre's innocence before raising him to the throne with her, but, fearing for her reputation and alarmed lest she be accused of connivance, has not the courage to prove it by confessing her presence with him in the grove of Diana on the fateful night. Nicostrate succeeds in raising a large army; Evandre's situation becomes critical. Carmante decides to confess; Evandre threatens

[8] Vol. III in the *Œuvres complètes*, 576 pages. Only the *Exilez*, the *Annales galantes* and the *Journal amoureux* compare with it in length.

[9] The prophecy of the Oracle is fulfilled in reverse chronology, it will be noted; Mlle Desjardins is hardly scrupulous about such details.

to kill himself rather than let her stain her *gloire*. At this point Arcaste, Palans' sister and betrothed of Nicostrate, confesses that Nicostrate himself is the murderer, having been provoked to the regicide by her ambitious desire to put the two of them on the throne. She betrays the crime to revenge herself on Nicostrate, who has fallen in love with a common shepherdess and wishes to marry her against her will and make her queen. Evandre's innocence is fully proved, but to avenge himself on Nicostrate he captures the city of Stymphale in which Nicostrate has entrenched himself. Both Nicostrate and Arcaste commit suicide rather than fall into Evandre's hands.

Evandre marries Carmante and ascends the throne; Timoleon marries Perselide. Timoleon, the rightful king of Syracuse, renounces his right to the throne so that the island home of Theocritus may remain free. Evandre removes his government to Latium and there brings the arts and sciences to such full bloom that he is honored as a son of Mercury. In honor of Carmante the festivals bearing her name ("Carmentales") are invented, and after her death she is honored as a prophetess because of her verses called "Carmes."

Haureau was the first to point out, in 1852, that the germ of the argument of *Carmante* was probably found by Mlle Desjardins "dans quelques vers de Virgile."[10] Kretschmar quotes the passage from the *Aeneid*, as does Chatenet, who adds, "Ce n'est pas du tout la même chose, comme on le voit."[11] Mlle Desjardins appears to have found in Vergil, Servius' commentary, and other classical sources most of her names and the bare idea of her personage Carmante; the rest is imaginary invention in the tradition of her first masters, d'Urfé, Gomberville, La Calprenède, and Scudéry.[12] Both *Cassandre* (1642-1645) and the *Grand Cyrus* (1649-1653) had dealt partially with Greek subjects, and though none had treated, like *Carmante*, incidents in the founding of Rome, the recent *Clélie* (1654-1660) had for its setting the early Rome of the monarchy. Du Verdier had published as early as 1627 a novel entitled *Les Amours et les armes des princes de Grèce*.

The year before the appearance of *Carmante*, Mlle Desjardins had

---

[10] *Op. cit.*, p. 34.

[11] Kretschmar, *op. cit.*, p. 40; Chatenet, *op. cit.*, p. 219. The passage occurs in Book VIII, lines 333-341. Evander at Rome gives among other reasons for his coming there the "warnings of my mother, the nymph Carmentis," and points out the Carmental gate, "tribute to the nymph Carmentis, soothsaying prophetess, who first foretold the greatness of Aeneas' sons and the glory of Pallanteum."

[12] Servius in his remarks on the foregoing lines from the *Aeneid* mentions the festivals called *Carmentalia*, the oracles called *Carmina*, and states that Carmentis was first called Nicostrata (cf. the Nicostrate of *Carmante*). "Palans" probably derives from "Pallantius," the name applied by Ovid to Evander (*Fasti*, v. 647). Timoleon and Theocritus are obviously anachronistic additions from other sources, doubtless Plutarch or Suidas.

expressed, in the preface to *Anaxandre,* her own and her epoch's growing
dissatisfaction with the formulae of the heroic novel. She wrote:

> L'Art Militaire n'est pas à l'usage des Dames. . . . Vous prendrez plus de plaisir à
> . . . entendre reconter le Siege d'un Cœur, que celuy d'une Ville.[13]

This tendency to discredit the whole plan of action of the heroic novel
and to concentrate on what had been only an added delicacy borrowed
from the *Astrée,* that is, the "love interest," may be seen already in
the *Grand Cyrus.* As pointed out earlier, Mlle Desjardins herself, after
writing the first 175 pages of *Alcidamie* (1660) in pure heroic style, had
abandoned her central story and "completed" her novel with a series of
nouvelles in which the psychology of love becomes more important than
heroic action. *Anaxandre* continued the new technique. *Carmante,* however, though it contains many passages and episodes of amorous psychology, represents in many ways a retrogression on the part of Mlle
Desjardins. There is, as we saw, a complicated plot; there are sea voyages,
pirates, both men and women in disguise, claimants struggling for the
throne, political intrigues, and those prerequisites of the heroic novel,
the plunging *in medias res* and the besieging of a town.

Despite these heroic trappings, *Carmante* was apparently meant to find
approval with a public which was gradually demanding a more realistic
atmosphere in its fiction. In her *Avis* the authoress insists that she knows
how to depict only "des hommes ordinaires," and that such are the heroes
of *Carmante.*[14] This is the same theme which she developed later in her
historical novels and which became almost her fundamental literary tenet:
"On est homme aujourd'hui comme on l'estoit il y a six cents ans . . . et
on aime comme on s'est aimé."[15]

How do these "hommes ordinaires" conduct themselves? Very much,
alas, in the traditional style of heroes of the novel. Evandre is "le
Prince du monde le plus magnanime" (p. 26), and in battle he is as
"vaillant" as any peer of Charlemagne, and has to restrain himself to
keep from killing off the entire enemy singlehanded (p. 538). Except
in his love relations, he is, like the other characters ("le fameux
Théocrite" and "la divine Carmante," for example) an abstract, perfect

---

[13] Unpaginated dedicatory letter (see Ch. VI, above).

[14] The *Avis* is unfortunately missing in the collected works; the above phrase is
quoted by Dallas, *op. cit.,* p. 34, from an edition I have not been able to consult.

[15] *Les Annales galantes,* ed. of 1700, introductory letter, opposite p. 4. See Ch. V,
above.

embodiment of traditional virtues, just as Palans is an unmitigated villain. Only rarely does some small trait appear to relieve their glaring perfection: Evandre, seeing Carmante again for the first time since her marriage, finds that "son embonpoint avoit augmenté" (p. 27), and once indeed is unable even to watch a tourney because of a very unheroic headache.[16]

Under the stress of emotion, however, the heroes and heroines lose some of their puppet-like stiffness and give expression to their feelings in actions and words often worthy of romanticists. If the analysis of their states of mind is somewhat scanty, their objective manifestations of feeling leave little to be desired:

> Palans m'enlever ma Princesse? m'écriai-je tout hors de moi-même. O Dieux! qu'est-ce que cette Lettre m'annonce? Une vérité qu'on ne peut plus vous dissimuler, Seigneur, répliqua l'Écuyer. . . . Mais je n'entendis qu'à peine ces dernieres paroles, et la douleur et la surprise s'étoient emparées de mon esprit d'une telle sorte, qu'elle avoient ôté une partie de l'usage de la raison. Je me laissai tomber sur un siege comme si j'eusse été frappé de la foudre, et lorsque ce premier acces de ma douleur fut passé, je dis et je fis des choses qui arracherent des larmes à tous ceux qui m'entendirent. Je voulois aller en Argos, poignarder Tessandre . . . (p. 80).

Carmante is likewise subject to these violent emotional spells; when Evandre tells her he must leave her forever, "La belle Carmante fut si pressée de sa douleur à ces dernieres paroles, qu'elle pensa perdre l'usage de tous ses sens. . . ."[17] Evandre utters his impassioned words with "un transport si véhément" that Carmante is left no doubt "qu'il ne les pensât de la même maniere qu'il les exprimoit" (p. 276). Carmante is forced to blush at his speeches, pass her hand over her forehead, and leave her lover, though she usually finds an opportunity to give him some sign of her secret feeling for him. Sometimes this procedure results in a coy situation which appears quite ridiculous to modern taste, as in the following passage:

> À ces mots elle se leva, et voyant le Prince à ses genoux qui ne pouvoit se résoudre à les abandonner, elle serra doucement sa tête entre ses mains, et se laissant tomber sur sa joue, elle tomba si heureusement pour lui, qu'elle le baisa. Mais comme la honte qu'elle eut de lui avoir accordé cette faveur, lui eût rendu la vûe du Prince insupportable; elle se démêla d'entre ses bras, et . . . elle se déroba aux yeux de son Amant avec beaucoup de vitesse (p. 269).[18]

---

[16] "Il avoit eu une migraine furieuse qui l'avoit empêché de voir la course. . ." (*Œuvres*, III, 47).

[17] *Ibid.*, p. 86. Notice the repetitious cliché, "ces dernieres paroles," used also in the preceding passage. The passage continues, ". . . et j'en fus pénétré d'une telle sorte . . ." (cf. "d'une telle sorte" above).

[18] Carmante's reactions are always lively: "La Reine rougit à ce discours" (p. 268);

The pastoral element referred to earlier is most prevalent in the middle section of *Carmante,* where the minor characters in Arcadia assemble to while away the time in conversation and recreation. The following excerpt will show the *Astrée*-like flavor of these passages:

[Théocrite] fut contraint de se coucher au pied d'un arbre où le sommeil le surprit. Il lui avoit donné une heure entiere lorsqu'il en fut retiré par la voix d'un Berger et d'une Bergere qui s'accordant à une flute douce, chantoient un air champêtre fort touchant et bien inventé. Théocrite prêta l'oreille à ce concert rustique, et il entendit que le Berger commençoit de cette sorte.

MADRIGAUX EN FORME DE DIALOGUE
Licoris
Avant cet injuste caprice,
Qui vous fit me quitter pour un nouvel Amant . . . .
Cyparisse
Quand je faisois toute la flâme
Que ton cœur pouvoit concevoir;
Quand tu me donnois toute ton âme, . . etc.

Ah Bergere! interrompit Licoris à la fin de ce couplet; que ne m'est-il possible d'ajouter une foi entiere à la protestation que vous me faites dans ces vers! . . . Mais moi-même, interrompit Cyparisse, que ne puis-je prendre pour une feinte, cette inconstance dont j'ai veu des marques si éclatantes![19]

There is nothing new here, except possibly an unsuccessful attempt to give the situation a lighter touch, a slightly more subtle bantering tone, than in d'Urfé. Mlle Desjardins accepted the pastoral formula completely and without question. Fortunately, she used it little after *Alcidamie* and *Carmante,* but when she does employ it even in later novels, such as the *Exilez,* one finds the whole artificial technique preserved without change.

The military and political passages are colorless, devoid of interest, and full of clichés remembered from similar situations in La Calprenède. The following is a description of Evandre falling upon the enemy troops:

Le vaillant Evandre donnant donc sur des troupes épouvantées, et les chefs des Mégariens fondant avec impetuosité au milieu d'un camp où le nouveau Roi avoit déjà porté la frayeur et la confusion, il fut fait une telle boucherie de ces pauvres gens effrayez, que si la bonté du Roi n'avoit retenu la fureur du soldat vainqueur, il ne seroit pas resté un seul des vaincus en état de combattre . . . (p. 538).

For all her claim that she is concerned only with "des hommes ordinaires," Mlle Desjardins, in *Carmante,* at least, demands of her heroes not only

---

"Cette nouvelle attaque ayant irrité cette belle fille, elle avoit un rouge sur les joues, et un brillant dans ses yeux" (p. 334), etc.

[19] *Ibid.,* p. 99. Mlle Desjardins reproduced these "Madrigaux" in her *Nouveau recueil de pièces galantes,* 1669, one year after the appearance of *Carmante.*

that they conduct themselves like Evandre above, but also that they be of noble birth. One of her characters expresses her attitude in a passage which may well be compared with that on absolute monarchy quoted below in the discussion of the *Portrait des foiblesses humaines:*

Il faut être un grand Prince, ou un grand Conquérant, pour remplir le titre d'une histoire dignement, et quand je voi un homme d'une naissance médiocre, et dont la vie est ordinaire, raconter avec emphase ce qui s'est passé entre lui et sa voisine, il me semble voir quelqu'un redire comme prodige, qu'une brebis a fait un agneau. Tout le monde s'éclata de rire à cette expression de Philistion. . . . Il fit une peinture fort plaisante de ceux qui faisoient un Roman de toutes sortes d'avantures, et qui mettoient au nombre des incidents remarquables, les accidens ordinaires d'une vie obscure et triviale (p. 566).

It would be hard to find a more complete endorsement of the aristocratic system. What Mlle Desjardins meant by "ordinaire," as we may see in her historical novels, where she makes a genuine effort to achieve a kind of realism, was rather "contemporary." Her technique in making Evandre, Ovid, Solon, Alcibiades, and characters in French history like Bussy d'Amboise speak, is not dissimilar to that of John Erskine in the twentieth century. The interesting question is how much of the behavior of her characters may be traced to the influence of literary tradition, and how much of it may be attributed to the authoress' own psychological analysis of the *milieu* in which she lived. In the historical works, we may say that in the main, since she was working in an almost untouched field — for the "historical" novels of La Calprenède and Scudéry were hardly taken seriously by any of her contemporaries—she drew the greater part of her psychology from her own observations and from the conceptions of her own day. In *Alcidamie* and *Carmante,* literary tradition dominates. In subsequent works, tradition and originality are mixed in varying proportions, with the balance but rarely in favor of the latter. The characters, except for one or two, such as the Marquise de Termes or Givry, rarely attain the stature of true individuals; whether Roman, Moorish, or French, they are only the artificially assembled, tradition-bound, superficial creatures which seem to have satisfied the average seventeenth-century reader's requirements for a personality or an individual. The personages in Mlle Desjardins' novels represent, for the most part, the social personalities which the average literate individuals of the time constructed for themselves, and in whose patterns they tried to force their natural personalities to live. The characters in these novels were for their readers in more ways than one a sort of ideal: ideal in their virtues, which were excessive and quite impractical, and ideal also in their superficial, elegant, witty, amorous natures. Though Mlle Desjardins holds her literary mirror toward a lofty realm, she inadvertently allows us to catch a glimpse of a nearer and more interesting world, that of the thoughts and actions of her own contemporaries.

Les Amours des grands hommes (1671)

"Le privilège des *Amours des grands hommes*," writes Derome, "était donné le 4 décembre 1670 à la dame des Jardins, veuve de feu sieur de Villedieu."[20] It appeared in published form in 1671, dedicated, like the *Fables* of the year before, to Louis XIV.[21] There were certainly five and possibly nine editions of it published, not counting those of the various collected editions of the eighteenth century.[22] One section, the *Amours d'Alcibiade*, was published separately in 1680.[23] Another, the *Histoire de Socrate*, was converted, around 1694, almost textually into a farce (see below). The *BUR* in 1776 analyzed two portions of the work (the stories of Solon and Alcibiades), changing many names and details, and placing them in an invented *cadre* in which none other than Cyrus, the son of the King of Persia, figures. A final comment reads:

Après avoir lu cet Extrait, on pourra nous faire le reproche, bien fondé, de n'avoir pas été fidèles au plan de Madame de Villedieu: mais nous espérons qu'on nous pardonnera, en faveur de la fidélité avec laquelle nous avons suivi l'Histoire Grecque. Presque tous les traits que l'on trouve ici, se retrouvent dans les Vies des Hommes Illustres de Plutarque. . . .[24]

We witness the perhaps unusual spectacle of an authoress corrected by means of her own source. Chatenet has given summaries of two of the stories (*Solon* and *Socrate*).[25] There are in all seven stories, totalling 448 pages:

Solon. Solon loves Orgine of Salamine, whom he cannot marry (according to Athenian law). He learns that Peisistratus, also in love with Orgine, holds her captive

---

[20] *Loc. cit.* Cf. the discussion of Villedieu's death in Ch. I, above.

[21] Mlle Desjardins was repaying Louis for the pension he had recently granted her; cf. Ch. I, above. Derome does not give the *achevé* of the work, but the first edition in the Bib. Nat. has 1671.

[22] A second Barbin edition of Paris, 1671; Cologne, Marteau, 1676; Paris, Barbin, 1678; Amsterdam, Hoogenhuysen, 1692; Lyon, Besson, 1696; and possibly La Haye, 1688 and Amsterdam, 1695, 1703, and 1710 (cf. Magne's bibliography). It occupies Vol. V of the 1741 edition of the *Œuvres*.

[23] According to Hauréau, *loc. cit.*

[24] *BUR*, May, 1776, pp. 90-145; quotation from p. 145.

[25] *Op. cit.*, pp. 210-215.

in his house. Solon's jealousy arouses Peisistratus' suspicions and the latter decides to take Orgine away from the city. Orgine however persuades a slave girl to go in her stead, and remains behind, revealing her trick to Solon. It then develops that the slave girl, Hyparette, is Solon's daughter, banished by him from Athens because an Oracle had predicted that she would bring ruin to the city. Overcome by the turn of events, Solon goes on the long journey during which he is supposed to have met Croesus. He formulates his famous laws, one of which repeals the ban against marriages with outsiders. Orgine receives a code of private "Loix d'amour" to govern her conduct. Whether Solon and Orgine are married or not, we are not told, for the "Auteurs secrets" from which the story is drawn, do not relate whether Orgine followed Solon into his voluntary exile.

Socrates. The young and beautiful Timandre has been entrusted to Socrates by a friend now dead. To allay the jealousy of his wife Myrto he has placed Timandre in the care of the woman astrologer Aglaonice. Socrates pretends that he is interested solely in the education of Timandre's mind, but his wife accuses him of self-deception and denounces the relationship as immoral and unworthy of the Sage. Alcibiades hears of Socrates' ward and has his curiosity aroused by Socrates' jealous concealment of her. Disguised as a Phrygian he calls at Aglaonice's house, but the latter pretends to be Timandre and Alcibiades leaves in disgust after Aglaonice has divined at his request the present actions of the famous Alcibiades, representing him to be at the moment cloistered with a renowned beauty. Overhearing Socrates congratulate Aglaonice on her protection of his ward from Alcibiades, Timandre is filled with curiosity to meet the well-known lover. She sends him a note, to which he replies curtly. Aglaonice, taken with Alcibiades' charms, also sends him notes, which he returns. At length, angered by the constant communications from the one he believes to be Timandre, Alcibiades sends his old nurse with a letter to Timandre refusing all commerce with her. The nurse, finding the true Timandre, is astonished to see her master turning down the favors of a young and beautiful girl, and tells him so on her return. Suspecting the trick played on him, Alcibiades has his nurse disguise herself as a *marchande de curiosités* and go to verify the identity of Timandre. When all doubt has been removed, Alcibiades makes a rendezvous with Aglaonice on the outskirts of the city, and, while she is away waiting for him, goes to Timandre, who receives him willingly. Meanwhile Socrates comes upon Aglaonice, finds the letter arranging the rendezvous, and uncovers the plot to deceive him. He hastens to Timandre's house, only to find the lovers already on rather intimate terms. Aglaonice goes to her books to seek the explanation in the stars of her failure in love, and Socrates resigns himself to the loss of his young pupil: "Ce fut le déplaisir que Socrate conçut de cette avanture, qui lui fit supporter la mort avec tant de fermeté."

Julius Caesar. Caesar, married to Pompeia, sister of Pompey, loves Pompey's wife Murcie. Cato's sister Servilia, who once was loved by Caesar, becomes jealous, and manages to reawaken Caesar's interest in her. Cato is angered and tells the story to Pompey. Pompey is at first inclined to laugh at Cato's concern for his sister, until he learns that Caesar also loves his own wife. This discovery by Pompey arouses the well-known enmity between the two great men.

Cato. Cato relates to Pompey how his friend Hortensius came to his house and made love to his wife Marcia. The latter, to get out of an awkward situation when

Cato found her writing a love letter to Hortensius, has signed—while Cato watched her—her sister-in-law Porcie's name to it, and told her husband that Hortensius was in love with Porcie and that she was acting as go-between for the two. Cato delivers the letter to Hortensius and upbraids him. Finally, however, he learns the truth, but instead of punishing Marcia, he makes out a contract releasing her and allowing her to marry Hortensius, whom he feels convinced she will later deceive as she has him. He seeks to humiliate her by his dignified indifference, but confesses to Pompey that he still loves her and yearns to go back to her. Pompey discourages him and tells Cato of his own love for a certain Flore, whom he has not allowed himself to seduce, out of regard for his friend Geminius who is in love with her.

Bussy d'Amboise. Bussy loves the widow of the Maréchal de Saint-André, but has two rivals, Ligneroles and Neufville. His former mistress, Château-Neuf, counsels him to overcome his rivals through generosity. Bussy succeeds with Ligneroles, whom he protects from the consequences of having divulged a state secret ("que le mariage de Madame et le Roi de Navarre . . . fut un ingénieux prétexte pour se défaire plus sûrement des Huguenots"—p. 147); Ligneroles gives up the Maréchale and even intercedes with her in favor of Bussy. When Bussy and the Maréchale meet in the *Salle d'armes* at Chantilly, she seizes a dagger and challenges him half seriously. They are overcome with emotion; Bussy protests that his relationship with Château-Neuf is innocent, and the Maréchale that hers with Neufville is only a device to make Bussy jealous. They enjoy great happiness until the Maréchale meets an untimely death: Jeanne d'Albret had given her, unknowingly, one of the pairs of poisoned "gans parfumez" which she had received from Catherine de' Medici, and which brought about her own death shortly afterwards.[26]

D'Andelot. D'Andelot loves the Amirale de Brion, who wagers he cannot win her in two months. The crafty courtesan Fontpertuis will be the judge of their wager. D'Andelot courts his mistress in various manners, once, for example, by telling her the story of a painting of a scene from the *Gerusalemme liberata*, in which Armida falls in love with Rinaldo. They meet at a ball, gamble together, have the usual misunderstandings about each other's relationships with other people. Fontpertuis helps d'Andelot win his suit, but not before there has been a general mix-up when Madame d'Aumale gives the Amirale a Chinese lounging gown like her own and the two women are mistaken for each other in the gardens, on the terraces, etc. After an exchange of letters and a reconciliation between the lovers, Fontpertuis spoils the situation by demanding as a reward for her services to d'Andelot a share of his favors. D'Andelot refuses, and Fontpertuis contrives to persuade the Amirale that he is unfaithful to her with Madame d'Aumale, thus turning her love for him into hate. At last d'Andelot explains his actions to Madame de Brion, and they again swear eternal love.

Alcibiades. Alcibiades loves Pericles' wife Aspasia, whom he pretends to give up when Socrates upbraids him. After many escapades, during one of which Alcibiades is rumored to have perished in a shipwreck, Pericles finds that Aspasia has been unfaithful to him with Alcibiades and dies of heart-break. Alcibiades' rival Théramène

---

[26] For this legend, see below. The Maréchale, as a matter of historical fact, died two years after Jeanne d'Albret (in 1574).

persuades the Athenians to declare war against Sicily. While Alcibiades and Niceas are away conducting the war, the people of Athens turn against the former, even accusing him of breaking all the statues of Mercury which were destroyed during the night before he left. They attempt to recall him, but he flees to Sparta. Aspasia hears that he has become the lover of the Queen of Sparta, and becomes herself the mistress of Théramène. Alcibiades, who, until he learns this news, has been faithful to his Athenian love, now accepts the advances of the Queen of Sparta and becomes her lover, during the absence of her husband. A son is born to them. When the King of Sparta returns he suspects Alcibiades, but bides his time until he can identify him with certainty as the father of his wife's child. A spy reports a night rendezvous of Alcibiades and the Queen, and the King issues orders that the Athenian be killed, but he manages to escape. "Je n'entends point," writes Mlle Desjardins, "de rapporter son retour dans Athènes, et ses glorieuses victoires, dont les Historiens parlent tant."

The source utilized by Mlle Desjardins for her Greek and Roman characters was the same as that to which the author of the analyses in the *BUR* turned later for his information—Plutarch. Her system was this: taking from the *Lives* her names and an occasional incident or bit of action, she invented around her figures a plot, almost entirely amorous in nature — as suggested by her title — in which, by a stretch of the imagination, they may have been involved. It is the same technique as that employed by La Calprenède in *Cassandre* and *Cléopâtre*.[27] Plutarch's life of Solon gave her the *données* of the rivalry between the lawgiver and Peisistratus—which were, of course, not based on any amorous competition — Solon's long journey and his legendary meeting with Croesus, his giving of the laws, etc. Orgine and Hyparette, around whom the action turns, are pure inventions of a mind saturated with the romanesque tradition of the heroic novel. Yet a new rationalization lies behind the emphasis on love and its effects: the belief, or pretended belief, that the great events of the past may be explained by the passions and amorous intrigues hidden beneath the cloak of history as it has been written down. The same theme is developed by Mlle Desjardins in the introduction to her *Annales galantes* of the previous year, and was later to be inserted into the body of the work itself—like the moral at the end of a fable—in the *Désordres de l'amour* (see Chapter V, above) and the *Portrait des foiblesses humaines*. Thus, the famous laws of Solon concerning marriage were created by him solely because, "voulant hâter

---

[27] See Ch. V, above, for a discussion of the seventeenth-century theories of the use of history in the novel. The popularity of Father Caussin's *Cour Sainte* and the wide use of it as a source for plays on graeco-roman subjects is another evidence of the widespread interest in such matters. See Hocking, *op. cit.*

les momens de sa félicité," he desired to clear the way legally for his union with a non-Athenian woman. Nor does the author blush to offer the reader—who doubtless accepted her premise as a conventional gambit —some hitherto unknown laws composed by the great Solon, concerning love and the proper conduct of lovers. This is part of their burden:

LOIX D'AMOUR

Qui veut aimer parfaitement
Doit se faire surtout une Loy du Mystere;
Des plaisirs de l'Amour, c'est l'assaisonnement. . . .

De l'excès de délicatesse,
Fait souvent, celui du bonheur. . . .

Dans les nouveaux Amans rien n'est plus ordinaire,
Que le vœu solennel d'éternelles Amours . . . etc.[28]

The story of Socrates greatly resembles the kind of satirical play about the pedant which was popular in the Italian theatre of the day. Its source may be a lost *novella* or *canevas*. The coherence and dramatic neatness of its plot is unusual for Mlle Desjardins, and increases the suspicion that it is not of her own invention. Perhaps the most interesting fact about it is that it became the textual source for a farce entitled *Le Docteur amoureux*, published for the first time in 1937. This farce appears to have been written almost certainly after 1683, and probably as late as 1694. It belongs to the *Théâtre italien*, and in it Socrates becomes a modern pedant, the Docteur Metaphraste. The other characters are similarly modernized: Alcibiades' nurse becomes the hero Lelio's valet, etc. A scene and a half of dialogue, a short song, and two scenes in pantomime (a serenade) were added to fill out the three acts of the farce, but its structure and speeches—with these exceptions—were copied directly from the work of Mlle Desjardins.[29]

The stories of Caesar and Cato are probably pure inventions. The characters and the semblance of historical atmosphere which surrounds them were doubtless taken from the obvious source, Plutarch's lives of Caesar, Pompey, and Cato. Plutarch mentions the strange contract by

---

[28] *Œuvres*, V, 25-26. Unlike most of the interpolations in verse of this nature found in Mlle Desjardins' works, these *Loix* were not reproduced elsewhere. Cf. Ch. II, above.

[29] *Five French Farces, 1655-1694?* A critical edition by H. C. Lancaster, assisted by the members of his seminar, 1935-1937, Baltimore, 1937, pp. 18-20 and 112 ff. The borrowing is discussed in my article "*Les Amours des grands hommes* of Mlle Desjardins and *le Docteur amoureux*," in *MLN*, LIII (1938), 344-347. See also Lancaster, *A History of French Dramatic Literature* . . . IV (II), 697-698.

which Cato ceded his wife to Hortensius, but does not explain it. Portia is referred to as Cato's sister. With these simple *données*, the imagination of Mlle Desjardins could have had little difficulty constructing the plot outlined above. The episode in which Marcia deceives Cato into believing a love letter she has written to Hortensius comes from her sister-in-law Portia, and persuades him to deliver it to her lover, seems to have suggested to an eighteenth-century critic that the central theme of the story was taken by Mlle Desjardins from Molière's *École des maris*, in which Isabelle escapes the wrath of Sganarelle by pretending her own amorous escapades are really those of her sister Leonor. The critic writes:

> Caton est le Sganarelle; Hortensius le Valère, Martia l'Isabelle, et Porcie la Léonore. Martia choisit Caton pour rendre les lettres amoureuses à Hortensius feignant que c'est de la part de Porcie sa sœur, etc.[30]

One cannot deny a certain similarity between the two works, but there is no evidence whatever of direct borrowing.[31] Cato, moreover, far from resembling Sganarelle, is rather an example of the new fictional type of the self-sacrificing, noble husband found in the *Princesse de Clèves* and in Mlle Desjardins' own *Désordres de l'amour*.

Plutarch's life of Alcibiades furnished most of the material around which Mlle Desjardins wove the last story in her collection: the turning of the Athenians against Alcibiades, his sojourn in Sparta, etc. Thucydides recounts the incident of the breaking of the statues of Mercury, and states that the crime was blamed by some on Alcibiades. Mlle Desjardins added his love for Aspasia (who becomes in her story the wife of Pericles), his rivalry with Théramène, the "Milesian" episodes of the false reports of death by drowning, the intrigue and affair with the Queen of Sparta, etc.[32] Though the authoress forswore treating of Alcibiades' return to Athens and his subsequent adventures, she returned to her character some fourteen years later, and added precisely this sequel.[33]

---

[30] The abbé de la Porte, *Histoire littéraire des dames françoises*, II, 48. The affair of the letter recalls also the complicated misunderstandings of the second act of *Dom Garcie* (1661) and of its Italian source (Cicognini).

[31] Cf. also Kretschmar, *op. cit.*, p. 54.

[32] Quinaut had written a play entitled *Le faux Alcibiade*, but Mlle Desjardins' story bears no resemblance to it.

[33] In the *Portrait des foiblesses humaines* (1685). The author of the summary in the *BUR*, May, 1776, pp. 90 ff., writes: "Les Amours d'Alcibiade, que Madame de Villedieu a placés dans le Portrait des foiblesses humaines, se trouvent encore dans les Amours des grands hommes, et y sont fort différemment tournés." The books appeared in the reverse order, and the stories, as stated above, concern two different periods in Alcibiades' life. Mlle Desjardins' chronology is so entangled that Pericles,

The two stories of Bussy d'Amboise and of d'Andelot belong rather to the *genre* of historical *nouvelle* treated in Chapter V, than to the *bloc* of graeco-roman and exotic novels and stories under consideration here. Their plots and atmosphere closely resemble those of the *Journal amoureux* (1669) and the *Annales galantes* (1670), with perhaps a slight foretaste of the more passionate, less *galant* conception of the *Désordres de l'amour* (1675). There is an effort to present realistically genuine feeling, beneath superficially *galant* speeches, which results in passages comparable to the best in Mlle Desjardins:

> Il y avoit dans Chantilly une sale et un cabinet d'armes. . . . Sur toutes choses, on y estimoit . . . un poignard tout semé de rubis. . . . La Maréchale voulut le voir. L'ayant vû assez de tems, et Bussy n'étant pas loin d'elle elle s'avança, vers lui, tira le poignard, et en portant la pointe d'un air menaçant, jusques sur le cœur de Bussy; À quel usage, lui dit-elle, ceci devroit-il être destiné? À percer le plus perfide de tous les cœurs, lui répondit-il en prenant la pointe du poignard et le tournant vers celui de la Maréchale. . . . Ah! Bussy, repartit-elle avec un air triste, mais amoureux, il n'en fut jamais un plus infidele. Que le vôtre, Madame, interrompit-il. . . .[34]

The historical documentation, like that of the works discussed in Chapter V, appears to have been taken from popular sources of the day.[35] Mlle Desjardins pretends, as in her other historical works, to a complete understanding of the inside story of all political events and intrigues, and freely invents anecdotes and situations to explain them. She also accepts the legends found in the works of the historians of her century (as did Saint-Réal that of Dom Carlos), and even embroiders upon them, as, for example, in the ingenious manner in which she allows the Maréchale to die, in the story of Bussy. She writes:

> On parla diversement de cette mort, mais trois jours après, celle de la Reine de Navarre étant arrivée, on en soupçonna les gans parfumez du Florentin; et dans les soupçons éclairés, on trouva que la Reine de Navarre avoit donné une de ces paires de gans à la Maréchale.[36]

The accusation that Catherine de' Medici had killed Jeanne d'Albret by

---

who dies in the *Amours*, is represented as still alive in the *Portrait des foiblesses humaines*.

[34] *Œuvres*, V, 197.

[35] D'Andelot is mentioned, though not extensively, by d'Aubigné (*Hist. univ.*, ed. S.H.F., III, 335; IX, 11 ff.), Anselme (*Hist. généal.*), and Brantôme (*Mém.*, ed. S.H.F., I, 222, etc.). Bussy is mentioned chiefly by Brantôme (*ibid.*, VI, 177-193, etc.), L'Estoile (*Journal*), de Thou (*Hist. univ.*), Marguerite de Valois (*Mémoires*), and Rosset (*Hist. tragiques*, 1615). Cf. Ch. V, above.

[36] *Œuvres*, V, 212.

some such device is found in Davila, d'Aubigné, Mézeray, and other historians. The closest parallel to Mlle Desjardins' version occurs in Mézeray:

. . . il y en eut qui dirent qu'elle [Jeanne] avoit esté empoisonnée par des gans et des collets qu'elle acheta chez un certain Parfumeur nommé René, Milanois de naissance. . . .[37]

The *Milanois* became "le Florentin," whose occupation as a perfumer doubtless caused the legend to acquire ultimately the picturesque flavor lent it by "perfumed gloves."[38] Extending Catherine's alleged crime to include the accidental death of the Maréchale, though it violated chronology by several years, could have cost only a slight effort to the imaginative Mlle Desjardins.

The *Amours des grands hommes*, therefore, is closely related to the historical-psychological fiction being written at the same time by Mlle Desjardins.[39] In general, the same principle underlies both *genres:* to account for past events of note by the love affairs which may have been concealed behind them. When her scene is classical, her characters and plots lose force and interest, largely because they tend to resemble characters in the pastoral and heroic novels of her predecessors. When her scene is the France of the sixteenth century, they acquire almost immediately a realism and a depth of psychology which belong more to the novel of the type to be produced by Mme de La Fayette and Saint-Réal.

Les Exilez de la cour d'Auguste (1672)

The *privilège* of the *Exilez* was accorded to "la Dame de Ville-Dieu" on February 6, 1672. The *achevé* is of March 24 of the same year.[40]

---

[37] *Op. cit.*, III, 245. Davila says Catherine had the poison administered to Jeanne "nella concia di certi guanti." D'Aubigné attributes the death to "un present de double ducats parfumez." Henri Carré in *Gabrielle d'Estrées, presque-Reine, 1570-1599*, says that a Florentine "banker," Zamet, an agent of Marie de' Medici, poisoned Gabrielle in a similar fashion. Richard Le Gallienne repeats this version in *From a Paris Scrapbook*, pp. 122 ff.

[38] The *Grand Larousse Universel*, under "Jeanne d'Albret," quotes the passage referred to above from Davila, in French translation, and the phrase "gants parfumés" is used in it, though it is not in the original. It may have been in a translation of the Italian historian consulted by Mlle Desjardins (one which I have not been able to consult appeared in 2 vols., Paris, 1657).

[39] Its theme appears to be echoed in Vaumorière's *Histoire des galanteries des anciens*, 1671.

[40] *Les Exilez*, edition of 1701, Extrait du privilège. Derome, *loc. cit.*, states that only the first volume appeared in 1672, and that the second volume was not published until February, 1673. He also quotes Barbin's remark "qu'il a ce livre depuis trois ans," which would place the composition of it around 1669.

Barbin published two more editions of it, in 1672 and 1675; Besson one at Lyons, in 1696; Brunet one at Paris, in 1701.[41] It appeared in all the collected works and was published à part as late as 1802, at Paris, as *Les Amours des principaux personnages du règne d'Auguste*.[42] There were several translations into English, in 1679, 1726, and 1729.[43] In the opinion of Magne, it is "son ouvrage capital."[44] The verses contained in it enjoyed some popularity, even into the eighteenth century.[45] Mme de Scudéry, wife of the writer Georges, wrote to Bussy-Rabutin about the work, praising it and making this comment:

> ... un petit roman qui s'appelle les *Exilés* qui est très joli. Il y a un endroit qui dit qu'une grande haine qui succède à un grand amour marque encore de l'amour caché; cela m'a fait souvenir de vous. . . .[46]

The *BUR* published "des extraits libres" of the work in 1776, departing radically from the original plots and including in the text many contemporary translations from the works of Catullus, Ovid, Tibullus, etc.[47] The work is in two volumes (pp. 276 and 298), divided into six *Parties*:

> *Partie I.* Ovid, "suspect à l'honneur et à l'amour de César," is exiled to "l'Isle de Thalassie" for "le crime d'avoir trop de charmes." Among his companions in exile are Hortensius and Tisenius Gallus, whose wife, Sulpicie, Ovid had loved in Rome. Ovid overhears two women talking and gets the impression that one of them, Roseline,

[41] This last is the edition I have used. Magne's bibliography also lists editions of Paris, 1684; Utrecht, 1684; and Leiden, 1703.

[42] According to Hauréau, *op. cit.*, p. 34.

[43] *The Unfortunate Heroes, or the adventures of ten famous men*, composed by Monsieur de Villa Dieu [*sic*], London, Herringman, 1679; *The Exiles of the court of Augustus Caesar*, London, D. Browne, 1726 ("from the French of Mademoiselle V"); *The Secret History of the Court of Augustus Caesar*, London, 1729. These translations are in the Library of Congress.

[44] *Op. cit.*, p. 372.

[45] Three pieces were reproduced in the *Recueil Barbin* of 1692, and two of these in the *Recueil* of 1752 (cf. Ch. II, above).

[46] In the Lalanne edition of the letters of Bussy, II, 92. Bussy replied: "Je suis d'accord avec Mlle Desjardins. . . . Je m'en vais mander qu'on m'envoie le roman des *Exiles* puisque vous le trouvez joli" (II, 95). The novel is not mentioned again. The passage referred to is on pp. 128-129; Aurelia insists that "la haine pour ce qu'on a tendrement aimé est une espèce de ruine, qui marque l'endroit de l'embrasement." Cepion himself confesses later that "la haine qui me reste [pour Aurelie] a des transports plus contraires à la tranquilité que le véritable amour" (p. 135). Bayle in his *Dictionnaire* says of the *Exilez* that "c'est un Roman qu'une illustre Dame trouva très joli." In a note he adds "Mme de Sévigné" and refers to Bussy's *Lettres*. It was, however, the wife of Georges de Scudéry who made the comment. For Mme de Scudéry, cf. the article "Sarraide" in Somaize, *op. cit.*, p. 213.

[47] *BUR*, May, August, and October, 1776. Mlle Desjardins' framework of Ovid's exile is used by the *BUR* chiefly as a pretext to quote the Augustan poets in translation.

loves him. In reality she loves Lentulus, who saved her and her brother [really Herennia and Herennius] from the Roman army, and it is her companion Junie who loves the poet.

Partie II. Hortensius tells Lentulus and Ovid how he refused to marry his beloved Aurelia because he thought Cepion to be her lover. Cepion arrives and explains his actions; he loves only Helvetie, niece of Maecenas, who has become a vestal virgin. Herennius reaches Thalassie with his slave-love Agarithe and tells how, when he went to Rome to secure her freedom, Augustus' daughter Julia fell in love with him and tried to persuade him to remain in Rome. He is interrupted by Lentulus, who comes in wounded. Tisenius had learned of Ovid's affair with his wife Sulpicie and had written to the poet asking for a rendezvous; Lentulus, intercepting the letter, had suspected wrongly that it had come from Herennia, had gone to the meeting place and there had been mistaken for Ovid, and wounded.

Partie III. The scene changes to Rome, in the house of Cicero's daughter Tullia, where a banquet is being held for such notables as Horace, Vergil, Cornelius, Agrippa, Julia, Terentia, and Augustus. Agrippa relates an old story of Ovid's attempts to win the favors of Maecenas' wife Terentia and the rivalry of Crassus, and how neither of the lovers could seduce her from virtue. Horace tells of a love affair in which he turned Tullia from Ovid. The feast lasts all night. When Vergil departs he goes to the home of Cornelius Gallus, who relates to him how he has incurred the Emperor's disfavor by pretending to be a prince of Egypt in order to satisfy the demand of his mistress Cytherea, a descendant of a Gallic prince and a woman with political ambitions.

Partie IV. Maecenas is requested by Augustus, who distrusts her, to remove his wife Terentia from Rome, and does so willingly when he discovers that his mistress Phaedra has fallen in love with Crassus. We then return to the home of Cornelius, where Vergil tells of his love for a certain Phila, who has lived disguised for fifteen years as a boy in the house of Cicero, to whom her dead father had entrusted her. Cornelius informs him that he has heard through Cytherea, a friend of Phila's, that Vergil has a rival.

Partie V. Arimant, the lover of Junie (who loves Ovid), has just returned to Thalassie. Herennius' beloved Agarithe tells how she freed her lover from the designs of Julia in Rome and how they finally reached Thalassie after many adventures. Arimant produces a written account of his adventures and gives it to Ovid to read, but he is broken off in the middle of his reading by the arrival of the newly banished Crassus. The latter relates how he met with Tisenius, who, thinking he has avenged himself on Ovid (though in reality it was Lentulus whom he wounded), was en route to Rome to punish Sulpicie for her unfaithfulness.

Partie VI. Julia has had her escaped lover, Herennius, captured and brought back to Rome. Despite the excitement Ovid finds time to make love to Junie. Phaedra, seeking to get over her unreturned love for Crassus, arrives in Thalassie with the news that Maecenas is dead and Crassus recalled to Rome. Cepion now hopes to persuade his Helvetie to give up her status of vestal virgin and marry him. Hortensius expects to be recalled when Cepion explains to Augustus the misunderstanding which had caused him [Hortensius] to refuse Aurelia's hand. These friends promise to work for Ovid's recall. Only Lentulus finds no hope, since his enemy Tiberius will have more power over Augustus, now that Lentulus' friend Maecenas is dead. Ovid then resumes the reading of Arimant's story, which tells how the author, as a slave in Tisenius' home, became the lover of Sulpicie. Tisenius has the misfortune to go to Rome on the same boat which carries back Herennius, and learns from him further evidence of his wife's unfaithfulness. Thus, leaving her "Amans de Thalassie" still "accablez . . . de divers chagrins," the author closes, promising at least another volume in the near future.

As the summary makes clear, the *Exilez* is a work in much the same style as the classical portions of the *Amours des grands hommes*, but with its stories woven together into a more unified pattern, making it, according to the standards of the time, a *roman* and not a collection of *nouvelles*. Its historical period, the reign of Augustus, and many of its characters had appeared in La Calprenède's *Cléopâtre* (1646-1657).[48] The *données* of Ovid's exile, as well as those of the semi-historical *décor* and events near Rome, are to be found in well-known classical sources.[49] For some reason, the real name of the place on the Black Sea to which Ovid was exiled in 8 A. D., Tomi, was changed by Mlle Desjardins to "Thalassie," a word apparently of her own coinage, designed to refer to an island in this sea.[50] Though Ovid is the central figure in the novel, the actual story of the cause of his exile is not presented, and only trivial earlier affairs attributed to him are related. We are told only that Ovid was exiled for being "suspect à l'honneur et à l'amour de César," and for having "trop de charmes." In her next work, however, the *Galanteries grenadines* (1673), the authoress took the trouble to work into the conversation of her characters a further comment on the Latin poet, with a slightly fuller and more accurate explanation of his exile; no doubt critical individuals had spoken to her on the subject and supplied her with information:

[48] The following characters appear in *Cléopâtre* and also in the *Exilez:* Ovid, Augustus, Livia, Tiberius, Julia, Horace, Vergil, Cicero, Lentulus. Desmaretz' *Ariane* (1632) had its scene laid in Rome and Syracuse at the time of Nero.

[49] Suetonius' *Augustus* mentions all the genuine historical personages to be found in the *Exilez:* Agrippa, Julia, Hortensius, Maecenas, Tiberius, Livia, Crassus, Augustus, Terentia, etc. Ovid's own *Tristia* tells of his exile (in a melancholy manner so different from the pastoral gaiety with which Mlle Desjardins depicts it, that one wonders if she could have read the poet's work). The non-historical characters were given common Roman names: Sulpicia, Herennius, etc. There is an "Arimant" in the *Astrée*.

[50] From the Greek word "Thalassa" one would expect in French "Thalasse." Tomi was well known in Mlle Desjardins' day (cf. Moréri's *Dictionnaire*) as the place of Ovid's exile; her new appellation must have been intentional. In one passage (II, 86) the word is written "Thessalie," probably a printer's error.

La conversation se tourne je ne sçai comment sur les malheurs domestiques de l'Empereur Auguste. . . . Les plus grands desordres de Julie . . . dit la Princesse . . . n'ont pas été pendant la vie de Marcel; Agrippa, son second mari, en souffrit plus que le premier, et elle ne fut répudiée que par Tibere. Il est vrai, Madame, repris-je, qu'on n'éclata contre elle, que dans ce tems-là; mais l'exile d'Ovide nous apprend qu'elle n'avoit pas attendu si tard à se revolter contre la tirannie. Les Historiens ne tombent pas d'accord, interrompit Molabut, de ce qui causa l'exile d'Ovide, on en dit une raison, que pour l'honneur des Souverains il est bon de ne pas publier. Et en effet, dans les livres qu'Ovide composa pendant son exil, il ne se plaint que d'avoir trop vû; ce sont ses yeux seuls qu'il accuse de ses malheurs, et il est aisé de conclure de-là, qu'on le perdit, parce qu'il pouvoit parler, plûtôt que pour avoir trop attenté. Mais suppose que son crime ne fut autre chose que d'avoir plû à Julie . . . etc.[51]

The structure of the *Exilez* is similar to that of the heroic novel. The stories making up the work are more uniform than those of *Alcidamie* and less military than those of *Carmante*. Amorous intrigue has supplanted all else, and the novel may well be called by the title given it in 1802, *Les Amours des principaux personnages du règne d'Auguste*. There are no sieges, no heroic exploits, and only one minor personal combat: only love and courtship, jealous misunderstanding, and unfaithfulness — in brief, *galanterie*. *Alcidamie* was composed of stories told by persons gathered in a single place; *Carmante* allowed greater room for pure narration by the author, and its scene moved about Arcadia, following the actions of Evandre, Nicostrate, etc. *Histoires intercalées* abound in the *Exilez*, and indeed constitute most of the work, but there are sudden and severe changes in scene from the shores of the Black Sea to the environs of Rome, and back again. Some characters tell their own stories, some have theirs related by others; one, Arimant, writes his down and has it read aloud by Ovid. The pastoral atmosphere of *Carmante* is replaced by a *cadre* of gallant verses, conversations, *collations,* etc. There are one or two disguises, lost love notes and personal ornaments, cases of mistaken identity, etc. In the stories whose action takes place at Rome, we find occasionally a touch of local color, if such a term may be used to describe the cold, barren notation of a custom, in this fashion: "J'étois un jour au Temple de la Concorde où vôtre belle Épouse offroit un sacrifice . . ." (II, 14)—or the rudimentary evocation of historical *milieu:*

---

[51] *Œuvres*, IV, 531. Ovid writes (*Tristia*, II): "Cur aliquid vidi? . . . Cur imprudenti cognita culpa mihi est?" Ovid had appeared as a sort of Hylas in Gilbert's *Amours d'Ovide*. The true explanation of the poet's exile is still a matter of dispute.

La Judée et la Capadoce vous demandent des Rois, les Armeniens se plaignent du leur, et nous apprenons par les Ambassadeurs des Parthes. . . . Laissons les affaires de l'Empire pour un autre tems, interrompit César, Terentia me trahit (I, 188).

The characters are psychologically simple, and characterized always by one chief quality: Ovid by his clever amorous technique (naturally, since he was the author of the *Art of Love*), Julia by her perverse and nympho-maniac passions, Sulpicie by her weak character and susceptibility to seduction, Tisenius by his genius for misfortune, etc.[52] Jealous accusa-tions or disappointed love provoke them to their greatest outbursts of feeling, which are marked chiefly by changes in the color of their faces and languorous, unhappy postures:

Phedre avoit changé plusieurs fois de couleur pendant ce discours. Elle l'interrompit d'un soûpir à cet endroit, et ne pouvant retenir quelques larmes qui malgré elle vinrent aubord de ses paupieres. Vous êtes un ingrat, me dit-elle, d'un ton de voix tout changé . . . (II, 16).

Il la trouva dans un état qui pensa desarmer son courroux: Elle avoit appris la disgrace de Crassus . . . et ce remord joint à la douleur de voir ses feux méprisez l'accabloit d'une tristesse mortelle. Ses yeux dont l'éclat faisoit ordinairement la plus grande beauté avoient une langueur touchante . . . et son corps . . . étoit negligemment couché sur un lit de repos, dont par sa posture et par son abatement elle sembloit avoir fait un tombeau . . . (II, 49).

Infidelle, s'écria-t-il . . . Phedre tourna languissamment les yeux du côté que cette voix étoit partie . . . Ha, Seigneur, lui dit-elle . . . (II, 50).

Nor do the great figures of history behave otherwise: Agrippa, Vergil, Cornelius, all of them remain preoccupied with jealous, faithless, or unattainable mistresses.

A passage of interest to the historian of ideas occurs when Volumnius is reproached for his prudish asceticism by a typical *mondain*. The argument utilizes several ideas relative to the *apologie du luxe* found later in Saint-Évremond, Mandeville, and Voltaire: the delights of an epicurean existence, the economic usefulness of luxury, and the explana-tion of austerity on psychological grounds as a defense mechanism against frustration and a rationalization of unfulfillment:

Dites, s'il vous plaît, par quels argumens vous pretendez destruire la superbe, et la volupté des Mondains. . . . Que trouvez-vous de dissoulu dans le siecle? . . . On y cherche à vivre commodement, et agréablement. Ne doit-on pas aux Dieux, ce compte des biens qu'ils nous ont departis? Se vous aviez donné à l'un de vos domestiques

---

[52] Raynal, *op. cit.*, p. 199, writes of the *Exilez:* "La psychologie y confine à la pathologie." The statement seems exaggerated.

quelques terres à faire valoir, luy sçauriez-vous bon gré d'en laisser la moitié en friche? . . . La mer nous offre des poissons, il faut les faire pescher. La terre nous offre des fruits, il faut les cueillir. Chaque élément, chaque saison, fournit à l'homme de quoy rendre la vie plus delicieuse. Tout cela ne se fait point en vain. . . .

. . . Vous appelez un vray repos . . . ce chagrin que vous venez d'étaler contre tous les hommes? L'humeur satyrique dont vous estes devoré . . . vous peint l'univers sous des formes hydeuses. . . . Non, Volumnius, vous n'estes point tranquille, vous n'estes qu'aveugle sur vostre trouble intestin. . . . Vous estes plus esclave de vos désirs, que le voluptueux dont vous vous dites le fléau, ne l'est des seins. C'est pour leur obéïr que vous noircissez les actions les plus innocentes, et vous trouvez en cela vostre volupté, comme un autre homme la rencontre dans la satisfaction de ses sens.

Mlle Desjardins thus anticipates some of the most basic ideas of such potent works of the Enlightenment as the *Fable of the Bees* and Voltaire's *Le Mondain*.[53]

The style of the *Exilez* shows no improvement over that of *Alcidamie, Carmante*, or the *Amours des grands hommes*. It is more superficial and more filled with abstractions and clichés than that of her historical novels, and abounds in such phrases as "l'honneur de vaincre quelque Dame," "poursuivit Junie avec la même froideur," "une émotion dont je commençois à reconnoître le caractere," "un cœur véritablement touché," "une passion très sincere," "cette cruelle personne," "un nombre infini de soins," etc. Why Magne should call it her best work and speak of the use made in it of "les procédés de psycho-physiologie"[54] is difficult to understand, although its immense popularity certainly establishes it as one of the best known of her productions. Classical French drama had presented the actions of famous Greeks and Romans more or less within the limits of historical fact and given them the noblest emotions of which the century was capable; Mlle Desjardins, in her *galant* novels about them, would appear rather to have profited by contemporary interest in such subjects by vulgarizing them and reducing them to the size of the personalities of her readers, inventing, for these great and

---

[53] For a somewhat more extended version of this passage and further comment on its implications, see my article "Mlle Desjardins and the *apologie du luxe*," *MLN*, LVI (1941), 209-211. The citation is from Barbin's 1675 edition of *Les Exilez*, p. 271, and is unquestionably the reference intended by the abbé de la Porte when he mentions, without identifying it, a passage in *Les Exilez* which has "tant de rapport avec l'*Anti-Mondain* de M. de Voltaire, qu'on est porté à croire que c'est dans les écrits de Mme de Villedieu, que le Poëte françois a puisé l'idée de cette petite pièce" (the abbé de la Porte, *Histoire littéraire des dames françoises*, II, 21). The abbé exaggerates the resemblance and confuses Voltaire's title with Piron's *Anti-Mondain* of 1738.

[54] *Op. cit.*, p. 372.

famous heroes, tiny love intrigues suitable to the taste of the day. The parallel of John Erskine again comes to mind; no doubt substantially the same audience as his (in a less sophisticated day) read *The Secret History of the Court of Augustus Caesar*.

Les Galanteries grenadines (1673)

The *privilège* of the *Galanteries grenadines* was accorded to "la Dame de Ville-Dieu" on the same date as that of the *Exilez*, February 6, 1672.[55] Barbin published the work in 1673.[56] It was published at Brussels in the same year, in the eighteenth-century editions of the *Œuvres*, and separately in 1711 as *Les Avantures et galanteries grenadines*.[57] The *BUR* did not analyze the work, but dismissed it with these words:

> *Les Galanteries grenadines* contiennent des aventures que l'on suppose arrivées à ces Maures d'Espagne, que l'on a trouvé si intéressans dans le Roman de Zaïde et dans quelques autres. Madame de Villedieu leur a fait perdre un peu de cet avantàge.[58]

The novel runs to some 180 pages and is composed of a main plot interrupted by five much entangled subplots. I have arranged the synopsis so that each story may be read separately, and have indicated the point in the main story at which the *histoire intercalée* is introduced:

> *Histoire du Marquis de Caly et de la Princesse Moraysele.* Prince Muça, son of King Muley-Hassan of Granada, encounters near the palace at night the Marquis de Caly, a Spaniard, who is in reality Dom Manuel Ponce de León. The latter tells Muça the story of his love for the Prince's half sister, Moraysele, whom he saw first at a tournament, falling in love with her at sight. As victor in the tournament, he received a bracelet from Moraysele and a request to come to see her. To his disappointment he finds it is the elder Moraysele who has summoned him, and leaves to return to Spain. A slave follows him, gives him a scarf from the young Moraysele, and informs him the latter too wishes to see him. Disguised as a Turkish slave, Caly returns to the court of Granada and there pays court to the Princess, joining in the endless festivals and games. He saves the Princess from the inevitable wild boar [cf. *Polexandre*, *Alcidamie*, etc.], and they pledge eternal constancy. Moraysele comes to believe Caly guilty of infidelity and marries Prince Abdily, who shortly becomes King. Caly asks Muça to arrange an interview between himself and Moraysele; the Prince, who doubts Abdily's love for the Queen, consents. Caly, disguised as a seer, answers a series of amorous questions put to him by Moraysele. When the Queen has gone, a Mufti tells Caly the complete story of her *galanteries* and lies, which include

---

[55] Derome, *loc. cit.*
[56] Magne, *op. cit.*, p. 417.
[57] Magne, *loc. cit.*; cf. below.
[58] *BUR*, March, 1776.

the deception of several men whom she pretended to love. Caly falls to brooding, and the authoress laments that "cette inquiétude" did not constitute for him "un fidele avertissement." But the two are destined to meet again, with tragic results. The story ends with the promise of a continuation.

Histoire de Malique Alabez et de Cohayde. Malique relates while Caly and Muça are at court the story of Cohayde's unreturned love for him. Only when he learned that the girl had turned in despair to another of the same name as he, were his jealousy and love for her aroused. Fortunately Malique's homonymic Sosie is killed in a battle.

Histoire de Gazul et de la Princesse de Fez. Gazul, ambassador of Muley-Hassan to Fez, relates to Caly and Muça how he fell in love with Zaïde, daughter of Mecmed of Fez. For political reasons the two were forced to keep their love secret; but both were surprised at a nocturnal rendezvous and Gazul forced to give up his ambassadorship and return to Granada.

Histoire d'Abenhamet, d'Abendaraez, et de Zulemaïde. When Caly has finished his story, he sees two men dueling and stops them. They are Abenhamet and Abendaraez. The latter relates how Abenhamet scorned the love of Zulemaïde, who then turned to him, at last provoking Abenhamet's jealousy and bringing about their duel. Abenhamet promises not to resort to force and to try to win back Zulemaïde through demonstrations and proofs of his love.

Histoire de Hache. At this point the men rescue a maiden in distress from capture by bandits. She turns out to be Hache, daughter of the Governor of Ronda, a former mistress of Abenhamet, who has been promised by her father to Gomele. Hache seeks protection from her father with Muça, who grants it. Abenhamet is consumed with new love for her, thus provoking the jealousy of Zulemaïde, who though really in love with Abendaraez, cannot accept the loss of a suitor to another woman.

Tendre confession de cœur. As the party moves towards Granada, they are met by an unknown man, who relates the story of his great love for a woman who has left him, and for whom he seeks. Muça suspects that the unknown is really a woman in disguise, abandoned by a man; but the stranger begs the company to wait until their arrival in Granada before asking that the mystery be disclosed.

With its main story and most of its minor ones incomplete, the novel ends. The promised sequel was never written, probably because the work did not please a public acquainted with more ambitious and successful novels in the same *genre*, Mlle de Scudéry's (or her brother's) *Almahide* and the Segrais-Mme de La Fayette work, *Zaïde*.[59] There is evidence that she also had competition in the Moorish field from Mlle de la Roche, who translated the common source of these works, Pérez de Hita's *Guerras*

---

[59] *Almahide*, 1660-1663; *Zaïde*, 1670. The two simultaneous editions of the *Galanteries* in 1673 were not followed, as usually happened in the case of Mlle Desjardins' popular works, by others.

civiles de Granada, in 1683, and who wrote a Moorish *Almanzaïde* in 1674 and an *Avantures grenadines* at an uncertain date.[60]

That the *Guerras civiles* was the source of these Moorish compositions was recognized by the public of the eighteenth if not of the seventeenth century. The *BUR*, in its preface to an abridgment of Pérez de Hita's work, states:

Ce livre est la source de tout ce que nous avons de Romans François qui roulent sur les galanteries et les aventures des Maures de Grenade, tels qu'*Almahide*, de Mademoiselle de Scudéry; *Zaïde* de Madame de La Fayette; *les Galanteries grenadines*, de Madame de Villedieu; *les Avantures grenadines*, de Mademoiselle de la Rocheguilhem; *l'Histoire de la conquête de Grenade*, par Madame de Gomez, etc.[61]

The *BUR* mentions specifically a Spanish edition of the *Guerras* published at Paris in 1660[62] which must have circulated widely during the publication of *Almahide* (1660-1663) and which may have been utilized by Mlle Desjardins rather than the earlier but rare French translation of 1606.[63] No doubt the success of both *Almahide* and *Zaïde* gave Mlle Desjardins the idea of writing something in the same vein.[64] Unfortunately, her work did not please the public. The only favorable word we have of it comes from the romantic enthusiast, Neveu: "*Les Galanteries grenadines*, orientale digne de soupirer dans les amoureuses colonnades de l'Alhambra! . . ."[65]

---

[60] Lanson and the editor of the *Centro de Estudios Históricos* (1913) edition of the *Guerras civiles* list the Roche translation of 1683; the latter calls it "una adaptación más bien que una traducción." The *BUR* is of the same opinion: "Mlle de la Rocheguilhem en a peine donné une idée imparfaite" (January, 1778). Dallas and Williams list *Almanzaïde*; Wurzbach and the *BUR* list the *Avantures grenadines*, the *BUR* mentioning it in a list of novels drawn from the *Guerras*, among which figures Mlle Desjardins' work. The title listed by Magne, *Les Avantures et galanteries grenadines*, 1711, is apparently a combination of the *Galanteries grenadines* and Mlle de la Roche's *Avantures grenadines*.

[61] *BUR*, January, 1778.

[62] Also listed by Lanson and in the *Centro de Estudios Históricos* edition of the *Guerras*.

[63] The evidence of the composition of *Le Favory* seems to prove that Mlle Desjardins could read Spanish, or at least was able to avail herself of the original, perhaps with the assistance of a translator. Lanson and the modern editor of Pérez de Hita list the 1606 translation, which appears to have been unknown, at least at the time of the *BUR*. Kretschmar erroneously states that the first translation of the *Guerras* is of 1809, and that therefore "muss sie es im Urtext gelesen haben" (*op. cit.*, p. 70).

[64] This is the opinion of H. Koerting (*Gesch. des fr. Romans im XVII Jahrh.*, Leipzig, 1885), W. von Wurzbach (*Gesch. des fr. Romans*, Heidelberg, 1912, p. 380), and Cazenave (*loc. cit.*, and see below). *Zaïde* had seven editions before 1700.

[65] *Op. cit.*, p. 6.

Jean Cazenave, in an article on the Hispano-Mauresque novel in France, considers the *Galanteries* merely one in the series of works drawn directly from the *Guerras civiles*, and after discussing *Almahide* and *Zaïde*, makes these comments:

> On gagne peu à parcourir ce volume, où l'auteur s'est contenté de prendre dans les *Guerres civiles* les histoires amoureuses et les descriptions de fêtes. Toute la partie historique a disparu: il n'est plus question du siège de Grenade . . . il ne s'agit plus que des aventures galantes. . . . Tous les personnages de Pérez de Hita défilent sous nos yeux dans les *Galanteries grenadines*; mais ils se sont efféminés. Les chevaliers . . . ne sont plus que des courtisans parés et doctes; ils ne songent qu'aux plaisirs de l'amour et des fêtes brillantes. . . . Dans ces salons les maures et les Espagnols font assaut d'esprit, étalent leurs connaissances, proposant des énigmes à résoudre. . . . Le livre de Mme de Villedieu est un ouvrage de pure imitation, mal écrit et dont la galanterie quintessenciée rend la lecture fort ennuyeuse.[66]

This judgment seems substantially correct. All the characters are drawn from the *Guerras*, though they are sometimes paired off differently; and the existence in the original of festivals and courtly gatherings (cf. those of Chapters IX and X) seems to have encouraged her in her natural *penchant* for such things, visible in many of the novels already discussed. The little "Romances, Vers et Chansons, dont l'ouvrage est rempli, à la mode des anciens Romans espagnols,"[67] which reappear frequently in *Almahide*, are dropped completely by Mlle Desjardins. Reminiscences of the *Astrée* (the "Articles de liberté" of Hache [p. 592], a well-worn theme even for Marie-Catherine) and of the heroic novel, probably the *Grand Cyrus* (the "énigmes" and "réponses" on pp. 619 ff.), appear. Certain *traits de mœurs* creep in, for example, the lotteries (p. 537) popular at the time.[68] All the romanesque apparatus of disguises, lost and found letters and tablets, mistaken identities, etc., is used. A tourney is mentioned, and there is one single combat (between Caly and Alabez), which is also in the *Guerras*, and an *enlèvement* (Hache), also in the original (Chapter VIII). The great festivals of Pérez de Hita (*Guerras*, Chapters IX and X) are transformed into a sort of *comédie-ballet* (pp. 480 ff.), with music, a *collation*, and even "une machine roulante" for the stage (p. 483). Mlle Desjardins does not copy literally any of the lines or descriptions from the Spanish work, but rather takes it as a point of

---

[66] *Loc. cit.* Chatenet, *op. cit.*, p. 218, finds that "les descriptions et le merveilleux dominent," though there are few descriptions and no "merveilleux" whatever.

[67] *BUR*, January, 1778, p. 8.

[68] Cf. two plays on the theme, Montfleury's *Gentilhomme de la Beauce* (1670) and de Visé's *Intrigues de la lotterie* (1670).

departure to construct the Versailles-ballet sort of *tableaux* in which she had already had some experience (see Chapter II, above). She uses her own mottoes, costumes, etc., and most of her figures are cupids, while Pérez de Hita's are dragons, volcanoes, etc.

Jerome W. Schweitzer (in his *Georges de Scudéry's "Almahide,"* Baltimore, 1939, pp. 27-28) assigns *Almahide* to Georges de Scudéry, and considers the possible influence of that novel, itself an imitation of the *Guerras civiles*, upon Mlle Desjardins' *Galanteries grenadines*. In both works Ponce de León, who in the *Guerras* is only an *aficionado* of tourneys, becomes the leading character, disguising himself as a slave, saving the heroine from a wild animal, etc. Scudéry makes an *inconstant* of Abendaraez as Mlle Desjardins does with Abenhamet. Schweitzer uncovers no evidence, however, of direct borrowing by Mlle Desjardins from *Almahide*. The presence in minor episodes of the *Galanteries* of such names from Hita's work as Zulemaïde, Molabut, Alasire, and Zoroïre (not found in *Almahide*) proves that Mlle Desjardins must have been familiar with the Spanish original or a close translation of it.

The characterization, structure, and style of the *Galanteries*, as may be gathered from the foregoing, hardly merit extensive consideration. For all the Spanish and Moorish names and the use of a Spanish source, the result is almost indistinguishable from the series of *galanteries*, conversations, and relating of personal histories which we have so often examined in Mlle Desjardins, in *Alcidamie, Carmante, Les Exilez*, etc. In this distinctly minor work there is no trace of the genuine emotion which Mlle Desjardins sometimes sought to portray, not a single character whose motives or actions have the slightest psychological interest. Only pseudo-elegance, preciosity, excess of "wit," and superficiality are present, rendered almost unbearable by the artificial "Moorish" *décor*. It is not surprising that the public, with superior pseudo-exotic merchandise available in *Almahide* and elsewhere, did not like the book, and demanded no further editions of it.

Le Portrait des foiblesses humaines (1685)

The *achevé* of this work is dated "le 14 août 1685." It was published by Barbin. There was an edition of Desbordes, Amsterdam, 1685, one of Brunel, Amsterdam, 1694, and one of Baritel, Lyons, 1696; and the work appeared in all the eighteenth-century editions of the *Œuvres com-*

plètes.[69] Though its first publication occurred two years after her death, Mlle Desjardins is spoken of in the publisher's *Avis* as still alive, a fact which suggests that the *Portrait* was written and in Barbin's hands before October of 1683.[70] The *Mercure galant*, in mentioning Mlle Desjardins' death, states that Barbin still has certain unpublished works by her, naming the *Portrait* specifically.[71]

The work is comparatively short (117 pages) and divided into four separate stories. In the same sense as the *Désordres de l'amour*, it is a *roman à thèse:* but, whereas the former had attempted to show that love alone was the principal source of various historical actions, this time a greater variety of emotions and passions are proposed as causes—ambition, vanity, egoism, excessive high-mindedness, and even a neurotic dissatisfaction with life (in the story of Paul Émile). Like the *Amours des grands hommes*, the novel alternates between Greek and Roman settings; and, as mentioned above, some of the same characters appear (Pericles, Alcibiades, Lycurgus, etc.) :

The Empress Livia hates Germanicus' widow Agrippina because of her great virtue She uses Sejanus to bring Agrippina into disfavor with Tiberius: Sejanus wishes to have Agrippina's sister-in-law Livia divorced from Tiberius' son Drusus in order to marry her himself, and when Agrippina protests, denouncing divorce, Tiberius, construing her action as an insult to Augustus and his mother, a divorcée, has her thrown into prison. Her end accomplished, the Empress undermines the favor into which Sejanus has risen with Tiberius by persuading the Emperor that his favorite has political ambitions dangerous to his throne. Drusus dies and the Empress accuses Sejanus of poisoning him. Tiberius sentences Sejanus to death, but the latter kills himself. Thus high-mindedness has brought Agrippina into disgrace, and ambition and vanity have brought about the ruin of Sejanus.

Pericles fears that the ambitious Alcibiades, who is returning to Athens covered with fame and glory, can hurt his position, and so wishes to destroy him. He persuades his wife Dionie [Aspasia], whom he has stolen from the tyrant Thrasibule and secretly married, to seduce him. The plan is successful; Alcibiades recognizes Dionie as a former mistress, falls in love with her again, and gives up his ambitious plans. Socrates, disapproving of the relationship, has Dionie accused of treason in an effort to separate the lovers. But when Dionie is banished, Alcibiades follows her into her

---

[69] See Magne, *op. cit.*, p. 417; Derome, *loc. cit.*; and Bayle, *Nouvelles de la république des lettres*. November, 1685 (*Œuvres*, I, 485), who speaks of "la vivacité du style, . . . la délicatesse des pensées, . . . [et] la fidélité des peintures" of the *Portrait*, analyzes two of its stories, and states that "les remarques historiques sont mêlées avec des évenemens forgez à plaisir." The *Portrait* is also mentioned in the *Journal des sçavans*, Nov. 19, 1685.

[70] See Ch. I, above. Barbin pretends to have stolen the work, composed "par une espece de délassement d'esprit," and to be publishing it without the author's consent.

[71] *Le Mercure galant*, November, 1683.

ten-year exile, during which, after the death of both Pericles and Socrates, Athens comes almost to the point of destruction. Thus Pericles' egotistic ambition and Alcibiades' weakness for love are the source of all the ills of Athens.

King Euriston of Sparta wishes to marry his two sons, Polyclete the elder with Cléonice, the daughter of the dead statesman Evander, and Lycurgus the future lawgiver with Argélie, daughter of Codrus. Lycurgus loves his Argélie, but Polyclete loves her too and would rather renounce the throne (occupancy of which hinges on marriage to Cléonice) than give her up. King Euriston has Argélie sequestered in the temple of Minerva and there persuades her that Lycurgus does not love her, so that she consents to marry Polyclete. Thereupon Euriston himself marries Cléonice and they occupy the throne together. Lycurgus, in his hatred and jealousy of his brother, leaves Sparta and seeks consolation with Socrates in Athens. The sage teaches him to draw from his own troubles much wisdom, which he afterward employed in the writing of his famous laws. Once again excessive susceptibility to the passion of love has brought about great difficulties of state, and great personal unhappiness. Polyclete's disobedience of his parents' wishes is also blamed, but this too springs from stubbornness in love.

Paul Émile is unhappily married to Papiria, who is his opposite in every respect and who makes life difficult for him. He wishes to divorce her, but his stepfather dissuades him. When Papiria suddenly dies, several women are offered to Aemilius Paulus to replace her: a virtuous one, a rich one, a beautiful one, etc. He refuses all these to marry the divorced wife of Lucius, who, as an ex-husband, assures his friend that his former wife Servilie never contradicted him. In truth Servilie does not contradict Paul Émile, as Papiria had done, but instead demands complete independence and insists that her life be an endless round of pleasures. Through her frivolity and neglect of her domestic duties she brings the greatest unhappiness to her husband, who through his trifling discontent with a good and virtuous (if quarrelsome) wife is thus brought to ruin.[72]

For once, in the story of Livia and Agrippina, Mlle Desjardins refers specifically to a classical source, Tacitus. She writes: "J'ose, après Tacite Corneille, peindre l'Imperatrice Livie, dévorée de sa propre ambition, et si insatiable de louanges," etc.[73] From Tacitus and possibly from Suetonius' *Tiberius* also, the authoress took the slight basis of fact which underlies her story: Agrippina's high reputation, Sejanus' designs on Livia and his attacks on Agrippina, the Empress Livia's schemes to retain control of the throne by dominating Tiberius, Agrippina's downfall, Drusus' death, and the ruin of Sejanus.[74] Agrippina's arguments against divorce, with her statement that "quand même ces égaremens forceroient une femme à faire ce que vous faites" [her sister-in-law Livia is asking

---

[72] Bayle, *Journal des sçavans, loc. cit.*, chooses for analysis the stories of Livia and Paul Émile, applauding the moral drawn from them.

[73] *Œuvres*, I, 216.

[74] Tacitus, *Ann.*, iv., through vi., especially; cf. Suetonius, *Tiberius*.

permission to sue for divorce], "il faudroit qu'elle menât ensuite une vie si pure et si retirée qu'on ne pût l'accuser de s'être servie d'un faux prétexte pour manquer aux loix de sa gloire et de la foi" (p. 227), are all pure invention, but they throw an interesting light on what the authoress obviously regarded as a most praiseworthy attitude, despite her own marriage with Villedieu, who already possessed one wife, and with the Marquis de Chaste, a *divorcé*. The story of Agrippina is perhaps of all her classical stories the one closest to historical fact.

In her second story of Pericles and Alcibiades, Mlle Desjardins seems to have returned to Plutarch for her material. She represents Pericles as married to Aspasia, and invents the whole love intrigue of the latter with Alcibiades. Plutarch's *Lycurgus* indeed mentions his brother Polydectes, but the whole plot of the two girls, the rivalry of the brothers, etc., is invented. Likewise Plutarch in *Aemilius Paulus* states that the Roman divorced his wife Papiria (in Mlle Desjardins' story she dies) to marry someone else (whose name is not given), but the "inside story" of this maneuver is the product of the authoress' imagination.

The conception, style, and technique of the work are identical with those of the *Amours des grands hommes,* of which it may be looked upon almost as a sequel. Characterization remains at the same level, and her one attempt to create a strong personality in the Empress Livia fails; she is merely another treacherous woman like the Lindarache of *Alcidamie* or the Fontpertuis of the *Amours des grands hommes.* Perhaps the only passage of much interest in the book is the one in which King Euriston of Sparta speaks to his son Polyclete about the beauties and advantages of monarchy by divine right. Just as we may see in Agrippina's tirade against divorce a piece of justificatory writing designed to suit the opinion and attitude of the day, here we find a speech almost worthy of the *plus-royaliste-que-le-roi* defenders of the Sun King, such as Bossuet, with suggestions of Fénelon in one of his descriptions of the moral virtues of beneficent monarchy:

Euriston . . . peignit au Prince les douceurs dans la Royauté. . . . Ne vous imaginez-vous pas, lui disoit-il, la joye que doit avoir un homme de se trouver choisi des Dieux pour exercer leur ministere sur la terre? Que fait dans le Ciel le plus grand des Dieux, qu'un Roi parfait ne fasse dans son Royaume? J'avoue que la puissance divine est éternelle, et que celle d'un Monarque est passagere. Je conviens encore qu'un Souverain n'est absolu que sur ses sujets, et que Jupiter l'est sur toutes les créatures; mais ces exceptions faites, un bon Roi fait la félicité de son peuple, comme les Dieux font celle des hommes. La prosperité des gens de bien; et la punition des méchans, dépendent souverainement de lui. . . . Quand un Roi s'acquite dignement de ses légitimes devoirs, sa vigilance est une participation de la providence divine. . . . Les guerres justes qu'il entreprend, le font craindre: la Paix, qui les suit, le fait aimer. Ses moindres vertus sont louées, ses vices sont dissimulés. . . . Pourvu que ses legitimes devoirs occupent la première place de son cœur, ce qu'il goute ensuite de plaisirs, sont des plaisirs indépendans, qui ne sont troublés par aucune Loi humaine.[75]

Les Annales galantes de Grèce (1687)

The *privilège* for this novel was granted "le 9 août 1685," and the *achevé* is of "le 24 mai 1687."[76] Barbin, who had charge of Mlle Desjardins' literary estate, published the first edition, which was followed by Moetjens' edition at The Hague, 1688, Baritel's at Lyons, 1697, Guérier's in the same city, 1698, and by that of an unnamed editor in Paris, 1700.[77] It was, therefore, well received by the public.[78]

The *Annales galantes de Grèce*[79] occupies some 140 pages in the *Œuvres* of 1741. The work includes one main story and several minor ones:

"Assez d'Auteurs célebres ont pris le soin d'écrire les actions mémorables des anciens Grecs, . . . mais aucun ne s'est encore avisé de parler des Grecques fameuses," begins Mlle Desjardins.[80] Therefore we are told the story of Phronime, Princess of Crete at the time of the thirtieth Olympiad, "en l'an 1400 de la Création du monde." Megabise, Prince of the Minyae, after being saved from death by Praxorine, the Princess of Lacedemonia, comes to Crete disguised as a jewel merchant.[81] He falls

[75] *Œuvres*, I, 277-278. The Christian rationalization is quite visible behind the pagan terminology of "les Dieux," etc. Obviously, Mlle Desjardins is a tolerant subject, giving her King *carte blanche* as far as his private life is concerned, but she does emphasize, if not so strongly as Fénelon, the "devoirs légitimes" of the King.

[76] Cf. Derome, *loc. cit.*

[77] Cf. Magne, *op. cit.*, pp. 413-414; Hauréau, *op. cit.* The "Moetjens La Haye" edition of "1668" listed by Graesse (*loc. cit.*) is obviously an error for 1688, and Magne is mistaken in accepting 1668 as the date of first publication. The work appeared regularly in the eighteenth-century editions of the *Œuvres*.

[78] Times have changed. Mornet writes in the *Romanic Review* for October, 1937: "On peut écrire un gros volume sur la *Princesse de Clèves*, une longue étude sur le *Grand Cyrus*; on conçoit mal cinquante ou même cinq pages sur les *Annales galantes de la Grèce* de Mme de Villedieu."

[79] Analyzed by the *BUR*, November, 1779. For the title, cf. Mlle Desjardins' earlier work, the *Annales galantes*, and the discussion of that title (Ch. V, above). Vaumorière had published in 1676 a work entitled *Les Galanteries amoureuses de la cour de Grèce, ou les amours de Pindare et de Corinne*.

[80] *Œuvres*, VII, 377. Mlle Desjardins herself had of course devoted several novels to the notable actions "des anciens Grecs," in which certain famous Greek women, such as Aspasia, had appeared. Monime and Penelope had also figured in plays.

[81] In the *Amours des grands hommes* (Socrate) Mlle Desjardins had depicted a woman disguised as a *marchande de curiosités*. Similar disguises appeared in

in love with Phronime, and she with him. The King becomes enraged, and he orders Megabise to take Phronime out to sea and throw her into the water. This Megabise does in fact, but not before tying the heroine to a plank which he draws back into the boat, thus fulfilling the letter if not the spirit of the command. Together the lovers go to the island of Theras [or Caliste], the inhabitants of which are descended from the followers of Cadmus on his search for Europa. The *ras*, ruler of the island, makes a long defense of its chief practice, the abduction of wives from their husbands: the latter are kept constantly loving and charming to prevent their wives from accepting the offers of other men to abduct them. Theras tells of his unhappy passion for Olimpie, who can only love a man who is indifferent to her. Praxorine and her *suivant* Aristandre arrive on the island. Praxorine tells the story of how she saved Megabise's life in Lacedemonia by slipping into the prison where he was confined and allowing him to put on her clothes and escape. After tracing him to Crete and learning of his abduction of Phronime, she is still eager to win his love if she can. Meanwhile Polimneste, a local *seigneur*, falls in love with Phronime. Isicrate, a man who appears timid but who has had much amorous experience, tells his story. Another courtier, Léonide, depicts the *parfait amant*; there are many *conversations galantes* on terraces, etc. Polimneste interrupts a duel and the two combatants, Agete and Tersandre, tell the story of their rivalry for the hand of the ugly Deodamie, who by praying to Diana became beautiful, only to be tricked into marriage with Tersandre, to whom Agete had entrusted her. Hebe complains to the company of the unfaithfulness of her lover Adraste with a "belle Étrangere." Deodamie resumes the story of Agete, Tersandre, and herself. Then suddenly, as if bored and weary of her work, Mlle Desjardins writes: "Mais n'y a-t-il assez longtems que nous y séjournons [à Caliste]? Mes Lecteurs ne s'ennuyent-ils pas d'un si long séjour, et ne faut-il point les en délasser par quelques autres recherches?" (p. 513).

The authoress ends her works so often upon this note (*Alcidamie, Les Exilez, Les Galanteries grenadines,* etc.) that we may be justified in assuming that her sense of form, as far as completeness goes, was lacking, and that she did not always feel the same obligation to finish a novel or story which her contemporaries usually felt and which was to become practically a rule for later novelists. Some of her longest novels are "incomplete" in that their stories are not brought to an end: *Alcidamie,* for example. It is as if, having created what we might term a "state of fiction" for a given number of pages, the authoress felt at liberty to end it at will, and to compose for her readers, should they desire further reading matter, some completely different work.

The basis of the story of Phronime is to be found in Herodotus, who mentions the merchant Themison (Megabise) of Thera whom Etearchus of Axus attempted to use to get rid of his daughter Phronime by making

Montauban's pastoral, *Les Charmes de Félicie* (1654) and Boisrobert's *Folle gageure* (1653). Cf. Lancaster, *op. cit.,* III (I), 63, 369.

him promise to take her out to sea and cast her overboard. Tying a rope about her, he threw her into the water, thus fulfilling his promise; then he drew her back into the boat, later taking her to Thera. In both Herodotus and the *Annales galantes de Grèce* Phronime's stepmother is largely responsible for the King's cruel action. Thera is also called Caliste by Herodotus and its inhabitants are said to be descendants of those left there by Cadmus. The story of the Lacedemonian women entering prison and changing clothes with the imprisoned Minyae, thus allowing them to escape, is also related, and becomes the source of the Praxorine episode of Mlle Desjardins' novel. The budding love affair between Phronime and Polymnestes, only hinted at in the novel, is set down by Herodotus: Phronime became his concubine and bore him a stuttering son.[82]

Mlle Desjardins added to the material of her source scenes and actions in her usual style: the pastoral-gallant conversations at the court of Thera, and *histoires intercalées* in the pattern with which we have grown so familiar. There is nothing in the *Annales galantes de Grèce* which was not already in *Alcidamie, Carmante,* or the *Exilez.* Despite her avowed purpose of making the heroine her principal point of interest, the author neglected her almost entirely and dwelt chiefly on the episode of the false drowning, the conversations at Thera, and the trivial minor plots. The style of the work does not differ from the commonplace, dilute solution of d'Urfé and La Calprenède with which Mlle Desjardins began her fictional writings. The characterization is afflicted with the customary elegant, precious "psychology" to which she unfortunately devoted so much of her work, but which appears to have delighted her public and satisfied its literary taste.[83]

Les Nouvelles africaines (1687?)

The passage in the *Mercure galant* of November, 1683, which speaks of Mlle Desjardins' death, states that Barbin has several works of hers yet to be published, among them the *Nouvelles africaines.*[84] The exact date of its first edition is not known; but since the *Portrait,* which is also mentioned in the *Mercure,* appeared in 1685, and the *Annales galantes de*

---

[82] Herodotus, iv., 146-155.

[83] Magne, *op. cit.,* p. 123, note, writes: "Il est parlé élogieusement de Brébeuf dans le roman . . . de notre héroïne, les *Annales galantes de la Grèce.*" A careful reading fails to reveal such a reference.

[84] Cf. above.

Grèce, which is not mentioned, in 1687, we may surmise that it appeared in 1686 or after 1687, probably after 1687. It is a short work (118 pages) of little interest or importance, which Barbin would probably not have hastened to publish. There is no trace of any edition until it began to appear in the eighteenth-century collected works. The *BUR* analyzed it in March, 1776, calling it simply "more interesting" than the *Mémoires du sérail,* a work wrongly attributed to Mlle Desjardins.[85] Chatenet has likewise commented on the work, but very briefly.[86] The main plot is interrupted once by a minor plot, the action of which, so to speak, joins the main plot at the point of interruption:

Albirond must leave France because he has violated the law against duels. He leaves behind his beloved Uranie, and goes to Tunis, where he meets his old friend Mahemet Lapsi, in charge of the fleet of Tunisia. The latter tells Albirond of his love for one of his slaves, a Christian girl, and offers as a sign of his love to become converted to Christianity. Albirond goes to intercede for his friend, but finds that the slave Rahecma is really his own Uranie, who, thinking he had left France to follow a certain Genoese woman who had made overtures to him, had set out in jealous pursuit only to be captured at sea and imprisoned by Mahemet before Albirond arrived in Tunis. The Genoese woman, also a captive of Mahemet, catches sight of Albirond and invites him to a rendezvous which he declines.

A certain Dom Pedre appears on the scene and relates to Albirond how he fell in love in Spain with the lady Isabelle, how he saved her from a wild boar [once more!] only to have his rival the Marquis de Pignastel save her from drowning. A duel between the two rivals is interrupted by Isabelle's brother Dom Alphonse, who is favorable to Pignastel's suit until Dom Pedre saves his life, whereupon he agrees to a plan by which Dom Pedre will abduct Isabelle, marry her, and take her away in a ship. The Corsairs of Tunis have raided the ship and taken Isabelle prisoner, and Mahemet holds her with the other women in his apartments. Dom Pedre and Albirond thus unite to attempt to rescue their mistresses, but the Genoese woman discovers the plot and betrays Albirond to Mahemet, who in a fury issues orders for Albirond to be killed on sight.

Matters remain thus until Albirond emerges from his hiding place in the woods one day to save Mahemet from an attack of bandits. Mahemet, overwhelmed at this act of generosity, gives up Uranie to his rescuer and gives them his blessing. The outcome of Dom Pedre's attempts to free Isabelle is not related, though Mlle Desjardins promises to continue the story in another volume.

In the *Avis* to the above work, we find:

Cette histoire semble n'avoir pas besoin d'un grand éclaircissement; il suffit de dire

---

[85] The *Mémoires* are included in the collected works of Mlle Desjardins. They appeared "le 1 octobre 1670" and were the work of Deschamps (Derome). Mlle Desjardins does not mention them in her list of 1671.

[86] *Op. cit.,* pp. 221-222. See also Kretschmar, *op. cit.*

qu'elle est vraye. . . . Mahemet Lapsi est vivant, il n'a pas encore trente-cinq ans. Il n'y a aucun François qui ait abordé sur les Costes de Barbarie, qui n'ait reçu des marques de sa magnificence. . . . [Quant à] notre Albirond et notre Uranie . . . qu'importe qu'ils soient Monsieur un tel, et Mademoiselle une telle. Ils sont réellement des personnes de notre siecle. Il doit être permis aux gens qui écrivent, de taire ce qu'ils jugent à propos de cacher. . . . Je prépare au Public diverses Histoires, que je tâcherai de bien choisir, et qui seront toutes aussi véritables que celle-ci.[87]

The final pages of the story contain a passage curiously similar to this, a fact which suggests that the *Avis* may be an invention of the publisher, copied from Mlle Desjardins' work with slight changes, and printed at its head to attract readers:

Il n'est pas nécessaire de faire une Préface, pour persuader le Public que ces nouvelles sont autant de vérités. Mahemet Lapsi est encore vivant, et même assez jeune. Il n'aborde aucun Francois de qualité sur la côte de Barbarie qui ne reçoive des marques de la bien-veillance qu'il conserve pour notre Nation . . . (p. 578).

Both passages moreover refer to certain "lettres originales" written in French by Mahemet and seen by the authoress in Paris; the preface links them to two "Chevaliers de Malte" captured and freed by Mahemet, but the story states merely that they are letters "qui feroient honte à certains François" (p. 588). Whatever lies back of this remains a mystery.[88]

It seems probable that the *Nouvelles afriquaines*, like *Lisandre*, is a work of pure invention put forth as true in accordance with the growing taste for the "realities" of historical fiction. The main plot bears certain resemblances to the Scudéry *Ibrahim* (1641). There is an Isabelle in both, and she is a Christian slave, one in a Turkish seraglio, one in the apartments of an Arab. In each case the heroine is loved by her captor. Just as Ibrahim pretends to become a Mohammedan, Mahemet Lapsi wishes to be converted to Christianity. Both captors are at first friends of the Sultan and Corsair, respectively, only to become objects of hatred with sentences of death hanging over them. The Sultan of *Ibrahim* suffers a *crise de conscience* and frees Ibrahim and Isabelle just as Mahemet forgives Albirond and frees Uranie.[89] The Roxane of *Ibrahim* could have suggested the perfidious Genoese woman of Mlle Desjardins' story (Ibrahim, in fact, is a Genoese). Both works contain sea raids, *enlèvements*, etc. The episode of Dom Pedre, which has no counterpart

[87] *Œuvres*, VI, 471.

[88] The name Lapsi suggests the early "relapsed" Christians of Africa; but their sect was extinct long before the seventeenth century.

[89] The name Uranie may have been suggested by a character of that name in *Cléopâtre*.

in *Ibrahim,* appears to be really no more than a duplication, with slight variations, of the story of Albirond himself.

There is little to be said for the composition and style of the *Nouvelles afriquaines.* The work is comparatively free of preciosity, *conversations galantes,* and the like, but on the other hand it falls into the worse error of extravagant actions, wild coincidences, and "Milesian" melodrama. *Traits de mœurs* are few; in one passage, however, a parlor game of the time, the *Jeu de Famille,* is described. Each member of the company draws from a bowl a slip of paper which designates him Father, Mother, Son, etc., of a family, whereupon the rôles are enacted. The Father is

... très-avare, et il fait incessamment des remonstrances inutiles. Les femmes sont ordinairement jalouses, et d'une humeur contrariente. Les fils aînés sont prodigues et débauchés; les filles ont une impatience d'être mariées; les Domestiques sont ennemis secrets de leur Maître, et jusqu'aux amis qu'on met quelques fois dans le corps de la famille, y sement la division, et profitent du désordre qu'ils ont causé (p. 558).

The influence of contemporary comedy appears obvious here: we are in the world of Molière and his successors, exaggerated and caricatured to heighten the effect of stock comic situations. It is rather surprising to find such an essentially bourgeois game described by an authoress most of whose characters are courtly and aristocratic to the utmost, and who seemingly have no families at all, unless it is to have a king for a father or a princess for a sister. The stage, which exploited family situations before they reached the novel, undoubtedly suggested the idea of this upper-class game.

The *Nouvelles afriquaines* may well have been the last work written by Mlle Desjardins. The *Avis* (which she may not have written) speaks of other works in preparation. The *Nouvelles et galanteries chinoises,* the first edition of which appeared *chez* Baritel at Lyons in 1712, was attributed on the title page to "Mlle de Villedieu," but it is hardly likely that Mlle Desjardins could have been the author, since Barbin remained executor of her literary estate and did not publish it, as he would surely have done in the years following 1683. It was not mentioned, further-more, in the list of her works written for the *Journal des sçavans* in 1703.[90] No *éditeur* possessing a manuscript of an authoress so popular with the public would have waited nearly thirty years after her death to publish it. Catherine Ferrand died in 1692, and any manuscripts left

[90] *Journal des sçavans,* XLII, Dec. 17, 1703.

to her by her daughter would have found their way then at least into the hands of a publisher.[91]

The novels and stories treated above represent various tendencies and stages in Mlle Desjardins' literary evolution: the pastoral, the heroic, the *galant*, the exotic (Spanish and Moorish), even the pseudo-historic and didactic (the *Portrait des foiblesses*, for example). They contain few elements not found elsewhere in her works, and represent the average and sub-average achievements of her craft. Most of them were extremely popular at the time, and if we separate them from her historical fiction to show greater esteem for the latter, her contemporaries made no such distinctions. Written in a monotonous, insipid style, full of clichés, they reflect a simplistic psychology, a conventionalized sense of action and *décor*, and a complete acceptance of the literary tradition laid down by the best-known earlier novels of the century. One feels that their author was attempting less to create a work of art according to the dictates of her esthetic sense, than to concoct a familiar potion to please the palate of an employer whose taste she well knew and understood. None of the emotion or insight present in her best historical fiction and in the best of her verse, none of the realistic good sense and pleasant gift of satire visible in her Holland letters, none of the amiable talent for telling a story, found for example in the *Annales galantes*, appears in sufficient quantity in the foregoing works to lift them above mediocrity. The anatomical interest which scholarship may take in dissecting them and attempting to account for their heredity and physiology is excused only by a sort of socio-literary history. Here, in the midst of "classicism," flourished these florid, rococo novels and stories, without unity (many of them indeed unfinished), full of melodrama, coincidence, and extravaganza, but pervaded by a refined, snobbish preciosity of wit, excessively violent yet polite amorous relationships, and all that was understood by Mlle Desjardins and her fellow-authors in the terms *galant* and *galanterie*. The historian of culture who sees the age of Louis XIV as one populated exclusively by geniuses of the rank of Racine, La Fontaine, and Mme de Sévigné (and their admirers), may perhaps profit by a glance at the more ordinary talent of Mlle Desjardins and the taste of the public which it pleased.

[91] As Derome points out (*loc. cit.*), Mlle Desjardins' works remained the property of her mother until the latter's death, after which numerous editions of the most popular works began to appear.

CHAPTER IX

CONCLUSION: EVALUATIONS, INFLUENCE, AND FORTUNE

It is evident from the many quotations made from various works of Mlle Desjardins that, whatever her other merits, the style and literary technique of her writings were ill suited to survive the test of time. Though her contemporaries thought her "la dixième Muse," the "célèbre des Jardins" of divine talents, possessing "de rares lumières," "une manière d'écrire aussi galante que tendre," and a style "que peu de personnes ont eu . . . plus aisé," the most we may now allow her is a fairly rapid, sometimes vivacious style, with somewhat shorter phrases than her predecessors used and an occasional line or turn which can still give a faint pleasure in the midst of so much cliché and banality.[1] Only in the *Recueil de lettres de la Hollande* (1668), and then only in the portions which treat of her actual travels and the sights she saw, did Mlle Desjardins produce elegant, colorful prose which can still give the reader a keen sense of *choses vues et vécues*.

Her poetic skill may likewise be briefly dismissed. Mlle Desjardins imitated the "poetic" traditions of her day, traditions which have since been so discredited that the names of most of the poets of her period are nearly as obscure as her own: Segrais, Saint-Pavin, Charleval, de Cailly, Chapelle, Mme Deshoulières, Benserade. Poetry as they understood it was a formalized, unimaginative, epigrammatic expression of certain conventional emotions which Mlle Desjardins quite aptly termed "des pensées vives." There are few images, little color, no real effects of anguish or aspiration, but only lighthearted reproaches to the faithless lover in whose arms "j'ay demeuré pâmée." No doubt Mlle Desjardins did suffer from "excès d'amour," and felt the "tourments" of which her verses are full, but of these "longues douleurs" little, if anything, reaches the sensibility of the modern reader. Her pastoral verses and *vers de circonstance* deserve even less consideration, except for the occasional historical interest of such a piece as her description of the festival at Versailles on the night of the performance of her play *Le Favory*.[2]

---

[1] Jean de la Forge's *Cercle des femmes sçavantes* of 1663; Martin de Pinchesne, *op. cit.*; Loret's *Gazette* of June 26, 1660; de Visé, *Mercure galant*, November, 1683. Cf. Ch. I, above.

[2] Cf. Ch. II, above.

As for her plays, one can only say that aside from a few "beaux vers"[3] her tragi-comedy *Manlius* and her tragedy *Nitétis* are derivative, tedious, and almost completely lacking in dramatic force. Their more or less "classical" form seems artificial, and is sometimes spoiled by gross sentimentality, as at the end of *Manlius*. Her rhymes and phrases sound like second-rate Corneille, and the endless recurrence of banal tags like "Hé quoi," "courroux," "flamme," etc., quickly fatigues the reader. Her single comedy, *Le Favory*, was successful in its day and seems superior to *Manlius* and *Nitétis* in construction, style, and dramatic effect. In selecting the subjects of her plays, Mlle Desjardins was guided by the two main tendencies of the times: use of classical historical figures, and adaptations of Spanish *comedias*.[4]

The outstanding achievements of Mlle Desjardins were her shortening of the novel form (or, more precisely, her championing of the short novel, since it was not her invention), her use of historical subjects in an effort to evoke historical *milieu,* and her keen analysis of the psychology and emotions of certain of her characters. Mlle Desjardins was primarily a novelist and story-teller. Beginning with an heroic novel in the manner of Gomberville or La Calprenède (*Alcidamie*, 1661), she soon tired of its *aventures* and *longueurs*, and changed it midway into a sort of *recueil d'histoires galantes*. The concept of *galanterie,* which Mornet promises one day to study,[5] appealed to Mlle Desjardins from the time of its first appearance, and she became one of the principal exponents of its literature.[6]

Another type of novel which engrossed her attention and to which she devoted a great part of her time and talents, was the graeco-roman historical novel. Reducing the length of her novels to correspond to about one volume of such works as the *Grand Cyrus* or *Cléopâtre,* and applying to classical history the theories she had developed in her novels of sixteenth-century France, Mlle Desjardins produced a pseudo-historical novel of would-be realistic background, peopled by classical figures like those

---

[3] De Visé, writing of *Manlius*, in his *Défense de Sophonisbe,* 1663; in Granet, *op. cit.*

[4] Cf. Ch. IV, above.

[5] "Le rôle joué par la galanterie, par 'l'homme galant' dans la société française, de 1660 à 1700, n'a pas été étudié, et j'espère le faire connaître quelque jour" (Mornet in the *Romanic Review,* October, 1937, p. 215). Cf. Brunot's *Histoire de la langue française,* III, 237 ff.

[6] For the elements of the chronology of *galant* novels and stories, cf. Chapters V and VI, above.

already familiar in the drama and in such works as Father Caussin's *Cour Sainte,* involved in disorders of love not to be found in any historical account. Bayle reproached her for this "mélange de la vérité et de la fable," this mixture of "intrigues galantes" with "des faits historiques," stating that such a procedure affects the study of history and "fait qu'on n'ose croire ce qui est au fond croiable." He recognized, as late as 1699, the continuing effect of Mlle Desjardins' method "dans une infinité de Livres nouveaux."[7]

Mlle Desjardins' one venture into the "realistic novel," the *Mémoires de Henriette-Sylvie de Molière* (1672), resulted in the overlong and repetitious story of a *picara* of the upper classes, who moves through a series of implausible adventures with a good deal of smugness and an almost complete lack of humor. Traces of Mlle Desjardins' own life may be dimly perceived here and there, but the work is assuredly not the genuine autobiography Magne and Chatenet have held it to be, and, as a fictitious one, falls far short of what one might expect from a person whose private life was so varied and eventful.

In her *Journal amoureux, Annales galantes,* and *Désordres de l'amour* (1669-1675), historical novels concerned mainly with sixteenth-century France, Mlle Desjardins, following the lead of the popular *Princesse de Montpensier* of several years before, worked out a theory for the use of history in fiction which was, in the opinion of one critic, the foundation of the historical novels of such writers as Courtilz de Sandras and the abbé Saint-Réal.[8] Starting the *Journal amoureux* with the *donnée* of the *Princesse de Montpensier,* that is, that names of real historical characters lend an added interest to an invented story, she proceeded to construct a more realistic theory, by which historical facts as well as names must be real, and the invention confined to what may reasonably be supposed to have happened to the characters. Her insatiable predilection for the *galant* showed itself even here, for she promptly set out to explain various historical episodes, such as the Religious Wars, by a secret "histoire d'amour" which motivated the principal personages involved.[9]

It was in the writing of her historical fiction that Mlle Desjardins brought into being those "Héroïnes de Roman qui ne sont pas meilleures

---

[7] *Dictionnaire,* article "Jardins."

[8] Cf. Dulong, *op. cit.,* and see Ch. V, above.

[9] Cf. Ch. V, above.

que les femmes ordinaires," of which Bayle speaks.[10] Seeking to depict historical events (or at least *possible* events) and to give the reader an impression of reality, Mlle Desjardins was better able here than elsewhere to give vent to the emotions she had experienced or observed in life. Too formalized in her poetry, blighted with preciosity in her strictly *galant* productions, unsuccessfully expressed in the unreal atmosphere of her graeco-roman *amoureux,* all that she understood and felt about love found an outlet in the thoughts and emotions of the heroes and heroines of such works as the *Désordres de l'amour.*

To present this new type of hero or heroine to the public, to make the reader feel what she wished to inject into her characters, required a type of description of states of mind, reactions, desires, and fears, beyond the scope of traditional psychological analysis. Until the time of Mlle Desjardins, only the drama had effectively portrayed the effects of sorrow, love, and poignant disillusion, which she produced in prose fiction. With finer stylistic gifts, she might have given us in the *Désordres de l'amour* the masterpiece we now recognize in the *Princesse de Clèves,* whose theme is similar and whose conception may well have been influenced by the earlier work.

Such, in brief, is Mlle Desjardins' place in the literary history of the seventeenth century. It seems, despite her failure to write a masterpiece, an honorable place. She lacked not only great talent, but also the willingness to refuse to cater to the tastes of the large public which she enjoyed, and whose values and standards are reflected, not in the tragedies of Racine or the sermons of Bossuet, but in works like the *Exilez* and the *Annales galantes.* She was thoroughly of her time, and her popularity should put us on our guard against the common opinion that the entire literary public under Louis XIV had exquisite and infallible taste, or that it demanded only the best.

We have noted Bayle's observation, written after 1699, that the influence of Mlle Desjardins was still felt in the literary world. Saint-Réal and the other writers of historical fiction had incorporated her achievements in a living tradition. Twenty years after the appearance of the *Journal amoureux* and the *Annales galantes,* La Bruyère singled them out as typical of the works popular in a certain social *milieu.*[11]

[10] *Nouvelles lettres sur le calvinisme,* II, 735. Bayle continues: "Les Romans de cette Dame sentent fort la Nature."

[11] *Les Caractères,* Gds. Éc. edition, I, 289.

One of the earliest unfavorable comments on the style of Mlle Desjardins was made by the abbé Faydit in his *Télémacomanie, ou la censure et critique du roman intitulé "les Avantures de Télémaque"* (Paris, 1700). Faydit reproaches an authoress because her reading of *Don Quixote*, Père Gautruche, and the novels of Mlle de Scudéry and Mlle Desjardins has corrupted her style and turned it into that of the "auteurs et autrices galantes."[12]

Mlle Desjardins' popularity was evidenced by the large number of editions of individual works, and of her *Œuvres complètes* published in the first half of the eighteenth century. One of her novels was reprinted as late as 1802.[13] Her verses were reproduced in anthologies in 1725, 1741, 1745, 1748, 1752, 1773, and 1783.[14]

Mornet, in his noted article on the contents of private libraries in eighteenth-century France,[15] gives a frequency table showing the occurrence of various works in some 392 private libraries of the period. According to this index of popularity, the *Œuvres* of Mlle Desjardins rank 26th, preceded by such recent fiction as *Pamela* (2d), *Tom Jones* (3d), *Clarissa Harlowe* (4th), *Cleveland* (5th), *La Vie de Marianne* (9th), *Gil Blas* (13th), but followed at some distance by works which are now more famous: Mrs. Aphra Behn's *Orinocko, Manon Lescaut,* the *Œuvres* of Hamilton, the *Diable boiteux,* and the *Princesse de Clèves.* Mlle Desjardins, moreover, ranks *first* among the seventeenth-century French authors. The only works earlier than her own which rank above hers are such classics as *Daphnis et Chloé* and *Les Amours de Théagène et de Chariclée.*[16]

Voltaire speaks of her twice, both times with the utmost disdain. Once, in his correspondence, he denounces the ideas of Bayle, in his *Pensées sur la comète,* as having no more relationship among themselves than "les fades histoires de Mme de Villedieu."[17] In the *Siècle de Louis XIV* his judgment is the following:

---

[12] Cf. E. Crooks, *The Influence of Cervantes in France,* Baltimore, 1931, p. 35, and Maurice Bardon, *Don Quichotte en France au XVIIe et au XVIIIe siècle, 1605-1815,* Paris, 1931, I, 388.

[13] *Les Exilez.* Cf. Ch. VIII, above.

[14] Cf. Ch. II, above.

[15] Daniel Mornet, "Les Enseignements des bibliothèques privées, 1750-1780," *RHLF,* 1910, pp. 473 ff.

[16] I except Caylus' translation of Marini's *Cloandre fidèle.*

[17] Voltaire, *Œuvres,* Paris, 1878, XXXVI, 201.

Villedieu (Marie-Catherine Desjardins, plus connue sous le nom de Mme de).
Ses romans lui firent de la réputation. Au reste, on est bien éloigné de vouloir
donner ici quelque prix à tous ces romans dont la France a été *et est encore inondée;*
ils ont presque tous été, excepté *Zaïde,* des productions d'esprits faibles qui écrivent
avec facilité des choses indignes d'être lues par les esprits solides. Ils sont même pour
la plupart dénoués d'imagination; et il y en a plus dans quatre pages de l'Arioste que
dans les insipides écrits qui gâtent le goût des jeunes gens. Née à Alençon vers 1640,
morte en 1683.[18]

The harshness of this opinion cannot conceal the fact that, despite their
lack of merit, these works which pleased the public of the seventeenth
century, were, as the phrase *et est encore inondée* indicates, still entertaining and engrossing a part of the public of Voltaire's day. One
school of modern critics maintains, following Magendie's paraphrase
of La Bruyère, that, concerning the great masterpieces of literature, "tout
a été dit, et bien dit."[19] The argument is that scholars must now concentrate on the lesser works of the past. Whether this viewpoint is sound
may be debatable, but one task which certainly remains is that of studying the entire literary edifice of the past, from *grenier* to *bas-fond,* and
attempting to round out our knowledge of literary moments and *milieux*
by studying, now that the principal action has been observed, what was
going on backstage and in the *coulisses.*

One of the rare mentions of Mlle Desjardins between Voltaire and
the nineteenth-century critics occurs in Restif de la Bretonne, who wrote:

Dès mon enfance, en lisant les romans, j'eus envie d'en faire; mais je sentais bien
qu'il manquait quelque chose à ceux que je lisais (c'était surtout ceux de Mme de
Villedieu) et que ce quelque chose était la vérité.[20]

She was discussed by Goujet and by the abbé de la Porte, who repeated
more or less what the frères Parfaict had written of her earlier.[21]

In the nineteenth century various critics and historians of literature
occupied themselves with reconstructing the life of Mlle Desjardins and
discussing her work: Hauréau, Clogenson, Fournier, de Gallier, Le
Vavasseur, Morillot, Gazier. Auguste-Louis Ménard, Praviel, La Sico-

---

[18] *Ibid.*, XIV, 142 (italics mine). Notice that Voltaire singles out for favorable
mention not Mme de La Fayette's *Princesse de Clèves*, now regarded as the masterpiece of the period, but her lesser known and almost forgotten *Zaïde.*

[19] *Op. cit.,* p. 455.

[20] Quoted by Derome, *loc. cit.*

[21] Cf. Goujet, *op. cit.,* and the abbé de la Porte, *Histoire littéraire des dames françoises.* Goujet was the first to give a detailed account of her second marriage, which
he regarded as illegal. See Ch. I, above.

tière Neveu, Desnos, and others.[22] One of these, Édouard Neveu, in a monograph included in Baratte's *Poètes normands* (Paris, 1846), spoke of her works as "des adorables idylles, dignes du pinceau d'Ovide," and compared one of her mediocre novels, *Les Amours des grands hommes*, to a "lanterne magique." In true romantic style, he composed an epitaph for the authoress:

ÉPITAPHE DE MLLE DES JARDINS

En traits naifs et gracieux,
Elle peignit l'amour: elle fit encore mieux.
Dans sa jalouse humeur, Érato se désole,
N'osant plus désormais de sa terne auréole
Faire montre au sacré vallon.
Depuis que Des Jardins a jeté, tendre folle!
Le carquois de l'Amour sur le dos d'Apollon.[23]

In the twentieth century, serious scholastic investigation of Mlle Desjardins, which began with the writers of the *Moliériste*,[24] has been continued in the works of Pierre Brun, Querlon, Derome, Bertaut and Séché, Kretschmar, Magne, Dulong, and Lancaster.[25] Certain minor problems in connection with her work, such as the relationship between the *Désordres de l'amour* and the *Princesse de Clèves*, have received attention from specialists.[26]

It is my hope that the present work will complete these previous investigations into the life and works of Mlle Desjardins, and provide a source of information and comparisons for further research into the seventeenth-century novel and related fields.

[22] Cf. above, *passim*, and see Bibliography.

[23] *Op. cit.*, p. 7 of separate pagination of Neveu's article.

[24] Cf. especially Chapters IV and VII, above.

[25] Only the most important are mentioned here. Chatenet contributed to public awareness of Mlle Desjardins; Miss Dallas wrote briefly of her position in the history of the seventeenth-century novel. See Bibliography, and the discussions above.

[26] Cf. Ch. V, above.

BIBLIOGRAPHY

Included below are books and articles relative to the critical study of Mlle Desjardins. The list does not include editions and republications of her works, or anthologies, recueils, etc., in which pieces by her have appeared: for these, refer to the discussions of individual works. Other items not included here, such as historical works used by Mlle Desjardins as source material, background references, and the like, are also described bibliographically at the proper places in the notes to the text.

Adam, Antoine: "La Genèse des *Précieuses ridicules*," *Revue d'histoire et de politique*, January-March, 1939, pp. 14-46.

Anonymous: "Essai sur la littérature et les beaux-arts," *Asmodée Cenoman*, 1822.

Anonymous: "Mme des Jardins de Villedieu," *Annuaire d'Alençon*, 1808.

Ashton, H.: *Mme de La Fayette*, Cambridge, The University Press, 1922.

Aubignac, abbé d': See Granet.

Baldensperger, Fernand: "À propos de l'*aveu* de la *Princesse de Clèves*," *Revue de philologie française et de littérature*, XV (1901), 26-31.

Barbier, Antoine: *Dictionnaire des ouvrages anonymes et pseudonymes composés*, Paris, 1822-1827, 4 vols.

Baur, J.: *Un Compte-rendu des Précieuses*, Paris, 1877.

Bayle, Pierre: *Nouvelles lettres sur le calvinisme*, Amsterdam, Mortier, 1715.
Œuvres, La Haye, 1737 (including the *Nouvelles de la république des lettres*).
Dictionnaire historique et critique, Paris, Desœr, 1820, 16 vols.

Beauchamps, P.-F. G. de: *Recherches sur les théâtres de France*, Paris, Prault, 1735.

Beaunier, André: *L'Amie de La Rochefoucauld*, Paris, Flammarion, 1927.

Bibliothèque universelle des romans, Paris, July, 1775-June, 1789, 224 parts in 112 vols.

Boileau, Gilles: *Œuvres posthumes de M. B. . . . .* , Paris, n.d.

Boursault, E.: *Lettres de Babet*, Lyon, Bruyset, 1715-1720.

Bray, René: *La Tragédie cornélienne devant la critique classique*, Dijon, Darantière, 1927.

Brébeuf, Georges de: *Œuvres de M. Brébeuf*, Paris, 1664.

Brueys, David-A. de: *Œuvres de M. Brueys*, Paris, Briasson, 1735.

Brugmans, Henri C.: *Le Séjour de Christian Huygens à Paris*, Paris, 1935.

Brun, Pierre: *Autour du XVIIe siècle*, Grenoble, Falque et Perrin, 1901.

Buffet, Marguerite: *Nouvelles observations sur la langue françoise*, Paris, 1668.

Bussy-Rabutin: *Correspondance*, edited by Lalanne, Paris, 1858.

Cazenave, Jean: "Le Roman hispano-mauresque en France," *Revue de littérature comparée*, V (1925), 596 ff.

Chamard, H., and Rudler, G.: "La Documentation sur le XVIe siècle chez un romancier du XVIIe, les sources historiques de *La Princesse de Clèves*," *Revue du seizième siècle*, 1914, pp. 92, 289 ff., and 1917-1918, pp. 1, 231 ff.

Chappuzeau, Samuel: *Théâtre françois*, Paris, 1674.

Charnes, abbé de: *Conversations sur la critique de la Princesse de Clèves*, Paris, Barbin, 1679.

Chatenet, Henri: *Le Roman et les romans d'une femme de lettres au XVIIe siècle, Mme de Villedieu*, Paris, Champion, 1911.

Clogenson, S.: "Mme de Villedieu," *Athenaeum français*, July-August, 1853. Reprinted as *Mme de Villedieu*, Alençon, Poulet-Malassis, 1853.

Dallas, Dorothy: *Le Roman français de 1660 à 1690*, Paris, Gamber, 1932.

Derome, "le Capitaine": "Mme de Villedieu inconnue," *Revue historique et archéologique du Maine*, 1911, pp. 224-236.

Desnos, Odolant: *Mémoires historiques sur la ville d'Alençon et sur ses seigneurs*, 1787.

Article, "Orne," *La France*, 1834.

Despois, Eugène: *Œuvres de Molière*, Grands Écrivains edition, Paris, Hachette, 1873-1890, containing in Vol. II a critical edition of Mlle Desjardins' *Récit de la farce des Précieuses* and in Vol. IV the text of Marigny's *Relation des Plaisirs de l'Ile Enchantée*.

Dulong, Gustave: *L'Abbé de Saint-Réal, étude sur les rapports de l'histoire et du roman au XVIIe siècle*, Paris, Champion, 1921.

Faguet, Émile: "Un Critique homme du monde au XVIIe siècle (Valincourt)," *Revue des Deux Mondes*, May 15, 1909, pp. 372 ff.

Faydit, abbé: *Télémacomanie, ou la censure et critique du roman intitulé "les Avantures de Télémaque,"* Paris, 1700.

Fournier, Édouard: *Variétés historiques et littéraires*, Paris, 1856.

Gallier, Anatole de: "Le Roman dans la seconde moitié du XVIIe siècle: Mme de Villedieu," *Bulletin de la Société archéologique de la Drôme, 1882-1883*. Reprinted as *Mme de Villedieu*, Paris, 1883.

Gazier, Augustin: "Mme de Villedieu," *Bulletin du comité des travaux historiques et scientifiques*, 1883, No. 1, pp. 50 ff.

Goujet, abbé Claude-Pierre: *Bibliothèque françoise*, Paris, Hariette et Guérin, 1741-1756.

Graesse, J. G. Theodor: *Trésor de livres rares et précieux*, Berlin, Altmann, 1922, 7 vols.

Granet, abbé: *Recueil de dissertations . . . sur Sertorius* (including d'Aubignac and de Visé), Paris, Gissey, 1739.

Guéret, Gabriel: *La Carte de la Cour*, Paris, 1663.

Hauréau, B.: *Histoire littéraire du Maine*, Paris, Dumoulin, 1870-1877.

Huygens, Christian: *Œuvres*, La Haye, Nijhoff, 1888.

Jal, Auguste: *Dictionnaire critique de biographie et d'histoire*, Paris, 1867.

Journal des sçavans, Amsterdam, 1665-1753, 172 vols.

Jouast, Damase: *Nouvelle collection moliéresque*, Paris, 1879.

Koerting, H.: *Geschichte des fr. Romans im XVII Jahrhundert*, Leipzig, 1885.

Kretschmar, A.: *Mme de Villedieu, Leben, Romane, und Erzählungen*, Inaugural-Dissertation, Leipzig, 1907.

Lachèvre, Frédéric: *Bibliographie des recueils collectifs de poésie*, Paris, Leclerc, 1901-1905.

Disciples et successeurs de Théophile de Viau (Des Barreaux et Saint-Pavin), Paris, Champion, 1911.

Lacroix, Paul ("le bibliophile Jacob"): "Le Prologue du *Favori*," *Moliériste*, III (1881), 3 ff.

"Sur les ouvrages attribués à Subligny," *Moliériste*, III (1881), 273 ff. Edition with notes of the *Récit en prose de la farce des Précieuses*, in the *Nouvelle collection moliéresque*, Paris, 1879.

La Fizelière, Albert de: "De la liberté de la presse sous Louis XIV," *Bulletin du bibliophile*, 1858.

La Forge, Jean de: *Cercle des femmes sçavantes*, Paris, Loyson, 1663.

La Grange: *Registre*, Paris, Claye, 1876.

Lancaster, H. Carrington: *A History of French Dramatic Literature in the Seventeenth Century*, Baltimore, The Johns Hopkins Press, 1929-1940.

Five French Farces, 1655-1694?, Baltimore, The Johns Hopkins Press, 1937.

Langlet du Fresnoy, abbé Nicholas: *De l'usage des romans*, Amsterdam, 1734.

Langlois, Marcel: "Quel est l'auteur de *La Princesse de Clèves?*," *Mercure de France*, CCXC (1939), 58-82.

La Porte, abbé de: *Dictionnaire dramatique*, Paris, Lacombe, 1776.

Histoire littéraire des dames françoises, Paris, 1769.

La Sicotière, Louis de: "Mme Desjardins de Villedieu et ses relations avec Molière," *Bulletin de la Société historique de l'Orne*, 1883.

Le Pays, René: *Nouvelles œuvres de M. Le Pays*, Paris, 1715.

Le Vavasseur, G.: "Mlle Desjardins," *Bulletin de la Société historique de l'Orne*, 1893.

Livet, Charles: Article on *Les Mémoires de Henriette-Sylvie de Molière*, in *Moliériste*, I (1880), 305 ff.

Loret, Jean: *La Muze historique*, edited by Livet, Paris, Jannet and Daffis, 1857-1878, 4 vols. See also Rothschild.

Magendie, Maurice: *Le Roman français au XVIIe siècle de l'Astrée au Grand Cyrus*, Paris, Droz, 1932.

Magne, Émile: *Mme de Villedieu*, Paris, Mercure de France, 1907.

Le Cœur et l'esprit de Mme de La Fayette, Paris, Émile-Paul frères, 1927.

Marolles, Michel de: *Mémoires*, edited by Goujet, Paris, 1755.

Marigny: See Despois.

Martinenche, Erneste: *La Comedia espagnole en France*, Paris, Hachette, 1900.

Mélèse, Pierre: *Le Théâtre et le public sous Louis XIV*, Paris, Droz, 1934.

Répertoire analytique des documents contemporains d'information et de critique concernant le théâtre à Paris sous Louis XIV, Paris, Droz, 1934.

Ménard, Auguste-Louis: *La Fontaine et Mme de Villedieu, les Fables galantes présentées à Louis XIV le jour de sa fête, essai de restitution à La Fontaine*, Paris, Chavaray frères, 1882.

Mercure galant, edited by Donneau de Visé, Paris, Lyon, 1672-1717, 571 vols.

Michaut, G.: *Les Débuts de Molière à Paris*, Paris, Hachette, 1923.

Monceau, Paul du: "Correspondance," *Moliériste*, I (1880), 352.

Morillot, P.: *Le Roman français durant l'époque classique*, London and Toronto, 1921.

Mornet, Daniel: "Les Enseignements des bibliothèques privées, 1750-1780," *Revue d'histoire littéraire française*, 1910, pp. 473 ff.

Morrissette, Bruce A.: "*Les Amours des grands hommes* of Mlle Desjardins and *le Docteur amoureux*," *MLN*, LIII (1938), 344-347.

"Mlle Desjardins and the *apologie du luxe*," *MLN*, LVI (1941), 209-211.

"Marcel Langlois' Untenable Attribution of *La Princesse de Clèves* to Fontenelle," *MLN*, LXI (1946), 267-270.

Neveu, Édouard: "Mlle Desjardins," in Baratte's *Poètes normands*, Paris, 1846.

Parfaict, frères: *Théâtre françois*, Amsterdam, 1735-1749.

Pavillon, Étienne: *Œuvres*, Paris, 1750.

Pinchesne, Martin de: *Œuvres de Martin de Pinchesne (additions de quelques pièces nouvelles, faites depuis l'impression)*, Paris, n.d.

Pure, abbé de: *Idée des spectacles*, Paris, 1668.

Praviel, A.: "Mme de Villedieu et la *Princesse de Clèves*," *Revue littéraire*, 1898 (as cited by H. Ashton).

Querlon, P. de: "Mme de Villedieu et *Le Journal amoureux*," *Revue politique et littéraire*, March, 1904.

Ravaisson, Fr.-N.: *Archives de la Bastille*, Paris, 1866-1891.

Raynal, Marie-Aline: *Le Talent de Mme de La Fayette*, Paris, Picart, 1926.

Reynier, G.: *Le Roman sentimental avant l'Astrée*, Paris, Colin, 1908.

Richelet, Pierre: *Vie des auteurs françois*, Paris, 1699.

Les Plus belles lettres françoises, Paris, 1698.

Rigal, Eugène: *Molière*, Paris, 1908.

Robinet, Jean: See Rothschild.

Rothschild, Baron James de: *Les Continuateurs de Loret*, Paris, Morgand, 1833.

Rudler, G.: See Chamard.

Schweitzer, Jerome W.: *Georges de Scudéry's "Almahide,"* Baltimore, The Johns Hopkins Press, 1939.

Séché, A., and Bertaut, J.: "Une Aventurière de lettres au XVIIe siècle, Mme de Villedieu," *Mercure de France*, February, 1900.

Somaize, Baudeau de: *Dictionnaire des précieuses*, edited by Charles Livet, Paris, Bibliothèque élzévirienne, 1856.

Sorel, Charles: *Bibliothèque françoise*, Paris, 1664.

De la connoissance des bons livres, Amsterdam, Boom, 1672.

Tallemant des Réaux: *Historiettes*, edited by Monmerqué and Paris, Paris, Techener, 1854-1860.

Thierry, Édouard: "Le *Favory*," *Moliériste*, III (1882), 6 ff.

"Le *Misanthrope* avant la représentation," *Moliériste*, IV (1883), 131 ff.

Titon du Tillet: *Description du parnasse françois*, Paris, Coignard, 1727.

Toinet, Raymond: *Essai d'une liste raisonnée des auteurs qui ont écrit en vers français de 1600 à 1715*, Tulle, 1911-1913.

Valincourt, Jean Baptiste de: *Lettres à la Marquise de * * * au sujet de La Princesse de Clèves*, Paris, Mabre-Cramoisy, 1678.

Van Vree, P.: *Pamphlets et libelles contre Molière*, Paris, 1934.

Vertron, de: *La Nouvelle Pandore*, Paris, 1698 (Vol. II, article "Châte").

Visé, Donneau de: See Granet, and *Mercure galant*.

Voisenon, abbé de: *Œuvres*, Paris, 1781.

Williams, R. C.: *Bibliography of the Seventeenth-Century Novel in France*, New York, Century Co., 1931.

Wurzbach, W. von: *Geschichte des fr. Romans*, Heidelberg, 1912.

INDEX*

* An index of persons, periodicals, and books (including plays). Historical personages used by Mlle Desjardins merely as fictional characters are not included.

WASHINGTON UNIVERSITY STUDIES
(NEW SERIES)
LANGUAGE AND LITERATURE

WASHINGTON UNIVERSITY STUDIES

(NEW SERIES)

SCIENCE AND TECHNOLOGY

WASHINGTON UNIVERSITY STUDIES
(NEW SERIES)

No. 10. Collected Studies of Skin Diseases—Vol. III (Price, $2.00)
Edited by M. F. Engman, Sr., M.D.

No. 11. The Weight Field of Force of the Earth (Price, $1.50)....by William H. Roever

No. 12. Fundamental Theorems of Orthographic Axonometry (Price, $1.00)
by William H. Roever

SOCIAL AND PHILOSOPHICAL SCIENCES

No. 1. The Localization of Business Activities in Metropolitan St. Louis (Price, $2.00)..by Lewis F. Thomas

No. 2. Science and Humanism in University Education (Price, 50c)
by John D. E. S. Spaeth

No. 3. Three Philosophical Studies (Price, $1.00) Contents:
Spinoza and Modern Thought................................by Lawson P. Chambers
Existence and Value................................by George R. Dodson
The Realm of Necessity................................by Charles E. Cory

No. 4. Sociology and the Study of International Relations (Price, $1.25)
by Luther L. Bernard and Jessie Bernard

No. 5. A Survey of the Labor Market in Missouri in Relation to Unemployment Compensation (Price, $1.00)................................by Joseph M. Klamon
in collaboration with Russell S. Bauder and Roy A. Prewitt

No. 6. Types of Utility Rate Bases Under Depreciation Reserve Accounting (Price, $1.50)..by William S. Krebs

Annual Bibliography 1945-1946 (Gratis on application)

---

*Orders for any of these publications should be addressed to the Bookstore,
Washington University, St. Louis, Mo.*

9 781163 159170